Referent Markings in L2 Narratives

Referent Markings in L2 Narratives
Effects of Task Complexity, Learners' L1 and Proficiency Level

Yuko Nakahama

Hituzi Syobo Publishing

Copyright © Yuko Nakahama 2011
First published 2011

Author: Yuko Nakahama

All rights reserved. Except for the quotation of short passages for the purposes of criticism and review, no part of this publication may be reproduced, stored in a retrieval system, or transmitted in any form or by any means, electronic, mechanical, photocopying, recording or otherwise, without the written prior permission of the publisher.
In case of photocopying and electronic copying and retrieval from network personally, permission will be given on receipts of payment and making inquiries. For details please contact us through e-mail. Our e-mail address is given below.

From FROG, WHERE ARE YOU? @1969 by Mercer Mayer. Used by permission of Dial Books for Young Readers, A Division of Penguin Young Readers Group. All rights reserved.

Hituzi Syobo Publishing
Yamato bldg. 2F, 2-1-2 Sengoku Bunkyo-ku Tokyo, Japan
112-0011

phone +81-3-5319-4916 fax +81-3-5319-4917
e-mail: toiawase@hituzi.co.jp
http://www.hituzi.co.jp/
postal transfer 00120-8-142852

ISBN978-4-89476-535-1
Printed in Japan

Preface

Cross-linguistic influence (CLI), also known as language transfer, has long been recognized as an important element that influences second language (L2) learning. Since Odlin published his well-documented review of CLI studies back in 1989, many second language acquisition (SLA) researchers have continued to investigate this topic in various areas of language learning and at this point have amassed a great deal of evidence that CLI is in fact an operative factor in L2 learning.

The objective of this book is to explore the functioning of CLI on a new, relatively uninvestigated level. It aims to show that not only learners' L1 grammar, but also their conceptual frameworks are transferable to their L2 oral production. Differing perspectives may produce different types of structures, as various linguistic selections are made specifically to depict a speakers' viewpoint of a story, irrespective of typological distance between two languages. The present research demonstrates that capturing the world and conveying thought through the means that are made available in the speakers' L1 is not easily altered to the conceptual norm of the target language.

In this study, the relationship between the learners' proficiency level and L1 background, as well as the impact of different data elicitation methods were explored in referent marking in L2 Japanese. While many of the previous L2 narrative studies employed either film retelling or picture description tasks in their investigation of CLI, the current study employed both task types. The picture description task, or here-and-now task, was considered as the less complex task, whereas the film retelling task, or there-and-then task, was assumed to be a more complex task. By employing both of the most commonly used narrative elicitation methods, this study hopes to contribute to a better understanding of the relationship between task complexity and L2 development, and to allow generalisability and comparison to previous research. It also provides pedagogical suggestions, such as appropriate task design to enhance L2 learning, based on the findings.

I would like to close my preface by giving appreciation to those people who encouraged me to carry out the study, as well as my former graduate school assistants and the participants of the study who provided such intriguing data. I am especially grateful to Terry Odlin, who has given me endless support to tackle CLI since I was a master's degree student at Ohio State. My appreciation also goes to Leo van Lier, whose authentic approach to language learning I truly admire. The impetus not only for this L2 Japanese narrative project, but also the interactional study I am currently embarking on, as well as other projects at various stages of development, has emerged from our academic discussions. Scott Jarvis's kind comments to my inquiry of his 2002 study are greatly appreciated. I would also like to acknowledge Tadashi Sakamoto since his remarkable studies of *wa* and *ga* originally inspired me to investigate topic continuity. My thanks also go to Rusan Chen for his continuous support on statistical analysis, and David O'Donnell for thoroughly proofreading the final version of the manuscript. Finally, I would like to thank my family and friends for their unconditional love and support, without which I could not have finished the project.

This work was supported by *Kakenhi* (Project No. 15520330) granted by the Ministry of Education, Culture, Sports, Science and Technology, Grant-in-Aid for Scientific Research (C). I would also like to acknowledge that the publication of this work was made possible by generous funding from the *Keio Gijuku Fukuzawa Memorial Fund for the Advancement of Education and Research*.

Contents

Preface i
Tables vii
Figures ix
Examples x

Chapter 1 Introduction 1
  1.1 Introduction 1
  1.2 Operationalisation of the terms 12
  1.3 Organisation of chapters 16

Chapter 2 Literature Reviews 19
  2.1 Cross-linguistic influence 19
  2.2 Narrative 34
    2.2.1 Narrative as means of communication 34
    2.2.2 Picture storytelling: *Frog, Where are You?* 35
  2.3 Functional approaches to understanding language use 38
  2.4 Referent markings 40
    2.4.1 Topic continuity 40
    2.4.2 Perspectives and voice alternation 41
    2.4.3 Acquisition of referential forms 45
    2.4.4 Referent markings in L1 and L2 Japanese 48
    2.4.5 CLI studies of the acquisition of NP+*wa* and NP+*ga* 54
    2.4.6 Referent markings in Korean 58

2.4.7	Referent markings in English	61
2.5	Task complexity and its effects on narrative production	62
2.6	Research questions and hypotheses	64

Chapter 3 The Present Study 69
3.1	Method	69
	3.1.1 Participants	69
	3.1.2 Interlocutor	73
	3.1.3 Learners' proficiency levels	74
	3.1.4 Tasks (H/N and T/T tasks)	75
	3.1.5 Design	76
3.2	Analysis	77
	3.2.1 Coding	77

Chapter 4 Results 83
4.1	NS narratives	83
	4.1.1 L1 Japanese narratives	84
	4.1.1.1 Referent introduction	84
	4.1.1.2 Topic switch (Re-introduction of referent)	98
	4.1.1.3 Continuous mention of referent	101
	4.1.2 L1 Korean narratives	102
	4.1.2.1 Referent introduction	103
	4.1.2.2 Topic switch (Re-introduction of referent)	108
	4.1.2.3 Continuous mention of referent	110
	4.1.3 L1 English narratives	111
	4.1.3.1 Referent introduction	112
	4.1.3.2 Topic switch (Re-introduction of referent)	118
	4.1.3.3 Continuous mention of referent	122

4.2	NNS Narratives	124
	4.2.1 Referent introduction	125
	4.2.1.1 NP+*ga* for referent introduction in H/N narratives	127
	4.2.1.2 NP+*ga* for referent introduction in T/T narratives	132
	4.2.1.3 NP+*wa* for referent introduction in H/N narratives	134
	4.2.1.4 NP+*wa* for referent introduction in T/T narratives	135
	4.2.1.5 NP+*o* for referent introduction in H/N and T/T narratives	138
	4.2.1.6 The use of NP+*ni/kara* and the passive construction/expressions in H/N and T/T narratives	141
	4.2.1.7 NP+particle drop in H/N narratives and T/T narratives	154
	4.2.2 Topic switch (Re-introduction of referent)	159
	4.2.2.1 Zero anaphora in the context of topic switch	164
	4.2.2.2 Particle drop in the context of topic switch	166
	4.2.2.3 Re-introduction of the frog	168
	4.2.3 Continuous mention of referent	170
	4.2.3.1 The use of zero anaphora in the context of continuous mention	172

Chapter 5 Discussion and Conclusion 183

5.1	Discussion	184
	5.1.1 CLI evidenced in L2 narratives by Korean L1 speakers: Accelerated acquisition of NP+*ga*	184
	5.1.2 CLI evidenced in L2 narratives by English L1 speakers	186
	5.1.2.1 Particle drop in referent introduction and topic switch	186
	5.1.2.2 The use of definiteness marker, NP+*wa* in referent introduction	188
	5.1.3 Proficiency and CLI: Constraints on transfer	192
	5.1.3.1 The use of NP+*ni/kara* and the passive constructions by Korean L1 speakers	192

5.1.4 Task complexity and its effects on L1 and L2 storytelling	195
5.1.4.1 Task complexity and accuracy of referent marking	195
5.1.4.2 Task complexity and production of attenuated form	197
5.1.5 Conceptual transfer	198
5.2 Conclusion	202
5.2.1 Answers to the research questions	202
5.2.2 Summary of findings	204
5.2.3 Limitations and suggestions for further research	207
5.2.4 Pedagogical implications	210
Bibliography	219
Appendix	235

Tables

Table 2.1	Referential Forms of English Within Discourse Contexts	61
Table 3.1	Demographic Information of Participants	72
Table 4.1	Referent Introduction by JNS	84
Table 4.2	Topic Switch (Re-introduction of Referent) by JNS	98
Table 4.3	Subjects of Topic Switch	99
Table 4.4	Continuous Mention of Referent by JNS	101
Table 4.5	Referent Introduction by KNS	103
Table 4.6	Korean and Japanese Referent Markings	104
Table 4.7	Topic Switch (Re-introduction of Referent) by KNS	108
Table 4.8	Continuous Mention of Referents by KNS	110
Table 4.9	Referent Introduction by ENS	112
Table 4.10	Marking of the Main Characters for Referent Introduction in the H/N	114
Table 4.11	Marking of the Main Characters for Referent Introduction in the T/T	116
Table 4.12	Topic Switch (Re-introduction of Referent) by ENS	119
Table 4.13	Subjects of Topic Switch by ENS	120
Table 4.14	Ratio of Main and Peripheral Characters in the Use of Definite Article and Pronouns in Topic Switch	120
Table 4.15	Continuous Mention of Referent by ENS	122
Table 4.16	Referent Introduction by NNSs and JNS: H/N Narratives	126
Table 4.17	Referent Introduction by NNSs and JNS: T/T Narratives	126
Table 4.18	Number of the Occurrences of Passives by JNS and NNSs	146
Table 4.19	Patients of the Passive Structures in the H/N Narrative	150
Table 4.20	Patients of the Passive Structures in the T/T Narrative	150
Table 4.21	Topic Switch by NNSs and JNSs in the H/N Narratives	160
Table 4.22	Topic Switch by NNSs and JNSs in the H/N Narratives	160
Table 4.23	Use of Full NP and Zero Anaphora in the H/N and the T/T Narratives	161
Table 4.24	Ratio of Main and Peripheral Characters in Topic Switch	163

Table 4.25 Re-introduction of the Frog	169
Table 4.26 Continuous Mention of Referents in the H/N Narratives	171
Table 4.27 Continuous Mention of Referents in the T/T Narratives	172
Table 4.28 Number of the Occurrences of Japanese Third Person Pronouns	177
Table 4.29 Referents that were Referred to with Pronouns in Topic Switch	178
Table 5.1 Number of the Occurrences of Passive Expressions by All Groups	199

Figures

Figure 4.1 Percentage Use of NP+*ga* in the Context of Referent Introduction 127
Figure 4.2 Percentage Use of NP+*wa* in the Context of Referent Introduction 134
Figure 4.3 Percentage Use of NP+*o* in the Context of Referent Introduction 138
Figure 4.4 Percentage Use of NP+*ni/kara* in the Context of Referent Introduction 141
Figure 4.5 Numbers of the Occurrences of Passive Constructions / Expressions 146
Figure 4.6 Numbers of Occurrences of Passive Constructions / Expressions by All Groups 149
Figure 4.7 Percentage Use of NP+Particle Drop in the Context of Referent Introduction 154
Figure 4.8 Ratio of Full NPs and Zero Anaphora in the Context of Topic Switch 162
Figure 4.9 Ratio of Main and Peripheral Characters Marked in Topic Switch 163
Figure 4.10 Percentage Use of Zero Anaphora in the Context of Topic Switch 164
Figure 4.11 Percentage Use of Zero Anaphora in the Context of Continuous Mention of Referent 173

Examples

Example 2.1	Passivisation of an Intransitive Verb in Japanese	60
Example 2.2	Passive Structure in Korean	60
Example 3.1	Coding of Referent Introduction	78
Example 3.2	Re-introduction of Referents (Topic Switch) and Continuous Mentions	79
Example 4.1	Marking of the Main Characters with *ga* by JNS	86
Example 4.2	Marking of the Boy with *ga* and the Frog with *o* by JNS	87
Example 4.3	Marking of the Frog with *o* by JNS (#5)	88
Example 4.4	Marking of the Bees with *o* by JNS (#10)	90
Example 4.5	Marking of the Owl with *ni* by JNS (#2)	90
Example 4.6	Beginning of Storytelling by JNS (#4)	92
Example 4.7	Typical Beginning of a Folk Tale in Japanese	92
Example 4.8	Marking of the Main Characters with *ga* by JNS (#10)	94
Example 4.9	Marking of the Main Characters with *ga* and *ni* by JNS (#7)	94
Example 4.10	Marking of a Peripheral Character with *ni* by JNS (#10)	96
Example 4.11	Referent Introduction of the Main Characters by KNS (#10)	104
Example 4.12	Referent Introduction of the Main Characters by KNS (#8)	105
Example 4.13	Passive Expression Produced by a KNS (#4)	107
Example 4.14	Referent Introduction by ENS (#3)	113
Example 4.15	Referent Introduction by ENS (#4)	113
Example 4.16	Referent Introduction of the Main Characters by ENS (#5)	114
Example 4.17	Referent Introduction of the Main Characters by ENS (#8)	114
Example 4.18	Use of the Possessive Pronoun (ENG #4)	116
Example 4.19	Introduction of Peripheral Characters with a Quantifier (ENG #8)	117
Example 4.20	Introduction of Peripheral Characters with a Quantifier (ENG #2)	117
Example 4.21	Re-introduction of the Frog by ENS (#2)	121
Example 4.22	Zero Anaphora in Continuous Mention in the T/T by ENS (#5)	123
Example 4.23	Zero Anaphora in Continuous Mention in the T/T by ENS (#9)	123
Example 4.24	Referent Introduction of the Boy, the Dog and the Frog by ENG-Mid Level (# 9)	130

Example 4.25	Referent Introduction of the Peripheral Characters by ENG-Mid Level (#9)	130
Example 4.26	Referent Introduction of the Dog and the Frog by ENG-High Level (#9)	139
Example 4.27	Referent Introduction of the Frog by KOR-High Level (#6)	140
Example 4.28	Use of NP+*ni/kara* in the T/T by ENG-High Level (#9)	142
Example 4.29	Successful Construction of Passive Structure by KOR-High Level (#1)	143
Example 4.30	Use of NP+*ni/kara* in the H/N by KOR-Mid Level (#10)	143
Example 4.31	Attempt of Passivisation of Verb in the H/N by KOR-High Level (#2)	144
Example 4.32	Attempt of Passivisation of Verb in the T/T by KOR-High Level (#5)	145
Example 4.33	Opting Out to Use Passive Structures by KOR-Mid Level (#3)	145
Example 4.34	Bees as Patients in the Passive Construction by ENG-Mid Level (#6)	151
Example 4.35	Passivisation to Modify the Snowman by KOR-Mid Level (#2)	152
Example 4.36	Episode of Particle Drop by KOR-High Level (#3)	156
Example 4.37	Use of '*ne*' in Japanese	156
Example 4.38	Episode of Particle Drop by ENG-Mid Level (#7)	157
Example 4.39	Use of Zero Anaphora in Topic Switch in the H/N by KOR-Mid Level (#1)	165
Example 4.40	Particle Drop in the T/T by KOR-High Level (#7)	167
Example 4.41	Particle Drop in the T/T by KOR-High Level (#3)	167

Chapter 1

Introduction

1.1 Introduction

It is evident not only to linguists but also to lay people that language learning must involve complex processes and that understanding such processes is not an easy task. Language acquisition has been studied by many different groups of linguists from many different perspectives throughout the years. One of the many factors that have been argued to influence language acquisition processes is cross-linguistic influence (hereafter CLI). CLI, also known as language transfer, denotes the influence of the source language (i.e., learners' first language (hereafter L1) in learning a target language (i.e., second language (hereafter L2)). CLI is not limited to unilateral investigation from L1 to L2; some researchers study how learners' L2 influence their L1, or how learners' L2 influence their L3 learning and so on. In this book, however, I will examine the role L1 plays in the acquisition of Japanese as a second language (hereafter JSL). The investigation focuses not only on grammatical features but also on discoursal factors, specifically how learners manage to achieve coherence in L2 narratives, by exploring how referents are being introduced and maintained as topics in L2 Japanese oral narrative discourse.

Anecdotally, language teachers who have had students with a variety of L1 backgrounds must have noticed that some learners are good at certain things, be it pronunciation of some sounds or conjugation of certain verbs, while others have persistent problems in the same areas of language. Of course, this could well be due to individual differences in learning styles. However, when certain consistent non-target patterns (e.g., a particular foreign "accent") are shared by learners from one L1 background, but not by those from another background, then it is possible that CLI is playing a part.

In order to investigate CLI and understand more of its effects in second language acquisition (hereafter SLA), researchers such as Selinker (1969) compared data of learners' L1 and learner language (this will later be called 'interlanguage' by him) as well as their L2. While comparison of L1, interlanguage and L2 will help detect possible negative and positive transfer, Jarvis (2000) further argues the importance of locating the following factors in order to confirm CLI:

1) Similarities in the interlanguage performance of learners sharing the same L1 background;
2) Differences in the interlanguage performance of learners from different L1 backgrounds; and
3) Similarities between the L1 and interlanguage performance of learners of the same L1 background.

In addition to determining the extent to which these three elements are attributable to CLI in the learners' acquisition process of L2, a careful comparison of the differences between the learners' L1 and the L2 is essential. Furthermore, in order to investigate the relationship between the learners' proficiency levels and CLI, comparing language production of different L1 speakers at multiple levels of proficiency would be necessary. In sum, the crucial conditions for testing CLI in SLA are as follows:

1) In order to test the general tendency of CLI, it would be ideal to compare the interlanguage of at least two groups of learners with different L1 backgrounds. To be more specific, the chosen languages would include languages that are typologically distant from and close to the L2 in order to detect the effect of possible interference, and also language learning facilitation, from the learners' L1.

2) In order to be able to distinguish developmental errors from errors caused by the learners' L1, a comparison of learners from different L1 backgrounds and at different proficiency levels is crucial. By examining learners of different L1 groups from different proficiency levels, we can obtain information about the differing patterns of language development and draw a correlation to the learners' L1. For instance, if the learners' L1 shares the same linguistic features

as the L2, we might expect them to exhibit more target-like performance at an earlier point in their language acquisition, as compared to those learners whose L1s do not have corresponding features in the L2. In contrast, if learners from both L1 backgrounds exhibit difficulty with certain aspects of the L2, this would suggest that similarities do not result in positive transfer in the production of a particular pattern; such a finding might lend support to possible universal factors affecting L2 learning.

3) In order to locate differences and similarities between the learners' L1 and interlanguage, analysis of the learners' L1 is necessary as is analysis of the native speaker (hereafter NS) production of the L2 to determine what the target-like presentations of certain linguistic features are.

Bearing this concept in mind, to compare the CLI from L1s that are distant from and close to Japanese, English and Korean were chosen for the present investigation. Korean and Japanese are considered to be "each other's closest sister language" and resemble each other grammatically, as well as culturally (Sohn, 1999: 11). In terms of the origin of the languages, according to Sohn (1999) and Shibatani (1990), many scholars support the hypothesis that Japanese and Korean belong to the Altaic language family. Though they both exhibit many Altaic features, researchers have not been able to provide conclusive evidence to establish the association between the two languages or their connection to the Altaic family of languages (Hattori [1959] cited in Shibatani [1990]).

While we are unable to show historical and genetic connections between the two languages, their typological similarities are noteworthy. In contrast to Korean, English does not share a historical connection, structural or orthographic similarity with Japanese.[1] For the purpose of this study, typological similarities between languages will be considered in order to determine language distance. A comparison of the features investigated among Japanese, English and Korean languages will be discussed in greater detail in sections 2.4.4, 2.4.6 and 2.4.7 in Chapter 2 of this book.

The Foreign Service Institute (1985) of the U.S. State Department has long provided rankings of languages in terms of their difficulty for English speakers to learn. This ranking is taken to reflect structural similarities between English and other languages. According to their guidelines, both Japanese and Korean are in Category IV, indicating that they are of the highest difficulty level for Americans (English speakers) to learn. This language distance between English and Japanese itself, measured by the amount of time required to reach certain proficiency levels, might imply a variety of typological differences between the two languages.

The Foreign Language Service Institute likely made this categorisation, at least in part, by assuming the influence of CLI. In other words, if a learner's L1 and L2 are close to each other, the required length of study of the language would presumably be shorter. Conversely, if a learner's L1 and L2 are distant from each other, it should take a longer period of time to learn the language. Herewith, the learners' demographic information with regard to the length of study required to reach certain proficiency levels was obtained in the current study to ascertain the relationship between the typological similarity/difference of the languages and the length of study required to reach certain proficiency levels. The mean length of study of Japanese was calculated for the two proficiency levels of both the Korean and English groups, and will be summarised in the methodology section (see Table 3.1 in Chapter 3).

In the past, many researchers were doubtful of the role L1 plays in SLA due to the extreme interpretation of language learning by the behaviourists. As is well known, this school of thought simply captured CLI as the focal point of the contrastive analysis hypothesis (CAH) and then started to lose its credibility as SLA researchers questioned the validity of CAH as the most important element involved in L2 language learning. Because many aspects of L2 learning could not be explained by CAH, the effect of L1 transfer in SLA was downplayed by some researchers in the 1970s and early 1980s (e.g., Dulay and Burt, 1974a; Krashen, 1981), claiming that most learner errors were of a developmental nature. However, since then, many scholars have rightfully re-evaluated the role of CLI and there is now substantial research that indicates its importance in better understanding SLA (e.g., Jarvis, 2000, 2008; Jarvis and Pavlenko, 2010; Kellerman, 1995; Odlin, 1989, 2003, 2005; Selinker, 1992).

In his invaluable review book of CLI, Odlin (1989) showed that the influence of CLI may vary in different areas of L2 acquisition. Back when Odlin's outlook on CLI came out, some aspects of language had been claimed to be more susceptible to CLI than others, phonology and phonetics being the key entities that were most dramatically affected. Dulay, Burt and Krashen (1982) argued that the acquisition of syntax and morphology is not susceptible to language transfer from L1. However, the questionable theoretical or empirical arguments used by critics rejecting L1 influence have caused doubts to be raised about the validity of their viewpoints (Odlin, 1989). The main assumption of these critics was that there are language universals that govern language acquisition and that CLI does not exist because universal developmental sequences account for all L2 developmental phenomena. This claim would be challenged if studies showed evidence of interaction between CLI and developmental prototypes in SLA. In other words, if differing patterns of development are found between groups of learners with different L1 backgrounds, then the strong version of the claim of universal developmental sequences can be discarded. In fact, more recently, some studies have provided evidence of L1 transfer even in the areas of acquisition where CLI was thought to be rather uncommon. Details of such studies will be discussed in Chapter 2.

With regard to types of language transfer, Ringbom (1987) observes that linguists have primarily focused on the differences between the learners' L1 and L2, and argues for the importance of investigating similarities as well (1987: 33). Kellerman (1995) articulates the importance of investigating both the similarities and differences between a learner's L1 and L2. He interprets Andersen's (1983) famous principle, *transfer to somewhere*, to help explain that CLI is mainly instigated by similarities (rather than differences) between L1 and L2, and shared features between the two languages will likely transfer in the learners' L2. From this standpoint, Kellerman also identifies the need for additional focus on learning difficulty caused by differences between L1 and L2. In support of this point, he cites a study by Thomas (1989), which demonstrated difficulty in the acquisition of article systems by learners whose L1 lacks such a system. This is particularly pertinent to the current study because the English article system represents a complex, discourse level phenomenon involving tracking of given and new information as well as speakers' assumptions about shared background knowledge, uniqueness of the referent, and so forth (Chafe, 1994).

While some evidence of both negative and positive transfer has been found, as Odlin (1989) suggests, we need to examine the interlanguage of learners with more than single-language backgrounds. Especially needed are studies comparing languages both typologically very close to and distant from a given L2. There have not been many empirical studies which have attempted to systematically study transfer effects on learners from typologically diverse languages. They include Jarvis (1998, 2002), Jarvis and Odlin (2000) and Ringbom (1987), who investigated the acquisition of English by Swedish speakers and Finnish speakers, and Polio (1995), who examined the acquisition of zero anaphora in Chinese by Japanese and English speakers, and Helms-Park (2001), who investigated the acquisition of verbal vocabulary in English causative constructions by speakers of Vietnamese and Hindi-Urdu. In the acquisition of L2 Japanese, some studies (e.g., Hanada, 1993; Kurihara and Nakahama, 2010; Nagatomo, 1991) have compared learners whose L1s are distant from and close to Japanese. However, these studies had methodological drawbacks such as small and/or unbalanced sample sizes, thus we cannot claim with certainty that they confirm CLI in SLA. The goal of the present study is to fill this void.

In addition, the role of proficiency level as a variable in CLI has not been clearly established in the literature, in that the results of CLI studies vary widely as to whether transfer increases, decreases, does not change, or alters with proficiency (Jarvis, 2000). As is sensibly recognised by CLI researchers such as Odlin (1990) and Kellerman (1995), the lack of evidence presented from CLI studies in some domains of language could be attributed to the inadequate choice of proficiency levels of the participants of the study. These researchers posit the possibility that earlier studies were not able to fully demonstrate the effect of CLI because they tended to look mainly at learners of a high proficiency level, and developmental tendencies at earlier interlanguage/developmental stages may have been missed. More recently, Jarvis and Pavlenko (2010) list several possible reasons that explain varying findings of the relationship between proficiency and CLI. Jarvis and Pavlenko maintain that differing definitions of proficiency levels among the studies might be one factor that explains the mixed results. The present study uses the standardised test for determining the learners' proficiency level and examines JSL learners at both intermediate and advanced proficiency levels in order to respond to these issues.

While there is evidence that interlanguage grammar tends to exhibit less influence from the L1, compared to other language subsystems, several studies have clearly shown certain consistent L1 patterns in the acquisition of morphology and sentential word order (e.g., Jarvis, 2002; Jarvis and Odlin, 2000; Master, 1987, 1997, 2002; Nakahama, 2003, 2009; Odlin, 1990; Orr, 1987). Some of these studies will be reviewed in detail in Chapter 2. CLI has also been recognised in the area of study that investigates beyond word and sentence levels, such as discourse level, and pragmatics. A well-studied field beyond sentential level is pragmatics, especially in regard to interlanguage speech acts. This extensive area of research has clearly shown the influence of CLI (see e.g., Takahashi, 2000; Kasper and Schmidt, 1996 for overview). Compared to the field of interlanguage pragmatics, an area that still needs to be explored further (for both positive and negative transfer) involves how form-function mapping is practised at the grammar-discourse interface in an extended discourse. Examining how speakers transfer the ways in which they refer to events in storytelling activities (which Jarvis and Pavlenko (2010) called 'framing transfer') is one sensible way to study form-function relationships. Only a handful of studies have shown that framing transfer has effects on speakers' written and/or spoken discourse by studying transfer in both positive and negative directions (see e.g., Jarvis, 2002; Kurihara and Nakahama, 2010; Nakahama, 2009; Polio, 1995). These studies listed above placed an emphasis on real language use, thus, they used relatively uncontrolled narrative elicitation measures. They investigated how speakers continue/discontinue topics within the course of spoken or written narratives in a single type of condition; the participants in Jarvis (2002) and Polio (1995) considered retelling of a silent film, whereas those in Nakahama (2009) and Kurihara and Nakahama (2010) employed a description of a series of pictures as a data elicitation measure. These studies will be discussed in Chapter 2.

Hanada (1993) and Nagatomo (1991) investigated L1 influence in acquiring Japanese particles such as *wa* and *ga* (a topic and a subject marker, respectively) by comparing learners whose L1s have great variance (i.e., English, Korean and Chinese). Their investigation was limited to the accuracy rate of these markers on a cloze test, resulting in providing scarce qualitative analysis. In other words, they did not offer insights on how learners develop form-function mapping skills in more communicative language situations. The majority of the investigations of L2 Japanese particles have used rather controlled tests which do not focus on discoursal factors. Exceptions were found in studies by Watanabe (2003, 2011) who delved into learner use of '*wa*' in an extended narrative discourse but did not compare learners from different L1 backgrounds.

In explaining why interlanguage grammar has high resistance to CLI in comparison with other linguistic subsystems, Odlin (1990) points out that metalinguistic awareness on grammar by L2 learners might make them consciously pay attention to the forms in question, and as a result negative transfer is avoided when producing such forms. The difference in modes (spoken vs. written) might trigger differing performances among learners, as the former would be spontaneous, whereas the latter is normally planned by the writers. Nakahama (2010) explains that her routine explicit teaching on the use of the articles in L2 English might have resulted in somewhat successful performances of L2 English referential forms in written narratives by her EFL learners. Further, Nakahama argues that the superior performance in referent making by her learners, than that was found in other previous discourse studies such as Chaudron and Parker (1990), could be explained by the difference in modes. The written mode allows the learners to monitor what they produced, thus grammatical accuracy might be ensured, whereas oral narratives do not have this advantage. Whatever the case may be, it would be sensible to design a study that examines CLI in grammar-discourse interface in such a way that learners would not consciously attend to grammar itself, in order to find out the learners' ability to perform in context.

My choice of ecological (rather than unauthentic) data elicitation measures stems from the view I ardently share with functional approaches to understanding SLA. This is because functional approaches value examinations of not only language forms but their functions within contexts. According to Tomlin (1990), functional linguistics, as a discipline, can be segregated into four major sectors. They are the Prag school of functional linguistics, European functionalists movement represented by Dik and his associates (Dik, 1987), systemic grammar (major contribution by Halliday, 1985), and Northern American functionalists (e.g., Givón, 1983; Klein, 1990; Tomlin, 1987, 1990) embarking upon functional approaches to describing how language is used in context. Regardless of the specific linguistic features functional linguists from different schools paid attention to, they are all keen on capturing and describing how linguistic knowledge is carried out within interactive discourse. In other words, their concern was in examining 'language use' in real context.

American functional linguists, Givón (1983) and Tomlin (1990), maintain that tracking of referents in discourse has been recognised as a key element of discourse-level language use. Agreeing with this view, the current study intends to describe developmental patterns in the management of referents (how referents are introduced and maintained as topics of discourse). Moreover, in investigating the developmental patterns of referential form markings, the study intends to demonstrate not only *what* forms were used by the learners but also *how* and *why* they were used. As a result, it reveals both the learners' use of the forms themselves, as well as how they perform form-function relationships in

L2 oral narratives.

Different languages employ different systems to manage referent in discourse. Typologically similar languages such as Korean and Japanese utilise similar grammatical options to mark topic continuity and discontinuity, while typologically distant English uses different types of marking systems to indicate such functions. For instance, both Korean and Japanese use postpositional markers after the noun phase (hereafter NP) to mark definiteness and indefiniteness of the referents. To be more specific, NP+ *ka/i* in Korean and NP+*ga* in Japanese are generally used to mark new referents, while known referents are normally referred to as NP+*(n)un* in Korean and NP+*wa* in Japanese (Hinds, 1983; Shibatani, 1990; Sohn, 1994, 1999).[2] English, on the other hand, uses preposed markers (indefinite and definite articles) to encode new and known referents (Givón, 1983; Chaudron and Parker, 1990). In Chapter 2, a functional account of how topic continuity is expressed will be discussed in depth, by means of Givón's (1983) topic continuity scale and iconicity principle. And then the management styles of noun referents in narrative discourse will be compared among Japanese, Korean and English.

As one of the influential functional linguists, Klein (1990) points out that many SLA studies tend to restrict their focus on examining the acquisition of certain grammatical features (e.g., pronouns, passives, past tense) which make an appearance in learner discourse without attending to the function of these linguistic elements. And exploring how discoursal factors play a role in the choice of the features that learners produce seems to have been overlooked. This is evidenced by the fact that some studies only utilise cloze tests, multiple-choice type questions, or grammatical judgment tasks, in which context plays a minor role. Toyama (2006) also identifies the difficulty of testing and uncovering how learners develop discoursal abilities, such as the acquisition of topic marking particle, '*wa*' in Japanese.

However, as both language teachers and researchers, we should keep in mind that knowing how to use linguistic forms in communicatively appropriate ways is essential to producing comprehensible discourse (Givón, 1983; Klein, 1986). Focusing on decontextualised grammatical features, such as syntax at the sentence level as measured in grammaticality judgment tests, does not fully allow us to observe the function of the forms used in learner discourse. In the current study, narratives were chosen for the base of investigating how speakers achieve the connectivity of storyline via tactfully managing referent introduction and tracking without being interrupted in any way by the interlocutors.

Narrative discourse can be elicited in many different ways. Robinson (2001, 2003) suggests that employing different complexity of tasks would have some bearing on learners' narrative performance in terms of complexity, accuracy, and fluency in their L2 English. Robinson (2001) showed various factors that affect task complexity and list +/- here-and-now condition as one of them. He argues that making references to entities which is in sight (here-and-now) is easier than narrating in the context of displaced time and space (there-and-then). Robinson (1995) compares learner narrative discourse under two different conditions. Here-and-now context (H/N, hereafter), and there and then context (T/T, hereafter). The H/N condition task requires the speaker's to tell a story while looking at pictures, whereas the T/T task entails the speaker to look at the pictures and retell the story afterwards, in the past tense. As noted above, the latter task is considered to be more complex than the former, as the speakers would need to code, store and search the content of the story while looking at the pictures as well as retelling the story under the T/T condition, and thus cognitively more challenging than the H/N setting.

L2 narrative studies that investigated CLI and the acquisition of noun referent forms have presented mixed results. Given that these previous studies have used various stimuli for eliciting data, be they silent film retelling (T/T condition type data elicitation) or describing consecutive pictures (H/N condition type data elicitation), a definite conclusion cannot be drawn pertaining to the development of appropriate marking of noun referents.

For this purpose, the current study compares narrative discourse data that were elicited via picture description (H/N condition) and a retelling of a silent film (T/T condition). It is hoped that adding this variable (i.e., task complexity) would enable us to better understand what learners of different L1 backgrounds are capable of at different proficiency levels, in terms of managing referents in an L2 narrative discourse. With the findings of the study, pedagogical suggestions can be made, as to what kinds of tasks can be given to what stages of language learners. More discussions on the use of the picture story book and the silent film, including each story plot, will be provided in Chapter 3.

The aim of the present study, therefore, is to find out how task complexity, learners' L1 and proficiency affect the ways in which L2 Japanese learners manage referent introduction and tracking in their oral narrative discourse. I will employ qualitative analysis to explicate any patterns found in quantitative findings.

In summary, this study proposes to fill several gaps in our knowledge of SLA in the following ways:

1) The study will investigate CLI in the context of grammar-discourse interface. Grammar (i.e., syntax and morphology) is the area of language where CLI is less obvious, as compared to other areas such as phonology and lexicon. This circumstance could possibly be caused by the observed trend that classroom learners tend to develop a high level of metalingual awareness of grammar (cf. Ellis, 1994; Odlin, 1990). Given this possibility, it would be useful to fashion a study which investigates CLI at the level of grammar in a context that ensures that learners would not be consciously paying attention to grammar exclusively. Therefore, an oral narrative task (whose purpose is to convey a message to the listener) was chosen as the data elicitation method.

2) To respond to Odlin's (1989) original critique that a full investigation of CLI requires data from learners with typologically distinct L1s, CLI was examined by considering subjects from two typologically different L1 backgrounds. Specifically, a comparison of languages that are both typologically very close to and distant from the L2 was chosen in order to investigate both positive and negative transfer. By examining a relatively understudied language (i.e., Japanese), it is hoped that the results will be compared to and replicated with other languages in order to enhance the understanding of the second language learning processes.

3) Methodological improvements over previous studies were attempted in the following ways.

a) Many of the previous discourse oriented studies employed either a silent film or picture story book to elicit data for investigating referential forms in extended oral discourse in various languages. Differing data elicitation methods create difficulties in comparing the results of relevant previous studies. Previous studies showed that the complexity of task influenced the constructions in L2 English narratives, such as language complexity, accuracy and fluency. The current study attempts to discover if the influence of task complexity holds true on the performance in L2 Japanese narratives, in terms of referent marking.

b) The current study will examine language production of learners at intermediate and high proficiency levels in order to meet the concern that previous CLI studies may have missed important evidence of transfer because of their tendency to study learner production at only high proficiency levels (see e.g., Odlin, 1990; Kellerman, 1995). Furthermore, learners' proficiency levels were determined using standardised test (the Simulated Oral Proficiency Interview hereafter SOPI), to respond to Jarvis and Pavlenko's (2010) suggestion that many CLI studies have employed non-standardised tests to determine learners' proficiency levels.

c) To accomplish methodological rigour, well-balanced participant numbers among groups were ensured, and appropriate statistical tests were applied depending on the nature of the data.

4) Lastly, since the study aims to understand the use of language and how it develops with levels of proficiency, as well as the influence of task complexity on learner discourse, it should prove valuable in furthering SLA research, not only in theoretical terms, but also with respect to finding benefits for teaching and learning.

The following three major research questions will be addressed in the study:

> What kinds of referential devices are used by NSs of Japanese, Korean and English for introducing and tracking referents in oral narratives?

> Are there any developmental patterns in acquiring referent marking strategies in L2 Japanese narratives? If so, does the pattern of learning differ between the Korean and English L1 speakers due to CLI?

> Does task complexity affect referent markings in oral narratives? Also, does task complexity affect L1 and L2 Japanese narrative formation differently?

I will provide the operationalisation of the terms that are of importance to the study.

1.2 Operationalisation of the terms

As is discussed in an overall review of the functional approaches to SLA by Tomlin (1990), operationalisation of the terms is a problematic issue since pragmatic notions are difficult to define. For instance, some researchers divided referents into two classes, new referents and known referents, in their investigation of referential forms (e.g., Chen, 1986; Clancy, 1980; Kondo, 2004; Polio, 1995; Yanagimachi, 1997, 2000), while others studied referential form use in several contextual settings such as new, known and current (e.g., Chaudron and Parker, 1990; Jarvis, 2002; Nakahama, 2003, 2009, 2010). I will attempt to adopt the appropriate contextual definitions for coding referent markings in order to evaluate the results of my study with comparable previous literature. In this regard, I will attempt to operationalise the following terms.

Cross-linguistic Influence:
In this study, "cross-linguistic influence" will be used mainly to refer to influence caused by the similarities and differences between the target language and the learners' already acquired language(s) (adopted from Odlin, 1989). While CLI can mean forward transfer (from L1 to L2), lateral transfer (from L2 to L3) and reverse transfer (from L2 to L1) (see Jarvis and Pavlenko, 2010 for detailed discussion), in the current study, CLI signifies forward transfer. CLI is mainly used here in preference to "transfer", as the term transfer is closely linked with behaviourist theories of L2 learning (i.e., CAH), and is commonly perceived as interference from the L1, rather than facilitation. To rectify this concern, Sharwood Smith and Kellerman (1986) suggests a theory-neutral term, "cross-linguistic influence", by which they claim more extensive phenomena of language learning processes such as avoidance, borrowing and interference can be studied. In this book, the term, CLI, is used to denote either negative or positive language transfer, and wherever appropriate, the terms 'positive transfer' and 'negative transfer' are used.

Language Distance:
Language distance is usually determined by the typological differences and similarities between two languages. For example, language distance is perceived as being close between Swedish and English whereas it is considered distant between Finnish and English. Swedish and English are both Germanic languages and they both employ prepositional markers to denote locational nouns, whereas Finnish, a Finno-Ugric language, uses post-positionals to mark the equivalent entity. Comparable typological similarities are found between Korean and Japanese and comparable differences are found between English and Japanese, in that Korean and Japanese both use post-positional markings for NPs, whereas English utilises pre-positional markings.

Some researchers (e.g., Kellerman, 1977) consider psycholinguistic distance (distance determined by what a learner thinks about the distance between L1 and L2) in addition to distance captured as linguistic phenomenon. Learners' psychotypology (i.e., differences or similarities of L1 and L2 viewed by the learners themselves) could operate as one of the factors that constrain transferability from L1. However, in the current study, distance refers to actual typological distance between the learners' L1 and L2. I intend to show language distance from Korean and English to Japanese by way of how long it took the learners in the current study to achieve the same proficiency level (The results will be shown in Chapter 3).

Referent Marking:
In order to compare the results of the current study with the findings of the relevant literature (e.g., Jarvis, 2002; Nakahama, 2003, 2009, 2010; Yanagimachi, 2000), referents in the study refer to entities that are considered to be animate characters, and therefore entities such as houses, trees and rivers are not included within this classification. In the story used to elicit narrative in H/N condition (i.e., storytelling while looking at the pictures), the main animate characters are a boy, his dog, his pet frog, and other peripheral animal characters that appear in the pictures. In T/T condition (i.e., silent film retelling task), on the other hand, the personified main characters are a bear, a rabbit, a sheep, and peripheral characters such as a personified snowman and a scarecrow.

This study concerns how a referent is introduced and maintained as the topic of discourse, and topical position is assumed to equate with subject position (see Chaudron and Parker, 1990). Referent marking is comprised of three parts: 1) referent introduction, 2) referent re-introduction, and 3) referent maintenance.

First, the manner in which new referents are introduced into the discourse will be examined and this is called referent introduction. The first time a referent is introduced obviously involves a change of referent and thus aspects of the least continuous referent marking system. Second, in order to understand how participants move in and out of topic position, topic discontinuity is examined by tracking the re-introduction of referents in the subject position; the re-promotion of a referent to subject position is labeled as re-introduction of referents (or topic switch). Lastly, continuous mention of referent in the topical position following their re-introduction will be coded and referred to as continuous mention of referent. These are considered to be the most continuous referents, as they remain the topic of discourse after repromotion to subject position (i.e., re-introduction). The precise definitions of the referent introduction, re-introduction of referents (topic switch) and the continuous mention of referent, with detailed examples are provided in Chapter 3, where coding of the data will be discussed.

Form-Function Relationships:
Simply put, form-function relationships refer to the ways in which a language user's morphological and syntactic choices are determined or shaped by the meaning, purpose and pragmatics of language. For instance, topicality of an entity in discourse is normally denoted by a post positional marker, *wa*, in Japanese. Thus, the function (topicality of the entity in discourse) is demonstrated by the use of the form (*wa*). Another example of form-function relationships can be found in the passive constructions. The structure could be motivated by the speaker's intent of demoting the agent to the non-topical position, while keeping the focus on the patient in the subject position (see Bamberg, 1994). In the study, the term, 'function,' specifically denotes an interface of 'grammatical function' and 'discoursal function.' This is because form-function analysis closely investigates the intent of the speaker's conceptualisation of a story by examining the grammatical features that are used to mark various grammatical functions such as topic (NP+*wa*) and agent (NP+*ni/kara*) in order to encode the role that the referent plays in oral narrative discourse. Discoursal function in this study signifies purposes served by the grammatical forms within the frame of a storytelling activity.

Proficiency Level:
In this study, proficiency levels are determined using the ACTFL guidelines (Byrnes et al., 1986). The testing instruments were the SOPI and the results were scored by the investigator who was a certified rater of SOPI and another SOPI rater to ensure the high reliability of the data. The students whose levels were tested to be intermediate-mid and intermediate-high were grouped into 'intermediate level', and those whose levels were tested to be advanced-low, -mid, and –high were grouped into 'advanced level' in the current study. Detailed procedures of test administration, scoring and inter-rater reliability will be discussed in Chapter 3.

Task Complexity:
Robinson (2001, 2003) claims that task complexity has connections with cognitive issues that influence the task doer's cognitive challenge and argues that there are two subcategories of task complexity: resource-directing and resource-depleting. Robinson claims +/- here-and-now condition is one of the factors that have bearings on task complexity within the domain of resource-directing category. Following the study by Robinson (1995) which tested task complexity effects on L2 narratives by varying +/- here-and-now condition, the current study attempts to examine how +/- here-and-now condition affects L2 Japanese referent markings. While Robinson used the same series of pictures for the learners to 1) describe while looking at them (+ here-and-now conditionthe, or the H/N condition) and to 2) retell the story from memory (- here-and-now condition, or the T/T condition), the current study used a silent film for retelling the story from memory (the T/T condition) and a series of pictures for telling the story while looking at them (the H/N condition). There was a slight concern that the differing story plots between the two stories might have some effects on L2 discourse. However, the study examines not only the L2 Japanese narratives but also L1 narratives of Japanese, English and Korean, therefore differing results between the two tasks that might be attributable to the above-mentioned concern would be identifiable by analysing both the NS and non-native speaker (hereafter NNS) data. Further, the two stories were not vastly different from each other in that they involved the same number of main characters and similar miscellaneous characters. The study hopes to show if and how task complexity affects accuracy and complexity of L2 Japanese narrative discourse, and this might clarify previous findings of referent markings in L2 Japanese.

1.3 Organisation of chapters

The remaining chapters will be organised as follows. Chapter 2 will review the literature on CLI in general, on narrative development in its relation to referent markings, on the theoretical models of functional approaches to language production, in particular the work of Givón (e.g., 1983, 1984, 1995), and the literature on referent markings in Japanese, Korean and English will be introduced. Lastly, studies that discuss task complexity and its effects on L2 narrative productions will be established. In reviewing the relevant literature, I will attempt to show that there is a gap in the current CLI studies, a void that I intend to fill by conducting the current study. Chapter 2 closes with the research questions as well as hypotheses that correspond to each research question.

In Chapter 3, I will discuss the empirical methodology of the study, which includes demographic information on the participants and research design. This chapter will also include the coding method and discussions on how the data will be analysed.

Chapter 4 will present the results both qualitatively and quantitatively. In order to identify CLI from the learners' L1, narrative productions by the NSs of Korean, English and Japanese will be presented and discussed prior to those by the learners of L2 Japanese.

Chapter 5 will discuss patterns in the Japanese L2 narratives that appear to be caused by CLI, as well as how task complexity can affect CLI and play a role in learner discourse. Subsequently, I will present a summary of findings in the conclusion section. Lastly, I will discuss the limitations of the study as well as its pedagogical implications in the second language classroom.

Notes

1 Japanese and Korean have different alphabets: hiragana/katakana and hangul, respectively. However, they both utilise Chinese orthography, albeit the frequency of use differ between the two languages.
2 *Ga* and *wa* are Japanese particles used for marking new information and old information, respectively. Detailed discussion of these forms will be provided in Chapter 2.

Chapter 2

Literature Reviews

Chapter 2 consists of literature reviews on CLI, narratives, L1 and L2 referent markings, as well as task effects on narrative production. First, the central theme of the current study, CLI, will be examined thoroughly with a review of research dating back to the heyday when the CAH was believed to provide a convincing explanation and viable remedy for problematic issues regarding L2 learning. The CAH will be criticised for its behaviourist notion of language learning as a simple stimulus-response mechanism, and more importantly, the current state of CLI within the field of SLA will be discussed.

After a concise explanation of why narrative was chosen as a bona fide device to study discourse, I will discuss the literature on the functional accounts of language acquisition, especially regarding form-function mapping in referent markings. I will first explain models of functional approaches applied to discourse, in particular the work of Givón (e.g., 1983, 1984, 1995). After reviewing the theoretical models, the succeeding section gives a review, with focus on studies of referent markings (referent introduction and tracking) in L1 and L2 Japanese, Korean, and English. The role passive forms play in portraying the speakers'/writers' perspectives in narratives will also be discussed. Finally, being guided by the unanswered issues in the relevant literature, I will present research questions and hypotheses which have been derived from these issues.

2.1 Cross-linguistic influence

This section will begin with a brief historical view of CLI, followed by a discussion of some problematic issues involving CLI. Then I will review some critical studies that demonstrate evidence of CLI in areas of language previously considered unlikely to show the effects of CLI. The notion of negative language transfer (or "interference") was initially formulated by Weinreich (1953).[3] He used the term 'interference' to refer to any case of transfer. The varying nature of CLI in bilingualism can be classified by the terms "borrowing transfer" or "substratum transfer" (cf. Thomason and Kaufman, 1988, cited in Odlin, 1989). Borrowing transfer refers to the interference of the L2 on a previously acquired language, while substratum transfer is what is currently known as the interference from L1 on the acquisition of an L2. Weinreich's (1953) research appeared to have provided enough empirical evidence to Lado (1957) to formulate the notion of the CAH. Weinreich (1953/1968) delineates how language distance influences in language learning as follows: "The greater the difference between systems, i.e., the more numerous the mutually exclusive forms and patterns in each, the greater is the learning problem and the potential area of interference." (Weinreich 1953/1968: 1) Simply put, the CAH claims that a learner will have difficulty learning features of L2 that are different from his/her L1, but will experience ease in learning those L2 elements that are similar to his / her L1.

The CAH has been criticised for its overly simplified notion of equating linguistic difference with linguistic difficulty, and the criticism was especially geared toward the behaviourists' viewpoint on language learning that was widely promoted at the time. Behaviourists believed that language learning was parallel to simple habit formation. Thus, in their view of language learning, in order to acquire an L2 successfully, learners must be carefully trained not to bring old/bad habits, i.e., the characteristics of their L1, into the new language system. As a practical application, in language classrooms during the heyday of the CAH, many language teachers used audio-lingual methods in which learners merely repeated what teachers said, as language learning was viewed as a habitually formulated stimuli-response sequence. In such language classes, the focus was on accurate pronunciation and grammar, and the learners would not have time to formulate their own hypothesis in their interlanguage grammar *per se*, as they were supposed to respond to teacher utterances as quickly as possible. Although not all the advocates of Contrastive Analysis had behaviourist views (see Weinreich, 1953, for further discussions), this seemingly invalid equation of language learning with the acquisition of new "habits" naturally cast doubt in the minds of generative grammarians and cognitive psychologists (Odlin, 1989, 2003).

One of the most controversial characteristics of the CAH concerns the fact that learners sometimes make errors that could not be predicted by the CAH in that the errors were not solely accountable by the L1. For instance, both Spanish and English share the copular verbs (*be* in English, *ser* and *ester* in Spanish). The CAH advocates would predict that Spanish speakers would not have difficulty learning English copular verbs, especially because L2 (English) has a coalesced form (*be*) for its L1 equivalent (*ser* and *ester*), as Stockwell, Bowen, and Martin (1965) found that learning difficulty would be lessened when L2 has a unified form for its L1 equivalent. However, as Peck (1978) later verified, sentences such as "That very simple", instead of "That's very simple", occur in the English of native Spanish speakers, which illustrates an example of copular verb omission not predicted by the CAH. This illustrates that L2 language learning processes involve more than a simple process which can be predicted by a mere comparison between the L1 and L2.

In fact, earlier criticisms of the CAH discussed the view that it only focuses on the structural analysis of learners' L1 and L2 and predicts what kinds of errors learners would make due to the different structures between two languages without paying attention to the actual learner language. In other words, it does not consider the importance of language learning processes. In an attempt to address some of the contradictory findings of various CAH studies that were caused by the predictive nature of the CAH, Wardhaugh (1970) classified the CAH into two types: strong and weak versions of the CAH. The former emphasises the prediction of errors based solely on a structural comparison of learners' L1 and L2 without paying careful attention to the actual errors learners produce, whereas the latter focuses on first identifying the learners' errors and then explaining them by ascertaining similarities and differences between the L1 and L2. By taking the latter approach, researchers would better be able to find the sources of L2 errors.

Although the notion of a weak version of the CAH ostensibly sounds reasonable, the deficiency of this approach was highlighted by Schachter (1974) who claimed that, if the analysis was done on the errors actually made by the learners, we might miss the avoidance strategies taken by the learners. In her investigation of the acquisition of English relative clauses, Schachter compared Chinese, Japanese, Arabic and Persian learners' written discourse. It was found that more errors with relative clauses were made by Arabic and Persian speakers than by their Chinese and Japanese counterparts. This result was surprising, as both Chinese and Japanese constitute left-branching languages (i.e., nouns are pre-modified), whereas Arabic and Persian constitute right-branching languages, just like English. A close investigation of the data revealed that this lower error rate by Japanese and Chinese can be explained by the fact that Japanese and Chinese speakers produced far fewer relative clauses than their Arabic and Persian counterparts and, as a result, fewer total errors were produced by the Japanese and Chinese learners of English. Schachter argues that solely relying on explanations of the errors could not help us to fully understand language learning processes. In fact, avoidance, as well as over-use of certain structures, could be the results of transfer as the learners might avoid certain features and overuse other forms that have similar forms in their L1s (Ellis, 1994). As this argument shows, CLI is a very complex phenomenon that intertwines with other internal factors of language learning. Thus, it is apparent that only studying structural comparisons of learners' L1s and L2s could not provide us with a complete explanation of language learning processes.

By the time Wardhaugh (1970) formulated the weaker version of the CAH, the hypothesis started to lose popularity and was beginning to be replaced by error analysis. Corder's (1967) classic article "Significance of Learner Errors" inspired many SLA researchers. Whereas errors were considered 'unwanted' as they were thought to be caused by "old habits" from learners' L1 in the framework of the CAH, they now came to be seen as very important elements in learners' language as they provide learners, teachers and researchers with the evidence leading to insights into language learning processes. However, detecting the sources of errors and thereby bringing these potential insights into the study of second language learning has turned out to be fairly challenging. Odlin (1989) has pointed out the general difficulty of identifying the sources of errors. He provides an example of the acquisition of the article system in English by Korean L1 speakers and Spanish L1 speakers. The omission of an article in English could be caused by negative transfer in the case of the Korean speakers, as the Korean language does not have article systems. It also could be attributable to simplification in the case of the Spanish speakers as a part of the developmental sequences they go through, since Spanish does utilise an article system (though there are slight differences in the articles systems between English and Spanish)[4]. Due to the fact that not only Korean speakers, whose

L1 has no article system, but also Spanish speakers, whose L1 has an article system comparable to that of English, had problems with article usage in the production of L2 English, thus indicating that the omission of an article in L2 English would not qualify as CLI (see Andersen, 1977). The confounding results concerning the omission of an article by the speakers of both L1 backgrounds could be explained by an interaction of transfer and simplification (see Jarvis and Odlin, 2000 for further discussion).

In fact, as represented in the above example of the omission of articles, one of the more problematic issues that SLA researchers face is the fact CLI is often difficult to ascribe, since errors deriving from L1 frequently correspond with learners' developmental errors (Ellis, 1985, 1994). The difficulty in distinguishing errors caused by a learners' L1 from developmental ones can be illustrated in the following studies. Dulay and Burt (1974a) claim that only 3% of learner errors are attributable to the learners' L1, whereas Tran-Chi-Chau (1975) showed a much higher ratio (51%) of interference errors. This variation could be triggered by the fact that it is, in fact, difficult to determine whether an error is caused by the learners' L1 or intralingual processes (Ellis, 1994). Furthermore, the standardisation of a coding system of the errors among studies is necessary to make a valid claim about CLI.

Another complexity that CLI presents is that the weight of the influence of CLI seemingly varies in different areas of L2 acquisition. Phonology, phonetics, and lexico-semantics have been the conventional areas of language that seem most straightforwardly explained by CLI. On the other hand, researchers (e.g., Dulay, Burt and Krashen, 1982) have argued that learners' L1 plays a minimal role in terms of the acquisition of grammar (especially morphology) and have maintained their position that intralingual learning processes are hardly affected by learners' L1. Specifically, Dulay, Burt and Krashen list a series of studies (e.g., Makino, 1979; Milon, 1974) to support their argument and report that in the area of syntax and morphology, only 4 to 12% of the errors are of interlingual type for children and 8 to 23% for adults. They strongly argue that phonology and phonetics are the only area of language that is significantly susceptible to L1 influence.

However, several studies have shown the substantial role L1 plays in L2 acquisition at all levels of language: phonology, lexio-semantics, morphology, syntax, discourse, and pragmatics (see e.g., the collection of CLI studies in Gass and Selinker, 1983; and the overview of CLI by Jarvis and Pavlenko, 2010 and

Odlin, 1989, 2001, 2003, 2006). Studies that are of relevance to the present study are by Hakuta (1978) and Koike (1983). Hakuta examined a developmental order of grammatical morphemes by a Japanese girl who moved to the United States with her parents at the age of five. Despite the contention of the universal developmental morpheme (accuracy) order made by many researchers, including Dulay and Burt (1974a), the results of Hakuta's longitudinal study reveal interesting phenomena which can only be explained by L1 transfer from Japanese. It was found that the Japanese girl displayed a differing acquisition order from the 'natural order' claimed by Dulay and Burt (1974b) in that she took a long time to acquire morphemes which involve number agreement and definiteness/indefiniteness, whereas she acquired the possessive quite easily. Hakuta argues that this result was possibly caused by L1 transfer from Japanese because there is no concept of plurality marking in Japanese, whereas possession is expressed postpositionally to the noun with a particle, *no*, in the same word order as is found in English. Therefore, it was hypothesised that a morpheme which represents an already familiar notion will be acquired prior to a morpheme which represents a new notion.

The same conclusion was reached by Koike (1983) who found that the acquisition of morphemes which concerned numbers and definiteness/indefiniteness was delayed in the production of three Japanese children (ages 5, 7, and 11) during a period of their residence in the U.S. These results provide support for CLI, as discussed above. Dulay, Burt and Krashen (1982) disregard the findings of Hakuta (1978) due to its small number of subjects. Dulay, Burt and Krashen, instead, value the results of the study by Makino (1979) which examined the acquisition order of morphemes by 777 secondary school students (ages 13-15) and revealed that the order was similar to that which was found in the study by Dulay and Burt (1974b). However, despite their small number of subjects, the same results by Hakuta (1978) and Koike (1983) do not seem to be coincidental, and merit further investigation. A study by Spada and Lightbown (1999) revealed L1 influence on the developmental readiness in the acquisition of English question sentence structures by francophone children (age 11–12 years). They found that with grammaticality judgment tests it could be demonstrated that the way in which participants judged grammaticality was influenced by their specific L1 grammar knowledge, regardless of the developmental stages the learners had attained in their L2. In particular, the students had a tendency to accept questions at a higher stage (subject and verb inversion) when the subjects were pronouns, but not when they were nouns. Spada and Lightbown claim this result demonstrates CLI because in French pronoun subjects can move to a position following auxiliary words, whereas noun subjects may not make such a movement. In fact, they state that this L1 French question formation rule, as a demonstrable example of CLI, has been observed in L2 English learning across many studies (e.g., Zobl, 1979, 1995 cited in Spada and Lightbown, 1999). Overall, the study by Spada and Lightbown contributed to our understanding of the complexities of L2 learning as it was able to quite conclusively show an interaction between CLI and developmental sequences.

Whereas the role CLI plays in L2 grammar acquisition has been debated, it is a well-established notion that interlanguage pragmatics bear clear evidence of CLI. Namely, how non-native speakers (NNSs) manifest their linguistic knowledge in their L2 (both comprehension and production) is influenced by their L1 pragmatic knowledge (Kasper, 1992). This so-called pragmatic transfer can be divided into two subcomponents: sociopragmatic transfer and pragmalinguistic transfer (Thomas, 1983). The former refers to L1 influence on the social perceptions of communicative action (see studies by Cohen and Olshtain, 1981; Kubota, 1996; Nakahama, 1999; Robinson, 1992 for investigation of sociopragmatic transfer). The latter refers to the transfer of L1 structures when mapping syntactic forms to social function (see studies by Faerch and Kasper, 1989; Olshtain and Cohen, 1989 for a deeper investigation of pragmalinguistic transfer).

As mentioned briefly in the introduction of the manuscript, there are numerous studies that investigated CLI in learner discourse in the form of pragmatic manifestation of language, such as speech acts. However, thorough investigations of CLI by comparing L1s that are distant from and similar to a given L2, through the dimension of grammar-discourse interface in an extended discourse, are still scarce. Nakahama's (2009) and Polio's (1995) investigation of referent markings in L2 Japanese and L2 Chinese narrative studies serve as exceptions. Details of these studies will be reviewed in the subsequent sections. As discussed above, in some areas of L2 acquisition, the impact of the L1 has not been as clearly visible. For instance, some studies which were carried out from a universalist perspective claim that structural constraints exist in word order transfer (Rutherford, 1983; Zobl, 1986). Though accepting the fact that word-order transfer plays some role in the acquisition of syntax, both scholars are skeptical about the notion of negative transfer of basic word order (Odlin, 1990). For instance, Rutherford (1983) claims that transfer of the SOV pattern of Japanese language never occurs in Japanese learners' acquisition of English. Zobl (1986) is basically in agreement with the argument made by Rutherford that learners might rely on their L1 "parameters," but not on the basic word order (SOV in this case). Zobl notes that the central property of word order appears not to be susceptible to CLI, though making an exception for languages that allow more than one basic word order such as Dutch (Zobl, 1986). Odlin (1990) challenges these strong claims made by Rutherford and Zobl by providing 11 counter examples showing basic word order transfer (e.g., SOV sentences in Hawaiian Pidgin English).[5] However, Odlin admits that evidence for basic word order transfer is still uncommon and provides the following possibilities to explain the relative dearth of prevailing evidence of CLI in word order: potential universal grammatical constraints; inadequate attention to lower proficiency level learners; and metalinguistic awareness, which makes learners consciously attend to such features so that negative transfer is avoided. Taking this last hypothesis further, it might be possible to argue that word order is more perceptible to learners than other areas of language. Being in accord with Odlin's point, Ellis (1994) argues that it is possible that learners might have developed a greater level of metalingual awareness of grammar as compared to phonology and discourse. Therefore, this awareness may help learners to have more control over linguistic choices in their L2 at the level of grammar than at other language levels.

With this point in mind, what may be needed is a study that investigates CLI at the level of grammar in a context that ensures that learners will not be consciously paying attention to grammar itself. If cloze testing or grammaticality judgment testing is provided to elicit learner language, learners might be conscious of grammar and thereby transfer might be inhibited according to the hypothesis formulated by Odlin (1990) and Ellis (1994). Thus, if this hypothesis is accurate, eliciting learners' oral speech production (such as via oral narrative) might lower the learners' explicit awareness of grammar rules, as the goal of the task is to convey a story to a listener in a communicatively appropriate way. Therefore, such an experimental elicitation method may allow evidence of L1 transfer to emerge which was previously masked due to the grammar awareness heightening qualities of previously used elicitation methods.

Odlin's (1990) argument about inadequate attention being paid to lower proficiency level learners was supported by Kellerman (1995). He states, "[Most] research does not focus on the very earliest stages, and it is possible that by the time researchers arrive on the spot, the bird [i.e., L1 grammatical influence] has flown the coop" (Kellerman, 1995, p. 136, referring to Odlin, 1990). There are, in fact, many studies that have investigated CLI in interlanguage of learners at a relatively higher level of proficiency (e.g., Rutherford, 1983; Schachter, 1974). Schachter (1974) conducted a study in which she only used advanced level students when she examined the use of relative clauses in written texts by L1 Japanese, Chinese, Arabic and Persian students of English as a second language (ESL). Rutherford (1983) on the other hand, classified his subjects into 'beginners' in his study; however, the task they performed was writing an essay, a task hardly suited for beginning level proficiency. Thus, as Odlin (1990) speculates, the proficiency measure itself is doubtful, and the level of the learners might have been more advanced than the researcher claimed, and therefore the CLI evidence cannot be claimed as being obtained from the novice level.

A second interesting aspect involving CLI and proficiency level is that certain aspects of L1 may influence the learners' interlanguage at different stages of development. Wode (1983) argues for the developmental constraints on CLI, claiming that certain types of negative transfer can only happen after learners have attained a specific proficiency level, which might explain why Schachter (1974) limited her investigation to advanced level learners. For instance, Wode (1978) found that German speaking children initially displayed the universal pattern of language development (L1 acquisition = L2 acquisition). However, when they recognised the shared grammatical rules for negation of the 'be verb' or an auxiliary verb between L1 and L2 (English), they overgeneralised the rules to the main verb, and as a result produced ungrammatical structures. Wode claims that his subjects assumed that English and German operate exactly the same way in terms of negation, and therefore applied the same rules to all negation structures.

There have been a set of studies which found that novice learners rely on L1 (e.g., Major, 1986; Ringbom, 1987; Taylor, 1975), while another set of studies has revealed that transfer also occurs in the performance of learners at very high proficient levels (e.g., Coppieters, 1987; Kellerman, 1983, Klein, 1986). Major (1986) found evidence of phonological transfer in the acquisition of Spanish *r* by four English speaking learners. In his longitudinal type study, he found that CLI which was observed at the very beginning of learning diminished over time and developmental processes increased, then decreased, revealing complex L2 learning processes, which is known as the Ontogeny Model. Taylor (1975) revealed interesting results on the topic of not only CLI, but also overgeneralisation in its relationship to learners' proficiency levels. He had 20 Spanish speaking learners of ESL at two levels (elementary and intermediate) translate 80 oral Spanish sentences into English in order to analyse their errors in the auxiliary and verb phrase. He categorised the error types into those of overgeneralisation, transfer, translation, and indeterminate origin. The findings reveled that error types varied with proficiency level; the learners at the elementary level relied on L1 significantly more than their intermediate level counterpart, whereas the intermediate level learners' reliance on overgeneralisation strategy was significantly higher than the elementary level learners.

In contrast to the above studies, Coppieters (1987) revealed CLI in the language of near-native speakers of French. All of his 21 subjects had been initially immersed in French at the age of 18 or older. Measured by the grammaticality judgment test, along with post-interview about their grammatical judgment, it was found that the near-natives barely diverged from their NS counterparts on some structures, but showed substantial divergence on others, such as tense and aspect contrasts, which seems to have been influenced by the learners' L1 (English).[6] Furthermore, Klein (1986) states that the possibility of CLI is enhanced when learners acquire more knowledge about an L2, which suggests an interaction between higher level proficiency and CLI.

The studies of interlanguage pragmatics also presented mixed results concerning the relationship between transfer and a learner's proficiency level in the L2. Some studies (e.g., Maeshiba et al., 1996; Robinson, 1992; Takahashi, 1984) showed that learners at a lower proficiency level were more likely to transfer their L1 pragmatic strategies, whereas other research (e.g., Blum-Kulka, 1982; Olshtain and Cohen, 1989; Takahashi and Beebe, 1987) demonstrated a positive correlation between L1 transfer and proficiency level, that is, more transfer occurred when the proficiency level was higher.

Evidently, the issue of CLI and proficiency level is far from simple. In the present study, I will attempt to clarify the relationship between proficiency level and CLI by including learners at a relatively early stage of language development, as well as at a more advanced level. Furthermore, by using learners from more than one L1 background, the study will attempt to show not only the relationship between CLI and L2 proficiency but also the differing developmental patterns that might be influenced by the learners' L1.

Despite the fact that some researchers have claimed that syntax and morphology are areas of language that are not susceptible to CLI (Dulay, Burt and Krashen, 1982), other researchers have conducted studies which have shown support for L1 transfer. For instance, Master (1987) investigated the acquisition of the English article system by speakers of five different native languages. The accuracy of article use by learners whose L1 had an article system (Spanish and German) was compared to the accuracy of those whose L1 did not (Japanese, Chinese and Russian). The analysis revealed that the acquisition of the English article system differed markedly between learners from L1s with an article system and those without, showing an influence from their L1 especially at the beginning levels of proficiency. Specifically, the study showed that the learners with no article system in their L1 achieved a 90% accuracy rate of article usage in English, at a later stage of linguistic development, in comparison with the learners with an article system in their L1. Besides Master's study, the common findings in the related literature were that the difficulty of the use of articles persists, though their correct use does increase with proficiency (see e.g., Butler, 2002; Liu and Gleason, 2007).

In investigating Finnish and Swedish L1 speakers' acquisition of English, Jarvis (2002) demonstrated clear examples of CLI in the learners' choice of the definite article and article drop. Jarvis examined the English article system in its relation to topic continuity in written narrative discourse, comparing learners who were K12 level students (5, 7 and 9 years old). CLI seemed to be at play in Swedish speakers' interlanguage in that they displayed very few instances of article drop in their L2 English just like their L1, and it appeared that those few cases of the use of article drop resulted from the speakers' deliberate use of simplified register. On the other hand, there is some resemblance between the Finnish speakers' L1 and interlanguage, in that they tended to 'avoid' redundancy in marking referents with definiteness and indefiniteness (*the* and *a* for English, respectively) for the NPs, which (they thought) were already salient in the discourse. Specifically speaking, Finnish speaking EFL learners produced many occurrences of article drop, exceeding 15% in all levels irrespective of contexts, the average use was over 30%.

In replicating Jarvis's study, Nakahama (2010) examined L2 English written narratives by adult Japanese speakers at three different proficiency levels. The study revealed that there were very few cases of article drop even in the lower level learners' marking of the main characters, which was not predicted based on the findings of Jarvis (2002). In interpreting the differing results between hers and Jarvis', Nakahama argues for her learners' conscious attention to the article usages and the difference in age group of the learners between the two studies. Nakahama states that her participants were regularly exposed to practise of article usage both in class and in homework assignments, in conjunction with communicative activities. The participants in Jarvis' study, on the other hand, were accustomed to exclusively communication based activities and did not explicitly receive grammar practice, including in regards to article usage (Jarvis, personal communication, April 19, 2010). Further, given their young age, the learners in Jarvis' study, might not monitor their grammar even in their writing exercises, such as the written narrative task that they performed.

Comparing Finnish and Swedish L1 speakers, Jarvis and Odlin (2000) also examined possible CLI of morphology by investigating the acquisition of English spatial reference. According to Jarvis and Odlin (2000), Finnish is a Finno-Ugric language and has a complex nominal case system, with case expressed via suffixes on nouns and adjectives. It also has approximately 15 nominal cases and inflections, but most of them are normally used as postpositions. Swedish, on the other hand, is a Germanic language and thus contains morphological systems which are similar to English. For instance, Swedish has an ample system of prepositions for signifying spatial, temporal, and other relations. Finnish expresses spatial reference via cases (postpositionally) attached to nouns/adjectives for most of those spatial and temporal relations expressed via prepositions in both Swedish and English. The results show that differences were found between Swedes and Finns in terms of locative and directional expressions in English, showing possible CLI effects in the acquisition of English spatial reference.

The following two examples exhibit cases of CLI. First, referring to a scene in which the main character was sitting on the grass, Finns preferred the use of "on", while Swedes preferred the use of "in," a usage that corresponded to their L1 counterpart. Second, omission (zero preposition) was found in the production of Finnish learners, whereas the Swedish learner group did not use zero preposition at all. Logically, it is possible to explain the Finnish learners' omission of spatial prepositions in English as simplification. However, the fact that the Swedish learners did not produce zero preposition suggests that the Finnish learners' omissions do not represent a common simplification strategy that L2 learners typically utilise. Thus, even if the Finnish learners "simplified" the prepositional phrase by omitting a preposition, it is possible that simplification could be caused by L1 transfer in that the learners had no equivalent L1 form to resort to, and ended up omitting the form. Therefore, as Jarvis and Odlin (2000) suggest, omissions of preposition by the Finnish learners can be caused by simplification, transfer, or an interaction between simplification and transfer. All in all, this research by Jarvis and Odlin is significant in at least two ways. First, they compared different L1 groups that shared similarities and differences with respect to the L2, thereby making investigation of both positive and negative transfer possible.[7] Second, they were able to show some possible cases of CLI in an area where transferability was questioned by some researchers.

Another study was conducted to investigate CLI in the acquisition of ESL by learners whose L1s share both similarities and differences in relation to the L2 (Helms-Park, 2001). She examined the acquisition of verbal lexicon in L2 English causative structures by Vietnamese speakers and Hindi-Urdu speakers. According to Helms-Park, Vietnamese and English share the following features in the making of the causative structures: 1) both languages have a reasonable amount of direct, stem-sharing causative types, and alternation to the causative structures does not involve morphological change. Further, these stem-sharing types of causative are susceptible to a number of semantic constraints. 2) They both allow a wide range of periphrastic causatives, including *make, cause*, etc. On the other hand, Hindi-Urdu differs greatly from English in that it has a variety of types of direct, stem-sharing causatives and morphological changes as well as semantic constraints. Hindi-Urdu also shares similarity with English as well, in that it has only a limited number of suppletive causatives, whereas Vietnamese has numerous instances.[8]

Specifically, while both English and Hindi-Urdu have direct causatives for forced motion, in English the construction is normally formed with a preposition phrase (PP). However, Hindi-Urdu allows translated versions of English causatives with or without PPs. This difference serves a very important point in the investigation of CLI in this study. It was hypothesised in the study that in terms of this class of verb, Hindi-Urdu speakers would accept not only grammatical but also ungrammatical sentences. In contrast, it was expected that Vietnamese speakers would reject both grammatical and ungrammatical structures due to differences between L1 and L2 structures.

The results of the study indicated that, in general, CLI played a major role in the selection of the verbal lexicon in causative structures of L2 English. To give an example of positive transfer, as predicted, for the verbs that express internal mechanisms, the Vietnamese speakers produced more periphrastic causatives than their Hindi-Urdu counterparts. The differences between the two groups were significant only at the elementary and intermediate levels, and this might suggest that negative transfer (from Hindi-Urdu) was at play at the lower proficiency levels, but that the more advanced speakers were able to overcome the influence of their L1 and produce more target-like causative forms, in terms of this class of verbs. More importantly, acceptance of ungrammatical structures caused by the close yet subtly different rules between L1 and L2 was evidenced with the class of forced motion verb. As predicted, Hindi-Urdu accepted many ungrammatical structures even at the advanced level and the differences among proficiency levels were not great. The performance of the Vietnamese speakers, on the other hand, improved with proficiency, using fewer overgeneralised direct causatives in the same class of verb. Helms-Park argues that the Vietnamese speakers had an advantage over the Hindi-Urdu in their capacity to restructure their interlanguage grammar because they lack direct causative structures to discard.

In sum, Helms-Park's study was able to show both negative and positive transfer in a complex manner by investigating different types of verbs produced by learners of two different L1 backgrounds at three different proficiency levels. In particular, the study shed light on the previous CLI literature, in that it demonstrated that CLI can play a role in getting rid of 'overgeneralised' rules in verb lexical selections as proficiency increases.

Besides the studies discussed above, several other studies on the acquisition of syntax and morphology in ESL have displayed strong evidence of CLI. Odlin (1989, 2001) discusses in detail the studies that reveal CLI in the acquisition of syntax such as word order and relativisation.

Some researchers of JSL have also considered the importance of CLI in SLA. Especially pertinent to the current study are the review article by Sakamoto (2000) and the studies by Nagatomo (1991) and Hanada (1993), which investigated the effects of positive transfer in terms of the acquisition of morpho-syntax (e.g., a topic suffixal marker in Japanese) as tested via cloze tests. These studies will be reviewed in the subsequent section, where the literature on topic maintenance is discussed. In summary, research has shown that CLI may play a role in the acquisition of syntax and morphology, areas of language where language transfer is traditionally claimed to have little effect. In this study, I propose to investigate syntactic and morphological CLI in SLA, but focusing particularly on the interface of grammar and discourse, instead of limiting the investigation to certain sentence-level features. Although the number of studies that explore conceptual aspects of CLI is gradually increasing, research in CLI still tends to focus on an investigation of core linguistic elements such as phonology and sentence-level syntax, overlooking its interface with discoursal factors (e.g., form-function relationships). This might be caused by the fact that not only the learners, but also L2 researchers, had somewhat low levels of awareness for language at the discourse level. In fact, implicitness of discourse awareness — as opposed to some obvious metalinguistic awareness such as word order as discussed above — makes language learning and teaching more difficult for both learners and teachers, respectively (Odlin, 1990).

With these issues in mind, I will follow the principle called "thinking for speaking" proposed by Slobin (Berman and Slobin, 1994; Slobin, 1991, 1993). This principle claims that language acts as a "filter" on the ways in which we talk about events. According to Berman and Slobin (1994), experiences are filtered into verbalisable events a) through choice of perspective and b) through the set of options available in the particular language. This "filtering" could play a very important role in learners' L2 acquisition[9], which might be manifested by the choice of grammaticised items such as voice, tense, focus and topicalisation, to name a few relevant aspects.

Some evidence of 'thinking for speaking' transferring from a speakers' L1 to L2 exists. For instance, studies by Ringbom (1987) and Jarvis (1998) showed conceptual transfer of semantics (phenomena observed by lexical choice) from the learners' L1 (Finnish and Swedish) in their acquisition of L2 English. Conceptual transfer is also visible in pragmatic aspects of language acquisition via speech act realisation; many studies have shown that learners' perspectives in their native language/culture influence their L2 language production in a variety of speech acts (e.g., see Cohen and Olshtain, 1981 and Faerch and Kaspter, 1989).

Although the results might not be as salient as in the studies of the acquisition of speech acts or lexical choice, I will attempt to investigate how the learners' conceptual organisation of relating events in their L1 might influence the linguistic coding of their L2 narrative production in the current CLI study. With this premise in mind, I will take an integrated approach focusing on the grammar-discourse interface in order to examine perspective and forms chosen by learners.

What follows is a discussion of narrative, attempting to show how it provides a useful context for an investigation of form-function relationships in language development. Then, I will review studies examining referential form use in SLA.

2.2 Narrative

2.2.1 Narrative as means of communication

Storytelling is an integral part of how humans construct their social world through verbal interaction. Narrative involves complex processes in which speakers use various resources to show continuity of such elements as discourse referents, temporality and location, across a span of text to convey information to the listener. Whether spoken, written, or signed, storytelling is a universal activity. But the ways in which stories are told, that is, how knowledge and experience are interpreted into telling, vary among cultures (Cortazzi and Jin, 1994; Riessman, 1993). In other words, as Slobin (Berman and Slobin, 1994; Slobin, 1991) puts it, experiences are "filtered" through choice of perspective and through the set of options available in a particular language (Berman and Slobin 1994: 9, 12).

As language teachers we frequently encounter a situation in which grammatical error is not the only cause for making learner discourse non-native like. In fact, it is not uncommon to find learner speech that is grammatically accurate but is still incoherent to a NS of the language (Tyler, 1995). Knowing how to use linguistic forms in communicatively appropriate ways (form-function relationships) will facilitate coherent oral production, and what Gumperz (1982, 1992) calls contextualisation cues play a major role in this form-function relationship. Investigating certain grammatical features in an isolated manner such as examining syntax on a sentence level measured in cloze tests would not allow us to discover L2 proficiency as a whole. Investigation of an extended discourse such as a narrative, which involves form-function relations, would enable us to examine how speakers manipulate their knowledge of grammar in context, and how they construct conceptual representations of the narrative structure in the L2, which might differ from their L1. In this research, therefore, I chose oral storytelling as the primary means for exploring the form-function relationship in terms of how a referent is introduced and maintained in learner discourse. Although I will be examining certain linguistic structures and how they operate in discourse, I follow the interpretation of "structure" by Odlin (1989) as a unity of form and function. He states, "… nothing is a structure unless it has both a form (some definite pattern) and a function (some definite use)" (p.31). In that sense, it is not only the form we will be investigating, but also how it functions as a whole.

2.2.2 Picture storytelling: *Frog, Where are You?*

Many of previous studies employed silent films to elicit data for investigating referential forms in oral narratives (e.g., Clancy, 1980 for L1 English; Jarvis, 1998 and Jarvis and Odlin, 2000 for L2 English; Clancy, 1980, 1985 for L1 Japanese; Nakahama, 2003 and Yanagimachi, 1997, 2000[10] for L2 Japanese; Chen, 1986 and Polio, 1995 for L2 Chinese; Kim, 1989 for L1 Korean). The use of silent films in this manner might present issues to resolve. In Nakahama (2003), when the participants did not discuss certain scenes, it was not possible to determine if the gap was caused by their linguistic limitations, memory problems, or their active decision to eliminate the particular scenes. Furthermore, due to the fact that the participants described some scenes while omitting others, it was not always possible to obtain consistent data across the participants. Therefore, use of a picture book was considered as one of the data elicitation devices in the present study, so that the participants can have the pictures constantly in view such that their memory capacity is not challenged. Consequently, consistent data is more likely to be obtained (see Berman and Slobin 1994 for more discussion on the use of picture storybooks in comparison with other elicitation devices).

Bamberg (1987) took a thorough approach utilizing bottom-up and top-down processing strategies to analyse L1 narrative development by German children and adults, using the picture book *Frog, Where Are You?*, by Mayer (1969). The bottom-up strategy entails an investigation of linguistic items, with the focus on their functions in the narrative. Top-down involves examining how the overall discourse is hierarchically sectioned into narrative units.

Comprehensive studies involving these bottom-up and top-down strategies are scarce, both in L1 and L2 narrative development investigations. Bamberg took a functionalist approach in his investigation of L1 narrative. While he examined specific linguistic features such as referential forms and tense marking (features which are considered important elements for achieving coherence), he investigated how the use of certain features was motivated. In order to investigate this form-function relationship in narrative discourse, Bamberg appropriately considered "contextualisation cues" discussed in Gumperz (1982, 1992). Bamberg argues that "...it (cohesion) addresses the relationship between the linguistic portrayal in terms of the formal devices at the textual level and the intended story at the conceptual level of uniting events into units, and those units in turn into the whole" (p.14). He further argues that without local level cohesion, global coherence of a whole string of utterances could not exist and that "the notions of coherence and cohesion are not mutually exclusive" (p.15). His study gives a detailed description about the governing motivations of how, why, and where certain grammatical features are used in L1 narrative discourse. In addition to Bamberg's (1987) study, the frog story was investigated cross-linguistically in several (L1) languages (see Berman and Slobin, 1994 for a collection of studies). As discussed earlier, in their investigation of L1 narrative development by children at various ages, Berman and Slobin view language production as the "filtering" of experience through language for purposes of speaking (Berman and Slobin, 1994: 9). They claim that experiences are "filtered" into language via choice of perspective and options available in a particular language. This theory can be supported by a number of pieces of evidence observed in the investigation of contrastive grammar (e.g., Hawkins, 1985), contrastive rhetoric (Bar-Lev, 1986; Kaplan, 1966), and contrastive discourse analysis (e.g., Tannen, 1980).

Besides "filtering", Berman and Slobin maintain two other themes in their investigation of narrative development. They are: a) packaging and b) cognitive and psycholinguistic constraints in children's language. By the former, Berman and Slobin purport that in a coherent narrative, events must be packaged into hierarchical constructions, rather than simply as a linear chain of successive events (1994: 13). By the latter, they claim that younger children have fewer options to express their concepts cognitively, communicatively (since they cannot fully evaluate a listener's perspective), and linguistically. Although adult L2 learners would be fully developed cognitively, they too have communicative and linguistic constraints, especially at their early stages of language development. Thus, taking these perspectives into consideration in the examination of L2 narrative discourse would be highly useful.

Like Bamberg (1987), Nakamura (1993) and Nakahama (2009) examined the development of referential structure, using the frog story. Nakamura's investigation was of L1 Japanese (children of various age group ranging from 3 to 9, as well as adults), while Nakahama's was of L2 Japanese by adult learners. The focus of both studies was placed on the analysis of the use of the postpositional markers and zero anaphora. It was found that as children grow older (in Nakamura's study) and learners' proficiency levels increased (in Nakahama's study), they are able to map the appropriate linguistic forms with the appropriate contexts. These results coincide with one of the findings in Nakahama (2003) in her examinations of L2 referential forms in Japanese, using a silent film as a measure of narrative data elicitation. In Nakamura's study, while *ga* dominates the form of an introduction of referents in adults, the youngest children group (age 3) showed varied results. They mainly dropped postpositional markers (54% of all cases), possibly indicating they were not capable of distinguishing the property of postposition marking yet. Particle drop was also found in Nakahama (2003, 2009) by the speakers whose L1 did not have postpositional marking systems. However, older children (especially the 7 and 9 year old group) in Nakamura's study were able to use *ga* as a marker to introduce new referents in the narrative, and the increase in the use of *ga* was also evidenced in Nakahama (2003, 2009). Surprisingly, young children seem to prefer *ga* to *wa*, and until the age 5, *wa* hardly appeared at all in their discourse. This contradicts the findings relating to *wa* and *ga* found in Clancy (1985) for L1 Japanese, as well as for JSL, in that the acquisition order for adult L2 learners seems to be in the opposite order (see e.g., Doi and Yoshioka, 1990; Nakahama, 2003, 2009; Sakamoto, 1993; Yoshioka, 2005). The results of these studies will be discussed in a later section.

The production of zero anaphora by children in all age groups in Nakamura's study, on the other hand, resembled that of the adult native speakers for referring to highly continuous topics. This finding was supported by Kajiwara and Minami's (2008) study which revealed that children from six to 12 years old preferred to use zero anaphora instead of full NPs. However, the result disagrees with the findings of the acquisition of zero anaphora for third-person pronouns by low proficient L2 learners of Japanese (Nakahama, 2003;

Yanagimachi, 1997, 2000; Yoshioka, 2005). Thus it is quite possible that the rate and route of the acquisition of referential forms are different for children and adult L2 learners. In this study, I will use the picture storybook, *Frog, Where Are You?* and a short segment of the film *Winter Carousel* (see Chapter 3 for a description of the study). The film is compiled, along with other films, on the DVD entitled *The Cameraman's Revenge and Other Fantastic Tales* (Starewicz, 1934). The former elicitation means will facilitate a comparison of the results of the current study with those of Nakamura (1993), Nakahama (2009) and Yoshioka (2005), which investigated the acquisition of L1 and L2 referential form markings in Japanese. The latter elicitation measures will help us understand the effects of task complexity on L2 narrative structures.

The following is a summary of related studies that investigated the management of referential forms in different languages.

2.3 Functional approaches to understanding language use

Functional approaches to the study of language (both L1 and L2) are concerned with language use in context. Therefore, they place their emphasis on discoursal (contextual) motivations for the emergence of linguistic features, rather than merely studying the constructions of language in an isolated manner. In other words, functional approaches attempt to address the interactions between form and function in on-going discourse.

Functional linguists address forms as they relate to meaning-making in discourse. For instance, as Tomlin (1990) discusses, active and passive structures differ not only in their syntactic organisation but also in the discourse-level function that each structure fulfills. Generally speaking, passive structures are used in order to keep a particular discourse entity in focus and concomitantly to place other entities in the background. Tomlin further points out that a functional framework has to focus on the explication of linguistic patterns found in discourse interaction.

Like other functional linguists (e.g., Klein, 1986; Tomlin, 1990), Givón (1979) perceives syntax and morphology as being intertwined with discourse. One of his most important proposals (Givón, 1984) involves the "quantity universal" which states that "more continuous, predictable, non-disruptive topics will be marked by less marking material; while less continuous, unpredictable/surprising, or disruptive topics will be marked by more marking material"

(1984:126). In other words, if an entity remains in topic position, it receives little overt linguistic marking; in contrast, when a new entity is placed in topic position, it receives more overt linguistic marking. Applying a functional analysis to developmental issues, Givón (1995) makes a distinction between two types of language, pre-grammatical mode (which he also referred to as pragmatic mode in Givón (1979) and grammatical mode (also referred to as syntactic mode earlier). Givón (1995) argues that acquisition is characterised as a gradual development from pre-grammatical to grammatical mode, via a process of syntacticisation. In terms of syntax, he refers to simple/conjoined constructions as pre-grammatical, whereas he refers to complex/embedded constructions as grammatical. With regard to morphology, lack of morphology (and even obligatory morphology) is typical of the pre-grammatical mode, while abundant use of morphology is found in the grammatical mode. As far as functional properties are concerned, Givón claims that the pre-grammatical mode's rate of delivery is slow and requires more mental effort and contextual support, in opposition to the grammatical mode in which speakers process discourse effortlessly and without requiring heavy dependence on context. The final point is of particular interest to functionalism in language, as more advanced language speakers are able to use an abundance of strategies, be it more complex syntaxisation or contextualisation cues (see Gumperz, 1982), whereas less proficient speakers might appreciate contextual support such as visual aids to supplement their lack of language ability. Besides many investigations made by L1 researchers who used Givón's (1979) model (e.g., Traugott and Heine eds. 1991), several SLA researchers have found evidence for Givón's discourse processing model (i.e., a gradual move from pre-grammatical to grammatical mode) in L2 learning (e.g., Sato, 1988; Schumann, 1987).

Despite the fact that this comprehensive approach to understanding language use offers us the possibility of more precise information as to how learners manage to map form and function in their discourse, this type of approach is not without its problems. Several researchers (e.g., Chaudron and Parker, 1990; Tomlin, 1990) recognised that tracking referents plays a very important role in creating a coherent discourse and have explored the quantity universal further in their investigation of referent markings in L2 discourse. However, these studies have produced somewhat limited results in that, due to their emphasis on quantitative exploration, they might overlook important patterns in the appearance of some forms under investigation. In addition, since the functional approach is description-based, research based on this approach can be susceptible to empirical weaknesses (Tomlin, 1990). Furthermore, as is pointed out by Polio (1995), most related discourse studies present their findings only with descriptive statistics, such as means and percentages (e.g., Chaudron and Parker, 1990; Jin, 1994, Nakahama, 2003; Yanagimachi, 1997, 2000). The present study specifically attempts to increase the validity of the research findings through a careful research methodology with appropriate choices of statistical tests, together with a sufficient sample size, rigourous rating of subjects' proficiency levels, and detailed qualitative analysis for explicating the distributional factors of the findings.

2.4 Referent markings

2.4.1 Topic continuity

Describing human discourse as multi-propositional, Givón (1983) evaluates the importance of analysing language beyond the clause level. He called this larger discourse unit the "thematic paragraph" and maintains that it enables one to explore a complicated process of discourse continuity. Within the thematic paragraph, how a topic is continued or discontinued plays a key role in creating a coherent discourse. In order to code topic continuity and discontinuity, Givón (1983) formulated the cross-linguistic topic continuity scale. While the original scale (Givón, 1978, 1979) involved complex grammatical devices such as R-dislocation and Y-movement, he also provided a simplified version, which he called the "subscale." Following the subscale, the most continuous topics should be marked with a zero anaphora, followed by unstressed/bound pronouns ("agreement"), then stressed/independent pronouns. The most discontinuous topics should be marked with the NPs. Of course, this continuity model needs to be modified in order to meet specific language requirements. In some languages topic-marking morphology plays a key role in the grammatical coding of topic continuations/discontinuations. For instance, Korean (Hwang, 1983) and Japanese (Hinds, 1983, Shibatani, 1990) use suffixal markings to code continuity/discontinuity of the topic. Detailed explications of the suffixal markings and topic continuity will be discussed later. The information status of the topic NPs is usually divided into three types. For instance, Chaudron and Parker (1990) discussed three different discourse types, distinguished by the way that the topic NPs are realised in the speaker/hearer's mind. When the referent is mentioned for the first time, its status is coded as "new". Once the referent is known to the speaker/hearer, then it is considered a "known" topic. Finally, when the known referent reemerges to become the current topic, it is realised as the "current" topic.

Different terminologies were used by different researchers. Chafe (1987, 1994), for example, used "notion of activation state" to correspond to the notion of new-old information level. He identified what Chaudron and Parker called new, known and current as new, accessible and given, correspondingly. In his interpretation, when a speaker introduces an unknown referent to the listener, the newly introduced referent would be inactive in the listener's consciousness. However once introduced into discourse, the referent can be accessible since it is already in the speaker/listeners' consciousness semiactively. Additionally, referents may be accessible through activation of appropriate schemata. If the referent continues to be the centre of the focus/topic of discourse, its status becomes "given" since it is actively in the consciousness of the speaker/listener. Although different manifestations of the idea resulted in the different terminologies, the gist of the concept is generally the same across the literature.

Following up on Givón's topic continuity scale, as well as the quantity universal mentioned above, Chaudron and Parker (1990) state that introducing a new topic into a discourse requires more information in order for the listener to establish the identity of the referent, whereas referring to a current topic requires less information such as zero anaphora or unstressed pronouns (whichever is available in the particular language). Chaudron and Parker are not the only researchers who took on investigating the acquisition of referential forms. Givón's analysis of topic continuity, in conjunction with a typological investigation of subject and topic (Li and Thompson, 1976), inspired many other researchers to delve into this subject further in crosslinguistic studies (see e.g., Bamberg, 1987; Clancy, 1980, 1992; Fuller and Gundel, 1987; Hinds, 1983, 1984; Huebner, 1983; Jin, 1994; and Polio, 1995).

2.4.2 Perspectives and voice alternation

Choice of perspective also plays a role in determining what kind of grammatical devices one chooses in marking a referent (Berman and Slobin, 1994). For instance, in their cross-linguistic investigation of a narrative across several languages, Berman and Slobin point out that the differing perspectives would produce different types of structures. They relate perspectives with the notion of foregrounding/backgrounding, topic/focus and such. Specifically, Bamberg (1994) maintains that the passive structure is used to keep a main character in a foregrounded and topical position to make ones' narrative discourse fluent. In his German L1 narrative analysis, he found that voice alternation has an association with topic continuity in the discourse in that the speakers tactfully switch between active and passive voices in order to maintain the topicality of the main character. Similarly, but from a slightly different perspective, Cooreman (1983) states in her investigation of an L1 Chamorro narrative that the patient in the passive voice structure has a higher topical role than the object in the active voice structure. In fact, the agent serves the extreme non-topical role in the passive construction. This can be explained by the theory proposed by Shotter (1989) who states that language provides a variety of devices to position agents in discourse. As one of the examples to sustain his claim, he gives an example of the use of passive voice. The agent is de-emphasised in the passive construction, and the speakers are not merely stating the same thing by alternating active and passive voices; language represents how the speakers view the events in the discourse. In his analysis of L1 Japanese, Shibatani (1985) also maintains that the agent gets "demoted" or "suppressed" in the passive structure. This speculation seems to be upheld in L2 oral narrative studies by Nakahama (2003) and Yanagimachi (1997, 2000). They both found that the use of the passive structure served to demote the agent or continue the topicality of the patient.

In Yanagimachi's (2000) study, some NSs used the passive construction for "viewpoint fixation" (p. 122) purposes. He states that the speakers adhered to limited characters (main characters) fixing their viewpoints on them, rather than going back and forth to focus on different referents in the story. In other words, these NSs in his study attempted to maintain topic continuity by demoting the agent to the oblique case. Interestingly such an attempt was not found in his learner data, including even the advanced proficiency level. Nakahama's (2003) study resulted in findings similar to those found in Yanagimachi's NS data. Some NSs and a few advanced level learners in Nakahama's study produced passive constructions. This was expected since the acquisition of passivisation is observed late in the developmental phase (Pienemann, 1998). More interestingly, a qualitative analysis of Nakahama's study also revealed that the motivation seems to be derived from the same basis found in Yanagimachi. In Nakahama, those speakers who used passive structures kept their focus on the main protagonist throughout the story by maintaining him in the subject position and introducing the antagonists with the "by phrase" in Japanese ("NP+*ni*"). Thus voice alternation seems to involve narrative formation on the conceptual level from the perspective of topic maintenance, and warrants further investigation in understanding the development of coherent narratives in terms of how referents are introduced and tracked in the discourse.

Incomprehensibility of L2 Japanese discourse has often been linked to an incompatible way of viewpoint setting by the learners (e.g., Kim, 2001; Kurihara and Nakahama, 2010; Nakahama and Kurihara, 2007; Tashiro, 1995; Watanabe, 1996). Comparing Japanese and Korean NS discourse, Kim (2001) and Jung (2002) revealed the differing ways in which events are interpreted and introduced into language by the choice of voice and focus in the two languages. Just as was found in Nakahama (2003, 2009) and Yanagimachi (1997, 2000), the researchers maintain that Japanese speakers tend to focus their perspectives on limited key referents by repeatedly placing them in the subject position, and consequently many instances of passive construction are produced. Korean speakers, on the other hand, tend to focus on the actions rather than the characters. As a result, more active structures than passive ones are found, and the variability of the subjects is higher in Korean discourse.

The different manners of setting perspectives are not unique between Japanese and Korean. The ways in which viewpoint is set in story formation varies among languages. Japanese is considered to be a so-called 'position centred' language, in that Japanese speakers tend to determine their perspective when telling a story and narrate from the viewpoint of the main characters throughout the retelling. English speakers, on the other hand, focus more on fact, rather than setting their viewpoint on certain characters (see Mizutani (1985) for further discussion on 'position centred' versus 'fact centred'). In other words, English speakers view the story from a neutral perspective and relate the events accordingly. As was shown in Kim (2001) and Jung (2002) above, Koreans seems to take a similar stance to English in terms of viewpoint setting in storytelling. This major difference between Japanese and English/Korean by itself would cause learners of Japanese some difficulties in narrating a story in a comprehensible manner in their L2.

Chinese seems to be a member of the 'fact centred' language group given the findings of the previous studies. Studies have shown that narrative discourse produced by Chinese learners focuses on many characters, thus making their L2 Japanese narrative rather unnatural and difficult to comprehend (e.g., Kurihara and Nakahama, 2010; Tashiro, 1995; Watanabe, 1996). Though the Korean speakers' L2 Japanese oral production was closer to the Japanese NSs compared to the Chinese speakers in the above mentioned studies, there were still frequent subject shifts among referents in the L2 Japanese discourse produced by the Koreans. For instance, Kurihara and Nakahama (2010) investigated the viewpoint shifts in written narratives by Japanese NSs and advanced level Chinese and Korean learners of Japanese. Viewpoint was measured by voice alternation, giving/receiving-related expressions, motion verbs, self expressions, sub-emotive expressions and emotive expressions. The researchers revealed that while the Korean learners of Japanese displayed a similar pattern to the Japanese NSs in that they fixed their viewpoint on one major character at a time. However, a considerable difference existed between the Japanese and Korean speakers in that the Koreans tended to shift the viewpoint between two major characters within the same episode. The Japanese NSs' viewpoint shift occurred when an episode moved from one to the next. There were only two cases of viewpoint shifts within the same episode by the Japanese NSs, and in both cases, the writer inserted 'direct speech' by one of the major characters before he/she shifted the viewpoint. This technique made their narrative flow better than it would have otherwise.

Aramaki (2003) investigated Chinese, Korean, and English speakers' perceptional knowledge and performance of auxiliary verbs of giving/receiving in L2 Japanese, which are considered to signify the speakers' viewpoints in the same way as passive expressions do. She found that there was no correlation between the participants' grammatical knowledge and the actual use of the giving/receiving auxiliary verbs; indicating that having the grammatical knowledge by itself does not guarantee the production of contextually appropriate giving/receiving auxiliary verbs. These results suggest the difficulty in acquiring not only the forms but also the functions, and as the author rightly argues, how to use the form in contextually appropriate manner (i.e., form-function mapping) needs to be introduced to learners. Aramaki's study gives a pedagogical directive for incorporating activities that promote grammar-discourse interface as well as consciousness-raising of the learner awareness of proper grammaticalisation of concepts that is appropriate in the target language.

As was discussed above, differing perspective alignments between Japanese and English/Korean are expected, which might be displayed via the use of passive structures in L1 narratives. Therefore, possible negative transfer of this L1 perspective of storytelling from English and Korean will be examined in terms of the use and non-use of passive structures in their L2 Japanese narrative discourse.

2.4.3 Acquisition of referential forms

Numerous studies have investigated the acquisition of referential forms in ESL (e.g., Chaudron and Parker, 1990; Butler, 2002; Fuller and Gundel, 1987; Gundel and Tarone, 1983; Huebner, 1983; Jarvis, 2002; Kumpf, 1992; Liu and Gleason, 2002; Williams, 1988, 1989). Besides English, studies of L2 French (e.g., Fakhri, 1989; Gundel and Tarone, 1983; Hendriks, 2000), L2 Chinese (e.g., Jin, 1994; Polio, 1995) and L2 Japanese (e.g., Nakahama, 2003, 2009; Yanagimachi, 1997, 2000; Yoshioka, 2005) have been reported.

Some investigations (e.g., Fuller and Gundel, 1987; Gundel and Tarone, 1983; Jin, 1994; Kumpf, 1992) were carried out to find out whether one's L1 has an effect on the acquisition of referential forms by studying learners of different L1 backgrounds, taking into account topic/subject prominent typologies. The results of these studies were confounding. For instance, in their investigation of referential forms in ESL, Gundel and Tarone (1983) and Kumpf (1992) found that the learners whose L1 was topic-prominent (Chinese in the Gundel and Tarone study, and Japanese in the Kumpf study) produced more full NPs than the learners whose L1 was subject-prominent (Spanish in both studies). In the same study, Gundel and Tarone (1983) also examined referential forms in L2 French by English speakers and found frequent use of zero anaphora in the direct object position by L2 French speakers. The researchers found this result rather surprising since overproduction of zero anaphora by those learners whose L1s were topic prominent languages was expected, as zero anaphora is one of the typical features of a topic-prominent language. In Gundel and Tarone's study, it was expected that Chinese speakers would produce errors in their English L2 omitting object pronouns due to negative transfer, whereas their Spanish speaking counterparts would not, as object pronouns are obligatory, just like English. Despite their prediction on the basis of transfer from L1 to L2, the results were quite the opposite, in that the Spanish learners of English made more errors in the omission of object pronouns than their Chinese counterparts.[11]

These studies failed to show CLI in the use of one topic-prominent feature (i.e., zero anaphora) in L2 development, however, other studies (e.g., Huebner, 1983; Rutherford 1983) claim that learners transfer topic prominence features from their L1 to L2 (English). However, seeing comparable performances of zero anaphora among the learners whose L1s are topic-prominent and subject-prominent, Fuller and Gundel (1987) claim that the appearance of zero anaphora can be described as an early universal topic prominent stage. This latter position cannot be conclusively accepted, since Fuller and Gundel (1987) only investigated English language acquisition, and unless the acquisition of topic prominent languages by learners of subject prominent languages is also studied, a strong claim cannot be established.

This weakness in the claim motivated Jin's (1994) research examining the acquisition of a topic prominent language by learners of a subject prominent language. The main purpose of his study was to investigate whether the appearance of topic prominence is a part of the universal developmental stage or is attributable to transferable typology. Forty-six NSs of English learning Chinese at four different proficiency levels were the participants in his study. The results showed that there was no universal topic prominent stage. In fact, subject prominence in the learners' L1 transferred to Chinese interlanguage and the emergence of subject prominence decreased as proficiency level increased. Lastly and most importantly, this study demonstrated that not only topic prominence but also subject prominence is a transferable feature in SLA.

While Jin's (1994) study was significant in that it was the first study investigating transferability of subject prominence in the acquisition of topic prominent languages, his claim of L1 transfer cannot be considered definitive since his study examined learners of the same L1 background (see Odlin, 1989 for a relevant discussion). Polio (1995) thus conducted another study to examine this concern by varying learners' L1 backgrounds in her study. She investigated the acquisition of zero anaphora, one of the topic prominent features in Chinese, by learners from two different L1 backgrounds, one that only allows zero anaphora to a very limited degree and the other which allows zero anaphora freely (English and Japanese, respectively).

Comparing the L2 Mandarin Chinese production of 21 speakers of Japanese and 21 speakers of English, Polio found that the occurrences of zero anaphora increased with L2 proficiency, a result which coincides with the findings of Jin

(1994). Furthermore, it was also found that there was no significant difference between the Japanese and English speakers' use of zero anaphora in Chinese, possibly indicating there was no positive transfer from Japanese to Chinese. Instead of entirely disregarding positive transfer from Japanese L1 to Chinese L2, Polio posited the following hypotheses in order to account for the insignificant differences between the L1 groups of English and Japanese. First, most of the Japanese speakers had studied English, and thereby were influenced by the systems of the English language. Second, the insignificant results of the nonparametric statistical test she used (Kruskal-Wallis tests) are not robust, as this is a conservative test for identifying significance. Lastly, in contrast to English speaking learners of Chinese, Japanese speaking learners of Chinese at all proficiency levels tended to use full NPs in their L2 Chinese production.

Polio's study also revealed that the learners tended to use pronouns, instead of zero anaphora, when the conjoinability of clauses was unclear. In other words, they were prone to use zero anaphora for a referent used in the immediately foregoing clause. This particular result was consistent with that of Muñoz (1995) in that with regard to the use of zero anaphora in English by Spanish speakers, the learners did not produce zero anaphora at the discourse level but did so at the syntactic level. To be specific, except for the beginning level learners who produced no instances of zero anaphora, the occurrences of zero anaphora were restricted to the subjects in conjoined clauses, just as were found in the NSs' production of zero anaphora. Muñoz explains that this could be attributable to the fact that the subjects were instructed foreign language learners and therefore they opted not to use ungrammatical (in the prescriptive grammar sense) but descriptively acceptable zero anaphora. She also explored the possibility that there could be a task effect present in that the participants wrote narratives in a highly controlled manner. Further investigations are needed to achieve a more comprehensive understanding of this specific topic prominent feature (i.e., zero anaphora) and the role positive transfer plays. It would be preferable that such investigations include learners whose L1 has analogous linguistic systems with the L2. In fact, in their investigation of CLI, the previous studies considered the possibility that they were examining languages that might not be 'close enough' to the target language.

For instance, as mentioned above, Polio (1995) regarded Chinese and Japanese as sharing topic-prominent features. Although both Chinese and Japanese are languages that allow zero anaphora when the topic continuity is high, Japanese allows suffixal topic-marking particles (e.g., Givón, 1983; Hinds, 1983; Kuno, 1973; Shibatani, 1990), while Chinese does not have such markers to encode topics. Korean, on the other hand, not only shares the same typological characteristic of both subject/topic prominence as Japanese, but also marks the topic via a suffixal topic-marking device (e.g., Hwang, 1983). In fact, some researchers (e.g., Li and Thompson, 1976) classify Japanese and Korean as both topic and subject prominent languages, whereas they categorise Chinese as a language of only topic prominence. In addition, with respect to encoding references in discourse, Chinese utilises personal pronouns like English, while such occurrences in Japanese and Korean are very rare. Thus, regarding Japanese and Chinese as similar languages solely due to the fact that both languages allow zero anaphora seems somewhat far-fetched. Considering this line of reasoning, instead of comparing languages that have diverse features, it is crucial to compare languages which have typological parallels for marking referential topics before we can close the book on positive transfer in this area of language acquisition.

There have been, in fact, a few small-scale studies that have compared the acquisition of the Japanese postpositional markers, *wa* and *ga*, by L1 speakers of English, Chinese and Korean (e.g., see Sakamoto, 2000 for a review of these studies). The results of these studies show potential in that Korean learners of Japanese displayed superior performance with respect to these particles, an outcome expected in typological comparison between Korean and Japanese. These studies will be discussed in depth in section 2.4.5.

2.4.4 Referent markings in L1 and L2 Japanese

This section will review studies investigating referential forms in narratives in L1 and L2 Japanese. Clancy (1980) studied 20 L1 Japanese and 20 L1 English narratives, focusing on the use of referential forms, using the film "Pear Story". "Pear Story" is a silent film that has been used by many researchers in linguistics. In her Japanese L1 data, only two referential options were found, namely, full NPs and zero anaphora. In other words, there were no occurrences of the third person pronouns *kare* (he), *kanojo* (she), or *karera* (they). Clancy reveals that although there are some variations that are unique to Japanese and English, there is a universal tendency towards referential form selection (between explicit nominal reference and zero anaphora). She found that referential form selection was determined by the following factors: distance between the two mentions of the same referent, switching referents, episode boundaries, and different individual referential strategies in order to avoid ambiguity, as well as creating a point of view for the narration. When a character is introduced for the first time, a full NP is used and zero anaphora usually occurs once the character has become shared knowledge between the speaker and the listener. However, when the referent in the subject position is replaced by another referent, a full NP is to be preferred over zero anaphora. This is also the case when there is a change in theme (i.e., episode boundary).

Furthermore, Clancy (1980) also reveals that the main characters of a narrative tend to be referred to with more attenuated forms than peripheral ones, as the former tend to have a stronger impact on the speaker/listener's consciousness (see also Clancy, 1992; Fox, 1987; and Hinds, 1983 for comparable findings). This tendency, which Clancy (1992) later calls the 'ellipsis for hero' strategy was especially more evident when topic switching took place, compared to when the same character was referred to as a topic continuously. In other words, even when the speaker switched topics, in which the use of full NP is normally expected, they tended to use zero anaphora when the main character replaced the peripheral characters as a topic of discourse, but not vice versa. In the continuous mentions of topics, on the other hand, the speakers did not show significant differences in the use of zero anaphora depending on the status of the characters (i.e., main or peripheral status); they tended to use zero anaphora for all the characters.

Whereas the NSs of Japanese in Clancy's studies demonstrated coherent patterns to distinguish discourse context with the use of appropriate form choice, learners of L2 Japanese tend to have difficulty marking the referents with the right forms. For instance, Kondo (2004) reported NS judgements on the total of six advanced and superior level Japanese L2 speakers' narratives that were extracted from the Oral Proficiency Interview (hereafter OPI). The researcher found that the L2 learners made inappropriate form choices that lead to incoherent narratives, resulting in high incomprehensibility judged by the NSs of Japanese. For instance, in marking new and switched referents, Japanese NSs generally chose full NPs, whereas the form choices made by the advanced and superior proficiency level learners of Japanese were erratic; they sometimes used full NPs and other times ellipsis and pronouns. Although the number of narratives the researcher had the NSs of Japanese assess was rather small, the results of her study gives substantial evidence of the important role that the proper referent marking plays in creating a coherent narrative.

Recall that Givón (1983), summarising his cross-linguistic investigation of topic maintenance strategies, concluded that the most continued referent would receive the most attenuated form, i.e., zero anaphora. Thus, we could say that the main character is the core of a narrative, being frequently mentioned, and therefore being the most continued topic in the discourse, hence it is marked by zero anaphora. On the whole, in Clancy's (1980) L1 Japanese data, form-function relationships seemed to be at play in the choice of referential forms, in that form was determined by discoursal factors. While Clancy (1980, 1992) studied oral narratives, Hinds (1984) investigated both interview data and scripted oral narration, in terms of how referential forms are marked. Besides referential form choices between full NP and zero anaphora, he looked at morphological markers of topic prominence in Japanese. That is, he also examined how a referent is marked with suffixal markers such as *wa* and *ga*, in terms of how a topic is continued/discontinued. Although a rather less restrictive encoding system of topic continuation was found in the interview data as compared to the narrative data, Hinds found that when a referent is introduced for the first time (i.e., when the information is new), it is marked by *ga*, then followed by zero anaphora unless there are ambiguity issues or rival topics at play. If such cases occur, the referent would be marked by *wa*. Thus, in general, a new referent is marked by *ga*, a known referent is marked by *wa* or zero anaphora, and zero anaphora is used to refer to the current topic of discourse (Hinds, 1980, 1984, 1987).

Watanabe (2004, 2011) examined discourse functions of *wa* by L1 Japanese speakers in narrative data. In Watanabe (2004), L1 Japanese spoken and written narratives were compared, with regard to the use of *wa*. There were 15 pairs of Japanese NSs participants, thus total of 30 participants; and one of each pair watched five minute segment of 'Pingu' and produced spoken and written narratives. The 'hearer' of the pair produced written narratives based on the story that the speaker explained. The main findings of the study include that *wa* was produced twice as much in the written narratives compared to the spoken narratives; however, the proportional use of *wa* in referring to the central character was the same in both types of narrative modes. Furthermore, in referring to important inanimate entities, the writers used *wa* as much as in referring to the central characters; however such trend was not observed in the spoken narrative data. As Watanabe's study demonstrates, the use of *wa* was motivated by discoursal functions, and it varied in different modes (i.e., spoken versus written).

While NP+*ga* and *wa* are the foremost particles used for introducing a new referent and for referring to a known referent, respectively, Hinds (1983) also discussed the use of other types of postpositional markers. In his discussion of postpositional markers found in Japanese discourse, he divided these markers into two types, subject/topic marking particles, and object marking particles. Hinds argued that the former group includes *ga*, *wa* and *mo* (meaning 'also'), whereas the latter includes *o*, *ni*, and *ga*. *Ni* is used for verbs that involve contact. For instance, sentences such as 1) A *wa* B *ni au* (A meets with B) and 2) A *wa* B *ni noru* (A rides on B) would exemplify the characteristics of these postpositional markers. *Ga* in the object marking group is used for marking stative verbs, while *o* is used for nonstative verbs.[12] Hinds added that some particles which normally appear in the subject/topic position can appear in an object position, a situation which would obfuscate case relationships. For instance, the object of a verb can be marked by the topic marker, *wa*, when the NP is used for a comparison purpose, or by *mo* (also) in order to highlight the NP.[13] On the whole, if one is only concerned with how referents are introduced into discourse as topics originally, and then continue to be the topics, the pattern, NP+*ga* (→ NP+*wa*) → zero anaphora, is the most canonical sequence for continuity of the topics in Japanese discourse.

The same pattern, NP+*ga* → zero, was found in the study of Clancy and Downing (1987) which used short cartoon strips and silent films to elicit narrative data. This result was consistent with Japanese L1 and L2 data found in Nakahama (2003). In Nakahama, with respect to the narration of a Charlie Chaplin silent film, the most frequent pattern found by the NSs and advanced level learners of Japanese was NP+*ga* → zero anaphora to introduce a referent and maintain it as the topic of the discourse. Furthermore, NP+*ga* → NP+*ga* sequence was the second most frequently used pattern, which is consistent with the results found in Clancy and Downing. It seemed to be that NP+*ga* → NP+*ga* sequence was found when the speakers wished to reiterate mention of the character after getting interrupted by the listeners or wished to rephrase the introduction as was the case in Clancy and Downing's (1987) study.

Nakahama (2009), Yanagimachi (1997, 2000) and Yoshioka (2005) also investigated referential form use in L2 Japanese oral narratives. In Yanagimachi (2000), he examined oral narratives of learners of Japanese at three different proficiency levels: novice, intermediate, and advanced. Four different types of narratives were used in order to elicit different types of pronouns, that is, first, second, and third person pronouns. He used four different elicitation methods to trigger these different types of pronouns. For elicitation of first person pronoun, the learners were told to tell what they did the previous day in a narrative fashion, as well as retelling a story from a cartoon strip. Second person pronoun was elicited in the format of retelling a story from a short video clip. The interlocutor of the participants appeared in the short video clip, and the participants had to describe what happened to the interlocutor to remind him of the situation. For third person pronoun elicitation, a short video clip was also shown to the participants, and they had to retell the story after viewing the video. It was found that the acquisition of zero anaphora for first and second person pronoun positions in Japanese was acquired more easily by English speakers compared to third person zero pronouns.

Yanagimachi explains that the context of first and second person narratives had a more stable topic in that the theme of the narration was centred on one specific viewpoint. In other words, in both first and second person narratives the protagonists were "me" and "you", respectively, and once they were introduced with full NPs, they could be continued with zero anaphora naturally. Third person narratives, on the other hand, did not require such a viewpoint establishment. It was up to the speaker to determine who the protagonists were and take charge of narrating the events in a coherent manner. Interestingly, it was found that NSs tended to focus on a limited set of characters, treated them as protagonists, and used several strategies to keep the same characters in the position of the discourse topic. For instance, they used auxiliary verbs of giving and receiving and passive voice in order to keep the protagonists in the subject position, and, as a result, their narration remained coherent and comprehensible to the listener. Due to the fact that these speakers kept the same topic/referents in the subject position, treating them as the main discourse topic, they used zero anaphora continuously. In learner discourse, however, the use of zero anaphora (for third person narratives) at the lowest proficiency level was less frequent, mainly due to switching referents in the subject position. Furthermore, none of the learners at any proficiency level used passive construction and auxiliary verbs of giving and receiving, although the use of zero anaphora for the third person increased with proficiency.

The results of Yanagimachi (1997, 2000) are supported by the findings of

Nakahama (2003, 2009) and Yoshioka (2005). Partially replicating Chaudron and Parker's (1990) study of the acquisition of noun referential forms in ESL, Nakahama (2003) investigated the use of referential forms in L2 Japanese by learners whose L1 is English. The concept of a markedness scale and the three types of discourse context (new, known, current) in Chaudron and Parker's study was adopted in her study as well. The hypotheses tested derived from the results of Chaudron and Parker's research that learners from each proficiency level (beginning, intermediate and advanced in their study) could maintain a distinction between all three contexts (new, known and current), in terms of using structural forms to different degrees.

The findings of Chaudron and Parker were confirmed in Nakahama (2003) in that the learners were largely able to differentiate referential forms between discourse contexts. Moreover, the ability to do so correctly increased with proficiency, i.e., more advanced learners of Japanese were able to use proper noun referential forms for given contexts more frequently, when compared to their lower proficiency level counterparts.

Specifically, the advanced level learners of Japanese mainly used zero anaphora (89.5%) to refer to the topic in the current context, while 83 % of mentions for current topic were marked with zero anaphora by NSs of Japanese. Intermediate learners of Japanese, on the other hand, used more varied forms of marking for referents in the current context (56.0 % zero anaphora, 40.1 % NPs with *wa*, 3.9 % NPs with *ga*).

Similarities were found between NS and advanced level learners in other contexts as well. In new contexts (referent introduction), the majority of the NPs were marked by *ga* in the production of both advanced level learners and NS (71.4% & 90%, respectively), while intermediate level learners of Japanese used NP+*wa* to mark newly introduced referent most frequently (61.1%), instead of *ga*. In fact, the intermediate level learner discourse was flooded with *wa* regardless of context, displaying their preference of the use of *wa* over any other form. This result indicates that *wa* has become a part of their interlanguage grammar, and it may well support the previous claim that *wa* is acquired before *ga* (see Doi and Yoshioka, 1990 and Sakamoto, 1993). It was also found that learners at a higher proficiency level employed syntactic forms with different complexity to differentiate the coding of referential topics based on the discoursal context.

Nakahama (2009) and Yoshioka (2005) both employed the same picture storybook, *Frog, Where are you* in their investigations of L2 Japanese referent markings by L1 Korean and English, and L1 Dutch speakers, respectively. The common findings between the studies were that the appropriate use of indefinite markings of referents seemed to be difficult for the English and Dutch speakers to achieve at lower proficiency levels, whereas the Korean speakers achieved appropriate form-function mapping at an earlier stage of acquisition compared to their English counterparts.

Overall, the common findings include that the use of zero anaphora in Japanese (for third person narratives) was difficult for English speakers to perform at lower levels of proficiency, possibly due to the tighter restrictions on the use of zero anaphora in their L1. Nakahama (2009) considered examining Korean speaking learners of Japanese to find out how language distance plays a role in the acquisition of L2 referential forms. However, due to the fact that these relevant studies employed varied elicitation methods (i.e., silent film retelling versus picture description tasks); therefore, the results cannot be conclusive. In order to address this gap, investigating both learners whose L1 is very close to, and very distant from Japanese in both types of data elicitation (film retelling and picture description task) is necessary.

While zero anaphora indicates highest topic continuity, most discontinuous information (i.e., new information) will be marked with *ga* in Japanese discourse. Some studies have been conducted to examine the acquisition of *ga*, along with *wa*, a marker used for denoting old information in discourse. Those studies that investigated CLI in the acquisition of NP+*wa* and NP+*ga* will be reviewed in the section below.

2.4.5 CLI studies of the acquisition of NP+*wa* and NP+*ga*

The investigation of *wa* and *ga* has received great attention in the last two decades or so. In terms of the acquisition of topic prominent features such as *wa* (topic marker) and zero anaphora by English L1 speakers, it has been shown that the acquisition of *wa* takes place prior to that of *ga* (Doi and Yoshioka, 1990; Nakahama, 2003, 2009; Sakamoto, 1993; Yoshioka, 2005) and zero anaphora is difficult to acquire for the third person position and that the appropriate use of these forms increases with proficiency level (Nakahama, 2003, 2009; Yanagimachi, 1997, 2000).

A few studies have been conducted to specifically investigate positive transfer (from Korean to Japanese) in the acquisition of *wa* and *ga*. First, Nagatomo's

(1991) study found evidence of positive transfer from Korean to Japanese L2 in the use of *wa/ga*. He compared the use of *wa/ga* by Korean and Chinese learners of Japanese. A cloze test was used and the material was a classical Japanese novel. The proficiency level of the learners was not specified; however, it was stated that the learners' Japanese was good enough to comprehend the advanced text. Nagatomo claimed that there is a systematic variability in the use of *wa/ga* in native Japanese speakers' discourse, calling this the systematic variation model. Comparing the NS answers to that of the learners in his data, he found the following results. There is some systematicity in the use of *wa/ga* in both native and learner discourse. There is a high positive correlation between Korean learners of Japanese and NSs of Japanese in terms of the systematicity of the variation of *wa/ga* (correlation rate=0.81). The correlation between Chinese learners of Japanese and NSs of Japanese, on the other hand, was relatively low (=0.53). He claimed that this variability in the use of *wa/ga* was attributable to the different linguistic systems to mark the subject in Japanese and Chinese, relating this to the notion of markedness and unmarkedness in each language. Korean, on the other hand, uses a similar system to Japanese (that is, Korean has markers which are equivalent to *wa/ga*), and therefore Korean learners of Japanese must have considered *ga* as unmarked, while Chinese speakers would view such an item as marked due to the lack of a comparable form in their native language.

Nagatomo continues that Korean speakers were successful in using *wa/ga* since they transferred the notion of a topic/subject marking system from their L1 to the L2. Although this is a valuable study showing evidence of positive transfer, the study had some limitations, as the researcher himself states. First, the classification of the learners' proficiency level was nebulous. Second, the material used was a cloze test, which might not necessarily test what learners would produce in real life communication.[14] In addition, a study which compares the interaction of proficiency level and learners' L1, that is, an exploration of CLI on the language development, might be beneficial, since such interaction is still not established in the literature.

Another study that found some effects of positive transfer in the acquisition of topic/subject marking was Hanada (1993). She compared learners of Japanese whose L1s are Korean, Chinese, English, and another European language. The other variable in her study was the length of the learners' stay in Japan and the amount and variety of Japanese language study. She found that there was no positive correlation between the accuracy of the use of *wa/ga* and the length of stay in Japan for L1 speakers of Chinese and English. In terms of Chinese learners, actually a negative correlation was found; that is, the learners whose length of stay in Japan was shorter performed better than those learners who had been in Japan longer. However, in terms of Korean speakers, the longer the stay was, the better the utilisation of *wa/ga*. More importantly, it was also found that the Korean learners performed much better than both the Chinese and Indo-European L1 speakers at all three levels (length of stay: less than a year, 1-3 years, more than 3 years). Especially noteworthy was the fact that all learners except for those learners whose L1 is Korean, overly used *wa* in order to introduce new referents, which should be marked by *ga*. This incorrect usage of *wa* did not decrease as the length of stay increased in Chinese and Indo-European language speakers. Korean speakers, on the other hand, more or less acquired the usage of *ga* (89% accuracy rate among the learners whose stay in Japan was less than a year) and its usage was perfect among learners whose stay in Japan was 1-3 years.

This result can be explained by discussion of part of the results found in Helms-Park (2001). Helms-Park found that positive transfer played a role in the ridding of 'overgeneralised' rules in the verb lexical selections of his study. In Hanada's study, while some overgeneralised use of *wa* was found among the Korean L1 speakers whose length of stay in Japan is the shortest, these speakers were able to get rid of the pattern as the length of stay in Japan increased. Hanada speculated that due to the fact that the Korean language shares equivalent markers for *wa/ga*, the Korean learners could transfer the notion of the function of these suffixal markers to their Japanese L2, noticing their use in everyday living in Japan. Chinese and Indo-European language speakers, on the other hand, found it more difficult to get accustomed to how these forms function and therefore the length of stay in Japan did not have the same salutary effect on these learners. This claim was compatible with what Nagatomo suggested referring to markedness of the forms.

As was the case in Nagatomo's study, Hanada used a rather ambiguous definition of the learners' proficiency. She relied solely on the learners' length of stay in Japan and study of the language, without testing their "level" of Japanese. Thus, definitive conclusions cannot be drawn with regard to the relationship of CLI and the development of L2 Japanese.

Besides Nagatomo (1991) and Hanada (1993), there were other studies that examined the acquisition order of *wa* and *ga* by various L1 speakers (e.g., Iuchi, 1995; Nagatomo et al. 1993). Most of the studies seemed to arrive at the general conclusion that *wa* is acquired preceding *ga* irrespective of the learners' L1 backgrounds. However, the studies typically have a single independent variable, such as the learners' L1 background or proficiency level, and usually there is an imbalance in the number of subjects among the groups. Consequently, a controlled study that investigates how different L1 backgrounds influence the learners' acquisition processes would serve to fill a gap in the literature.

It is important to repeat here that both Nagatomo (1991) and Hanada (1993) employed a cloze test to elicit data. As was discussed in the introduction of this manuscript, it should be pointed out that discoursal factors ought to be emphasised in the examination of language acquisition processes because of their important role in language use (particularly when considering tracking referents and their topicality, which are clearly discourse level phenomena). By investigating oral discourse data, researchers are able to determine the contextual rationale for the production of certain linguistic features chosen by learners. Moreover, testing the learners on the sentential level does not necessary disclose their real capacity for language use.

Keeping this guiding purpose in mind, as Sakamoto (2000) rightly suggests, we also need to realise that there are some important elicitation methods that have not been used in CLI studies investigating *wa/ga*. He points out that while discourse data were collected to investigate the acquisition of *wa/ga* by English L1 speakers, the use of extended discourse data is not commonly done for Chinese and Korean L1 speakers. Since Sakamoto's statement, some studies have been conducted (e.g., Nakahama, 2009; Watanabe, 2011) to investigate the use of NP+*wa* by Korean L1 speakers in an extended narrative discourse. Watanabe (2011) compared the use of *wa* by the NSs of Japanese and Korean learners of Japanese, as well as the Korean equivalent of *wa*, (i.e., *(n)un*) in written and spoken narratives. His findings include that the Japanese participants produced almost twice as many instances of *wa* than Korean participants' *(n)un* in both written and spoken narrative data. Further, the frequencies of the production of topic marker (*wa*) resembled that of *(n)un* in their Korean NSs narrative discourse, suggesting CLI from L1. Watanabe explains that this part of the findings supports Shimojo and Lee's (2010) contrastive study of Japanese and Korean. They found that in the context which

Japanese topic marker, *wa*, was normally used, Korean often employed the subject marker, *ka/i*. In fact, Korean tends to de-topicalise the known referents, much more so than their Japanese counterparts.

Watanabe's (2011) research provides a clear example of CLI between typologically very similar languages on the level of discourse/grammar interface, and thus considerably contributes to the existing studies of *wa*. However, we are still in need of a study that examines interlanguage of learners with more than single-language backgrounds and to help clarify the relationship between CLI and proficiency in an extended discourse such as oral narratives elicited via differing methods. In particular, employing different types of data collection methods will strengthen the generalisability and validity of the findings thus far acquired.

To sustain this contention, it should be mentioned that in Yoshioka's (1991) study, different elicitation methods generated different results with regard to the acquisition order of *wa* and *ga* by English L1 speakers. In her study, the accuracy rate of the production of *wa* was 71.4%, whereas that of *ga* was 69.7%, and the difference was not statistically significant when the data were elicited via comprehension test. However in production tasks — an elicited imitation test and a free interview — different results were obtained in that the acquisition of *wa* preceded that of *ga*. Her study shows how a given data elicitation method can influence the results of a study.

The following two sections will review some studies that investigated referent management in Korean and English oral narratives to illustrate their analogous and differing language encoding systems, as compared to Japanese.

2.4.6 Referent markings in Korean

Similar to what was found in L1 and L2 Japanese oral narrative studies (e.g., Clancy, 1980; Hinds, 1983; Nakahama, 2003; Yanagimachi, 1997, 2000; Yoshioka, 2005), speakers' choice of referential forms in Korean is not only controlled by syntax, but also highly driven by discoursal factors (Clancy, 1997; Kim, 1989; Lee, 1987). In her investigation of Korean L1 narratives, Kim (1989) specifically examined how new referents get introduced into discourse and continued in the narration of the film "Pear Story". In addition, she compared human and nonhuman participants and their role as topics in the discourse. The results of her study showed that a full NP is always used for introducing a new referent, and 94% of them were marked with the nominative case marker, *ka/i*. The topic marker *nun* was never used for newly introduced referents. Kim claims that this is due to the fact that the listener did not see the film, and thus since the first mention of referents were new to him, they could not be established as topics of the discourse yet. Once the character is "established" as a topic, it gets marked with zero anaphora, thus high topic continuity is expressed with the use of zero anaphora, just as is the case in Japanese. Therefore, topic continuity can be simply summarised as in the following sequence: NP+*ka/i* (least continuous) → zero anaphora (most continuous). However, topic continuity is not the only motive for the choice of referential forms. Kim states that a full NP was used to resolve ambiguity of referents and the use of zero anaphora was triggered by discourse redundancy. For the latter, she claimed that the use of zero anaphora is obligatory for coreferential use within the sentence boundary. This distinction made on the discourse level in the use of full NPs and zero anaphora was also found in children's conversational data in Clancy (1997).

Clancy found in her case study of two young children (1;10 and 1;8 years old) that they tended to use full NPs when referring to absent referents, whereas zero anaphora was their choice for present referents. It could be said that these children tried to avoid ambiguity and used full NPs when referents were not in sight in order to be more explicit.

Kim (1989) also found that there were differences between how human and non-human referents were encoded in discourse. It was found that human referents were marked as topics more often than non-human ones, and this result is predictable from the animacy hierarchy (see e.g., Comrie, 1989 regarding the animacy scale). According to the animacy scale, human referents are highest on the scale, and there is a great likelihood that human referents will be the focus of discourse (e.g., Hwang, 1983; Yamamoto, 1996). Kim (1989) divided anaphoric devices into three types (nominal, pronominal, and zero anaphora), as is the common practice in discourse analysis. In her data, just as Clancy (1980) found in her Japanese oral narrative data of the "Pear Story" film, only two types of referential forms (NPs and zero anaphora) were used. In referring to characters already mentioned once, NP use was 33.9% of the time, while the rest of the mentions (66.1%) were done with zero anaphora. This result is similar to the distribution of the NPs and zero anaphora in Clancy's (1980) Japanese data. Clancy's data showed that 26.8% of already mentioned characters were referred to with NPs, while the rest (73.2%) were marked with zero anaphora.

As discussed in 2.4.2 above, voice alternation involves narrative formation on the conceptual level from the perspective of referent introduction and tracking. Grammatical formation of passive constructions in Japanese and Korean will be briefly examined below to illustrate the structural similarities between the two languages.

Passivisation of Japanese is expressed through assigning the passive suffix –*(ra)re*, and both transitive and intransitive verbs can take passive forms. The agentive marker (*ni/kara*) can be used depending on the focus of the discourse (i.e., whether or not the agent of the passive structure needs to be specified). Japanese passive is distinctive in that there is a semantic difference between the passive of transitive and intransitive verbs. Passivisation of intransitive verbs demonstrates that the subjects of the passive clauses have experienced some adverse effects, whereas passive clauses of transitive verbs do not normally carry this connotation (Shibatani, 1990). The following example shows the passivisation of an intransitive verb.

Example 2.1 Passivisation of an Intransitive Verb in Japanese

Taroo   wa   kodomo ni   naka–re–ta.
Taroo   TOP   child   by   cry-PASS-PAST
'Taro was adversely affected by the child's crying.'

(Shibatani, 1990: 318)

Korean passives are conveyed via derivational suffixes just like in Japanese. There are four variations in the passive suffix, *-i, -hi, -li* and *-ki*, and the stem-final sound determines which suffix to take. The agentive markers are *kkey, eykey, hanthey,* and *ey,* and which form is used depends on the animacy of the agent and the formality of the context (Sohn, 1999), as in the following example.

Example 2.2 Passive Structure in Korean

Ku   totwuk   i   swunkyeng   hanthey   cap–hy–ess–ta
The   thief   NOM   police   by   catch-PASS-PAST-DC
'The thief was caught by the police.'

(Sohn, 1999: 368)

This is an example of the passivisation of the transitive verb 'catch' in Korean.

Unlike Japanese, the Korean language does not have adverse passives expressed via passivisation of intransitive verbs, an aspect which bears a resemblance to English. It should also be noted that there are some verbs that do not take a passive suffix; these are lexical passive verbs that have inherently passive meanings.

2.4.7 Referent markings in English

As discussed earlier, many studies have investigated the acquisition of referential forms in ESL (e.g., Chaudron and Parker, 1990; Fuller and Gundel, 1987; Huebner, 1983; Jarvis, 2002; Kumpf, 1992). Chaudron and Parker (1990) succinctly summarised how a new referent is introduced into discourse and maintained as a referential topic. According to the researchers, in English, the highest topic continuity would be encoded with a pronoun, while an already introduced but not current topic of discourse (medium continuity) would be coded with a definite article or a left dislocation with a definite article. The introduction of a new referent (least continuous topic) would normally be coded with an indefinite article or an existential with an indefinite article. These noun referential form encodings are summarised in the following table (partially adopted from Chaudron and Parker, 1990; page 46).

Table 2.1 Referential Forms of English Within Discourse Contexts

Refer to Current Topic	Introduce Known Referent as Topic	Introduce New Referent
Pronoun	Definite Article or Left Dislocation + Def. Art.[15]	Indefinite Article or Existential + Indef. Art.

In order to elicit the contexts of the current topic and new and known referents, the researchers employed the following data elicitation technique. First, the subjects were shown three pictures in which there is a consecutive action by one character, and another character who just passively appears in the pictures. These three pictures were shown at the same time, so that the subjects would realise the continuity of the story development. Then, as a continuation of the third picture, they are given one of three alternate pictures which depict 1) the current topic referent, 2) the known (but not the current) referent, and 3) a newly introduced referent. The subjects were given nine sequences of four pictures in all.

Though some unexpected results were found (for instance, 49% of the marking of current topic by NSs was done with a definite article and noun, instead of with pronouns), the participants roughly performed as expected (a result which is shown in the table above). Though the researchers did not remark on the unexpected result of NSs encoding of the current topic, it can be assumed that discourse flow was somewhat disrupted by the separate presentation of the fourth picture because the three consecutive pictures prior to the fourth one were presented all at once.

While this study attempted a highly controlled method to coordinate different discourse contexts, most of the studies of referential forms have used free narratives. However, there seems to be a consensus regarding how referential choices for the most continuous and discontinuous referent is marked. The least continuous referent is marked with full NPs and the most continuous referent is marked with pronouns. Clancy (1980), for instance, in comparisons of the referential choices between Japanese and English NSs' narrative discourse, found that pronouns were the major device (63.8%) for referring to the non-initial mention of the referents in oral narrative discourse in English.

With the results of the previous relevant studies in mind, the current study attempts to verify the existing findings of referent markings by using relatively uncontrolled data elicitation methods, as well as to compare the ways in which English NSs construct oral narratives with the methods of their Japanese and Korean counterparts.

2.5 Task complexity and its effects on narrative production

Lastly, I will discuss the theoretical motivation of the employment of two types of narrative elicitation method (film retelling and picture description task) in the current study. I will review Robinson's (2001, 2003, 2007) Cognition Hypothesis and related studies that examined the relationship between the task complexity and its effects on L2 narrative production. Robinson's Cognition Hypothesis of task-based language learning proposes that pedagogical tasks be sequenced in an order of increasing complexity. The Cognition Hypothesis predicts that high cognitive demands of tasks will (1) push learners to produce more accurate and complex L2 discourse so as to meet the greater functional and communicative demands and (2) facilitate increased attention to and memory for input and (3) cause input to retain longer, and (4) lead to automaticity and efficient development of the components of complex L2 production.

In delineating its concept, Robinson (2001) claims that task complexity has connections with cognitive issues that influence the task doers' cognitive challenge (e.g., doing simple addition as opposed to calculus). He further argues that there are two subcategories of task complexity: resource-directing and resource-depleting. It is hypothesised that the difference between these two categories lies in how resource is allocated during the task performance. Resource-directing variables involve cognitive conceptual demands (e.g., +/- no reasoning demands, +/- here-and-now) which direct learners' attention and effort in terms of conceptualisation by which their L2 system goes into operation. Resource-depleting variables (e.g., +/- planning, +/- prior knowledge), on the other hand, concern demands on learners' attention and effort without directing resources to any features of language code. Robinson argues that increased cognitive demands of tasks lead to learners' engagement with cognitive resources, and thus, the learners pay more attention to input and modify their output. He effectively links his theory to two existing hypotheses in SLA by arguing that higher cognitive demands facilitate the learners to 'notice' the gaps in discourse ('Noticing Hypothesis' by Schmidt (1990)) and to 'push' their output ('Output Hypothesis' by Swain (1995)).

In investigating one factor that he believes to influence task complexity within the domain of resource-directing category, Robinson (1995) compared +/- here-and-now condition in describing a series of events. He compared two types of L2 storytelling activities: describing a series of events in the present tense while looking at those pictures (+here-and-now), against retelling of stories from memory without pictorial support (-here-and-now, i.e., +there-and-then). He revealed that the more complex task (retelling the story under the 'there- and-then' condition) triggered more accurate but less fluent narratives. Accuracy was measured by the target-like use of articles in Robinson's study. The increased accuracy in T/T narrative condition measured by the target-like article use was also reported in Ishikawa (2007); other studies reported an increase in accuracy in the tasks with higher cognitive demands which was measured by error free T-Unit (Iwashita, et.al, 2001; Rahimpour, 1999) and the percentage of self-repairs and the ratio of repaired to unrepaired errors (Gilabert, 2007).

The T/T task requires the learners to store the information on the characters and the events, then put them together and reconstruct the story, therefore placing higher cognitive demands on the learners. In Robinson's (1995) study, not only higher accuracy but higher lexical complexity was observed in a task with higher complexity (i.e., T/T condition narrative). In explaining the higher grammatical accuracy in the T/T task, Robinson maintained that the more complex task motivated the learners to pay more attention to carefully connecting propositions, in order to make coherent narratives, and as a result the learners generated accurate uses of articles.

As was discussed before, most of the L2 narrative studies that investigated the acquisition of referential markings employed either picture narration tasks or silent film plot retelling. For instance, in the investigation of referent markings in L2 Japanese, a picture storybook was used by several researchers (Nakamura, 1993; Nakahama, 2009; Yoshioka, 2005), whereas a silent film was employed (Clancy, 1985; Nakahama, 2003; Yanagimachi, 1997, 2000). Therefore, a definite conclusion cannot be drawn from the studies with differing elicitation methods. With this limitation and the above mentioned task effects described above in mind, the current study attempts to compare the H/N narrative task via using storybook pictures and the T/T narrative task elicits via silent film viewing and retelling, with the hope of clarifying the previous findings of task effects, especially in the area of referent markings.

In sum, through the review of the literature in the field, it is apparent that a number of critical factors concerning CLI and developmental sequences of topic continuity have not been adequately explored. In order to fill this void, a quasi-experimental study was undertaken. In the beginning of this manuscript, these research questions were posed. They are repeated here with corresponding hypotheses related to each question.

2.6 Research questions and hypotheses

1. What kinds of referential devices are used by NS of Japanese, Korean and English for introducing and tracking referents in oral narratives?

Hypothesis 1(a): The most conventional form used for encoding referent introduction (most discontinuous context) by Japanese NSs will be the full NP with indefinite marking (i.e., NP+*ga*), while the most continuous topic will be coded most frequently with zero anaphora. Furthermore, topic switch will be achieved with full NP, rather than zero anaphora.

Hypothesis 1(b): In Korean, the marking for referents in the most discontinuous context will be done with NP+*ka/i* and zero anaphora for the most continuous context. Like Japanese, topic switch for Korean will also be achieved with full NP.

Hypothesis 1(c): In marking the equivalent forms stated in Hypothesis 1 (a) and (b) for English, indefinite articles (*a, an, bare*)+NP and pronouns would encode the most discontinuous topic and the most continuous topic, respectively. Topic switch for English will also be marked with the full NP.

Hypothesis 2: Besides the grammatical devices mentioned above, topic continuity will also be expressed via voice alternation (active and passive voices) in Japanese, Korean and English NS narratives. But the degree of passive form usage varies among the three languages; Japanese narratives are expected to show the highest occurrences of passive forms.

2. Are there any developmental patterns in acquiring referent marking strategies in L2 Japanese narratives? If so, does the pattern of learning differ between the Korean and English L1 speakers due to CLI?

Hypothesis 3: The target-like performance of referent introduction and tracking will increase with proficiency.

Hypothesis 4: The Korean and English L1 speakers will display differing acquisition paterns in referent markings. Specifically, Korean speakers will achieve target-like performance earlier than English speakers due to the typological similarities shared between Korean and Japanese.

3. Does task complexity affect referent markings in oral narratives? Also, does task complexity affect L1 and L2 Japanese narrative formation differently?

Hypothesis 5: L2 Japanese discourse under T/T condition will present more accurate and complex form choice for referential markings, as is predicted from The Cognition Hypothesis.

Hypothesis 6: L1 Japanese speakers' narrative discourse will not be affected drastically by task complexity.

Notes

3 There have been claims that Weinreich (1953) did not consider language influence in the field of SLA; however those statements were inaccurate. In fact, he had his intersts in all types of transfer, such as various kinds of language contact situations, as well as a variety of bilingualism (see Odlin, 1989, 2003, 2006). There was evidence that the instances of CLI presented in that book motivated Lado (1957) to explore this topic further and posit the CAH in the context of L2 learning (Odlin, 2006).
4 For instance, Spanish uses the indefinite article less frequently than English, as is seen in the following examples. *Mi hermano es demócrata.* (My brother is a democrat).
5 These cases include not only transfer from L1 to L2 (i.e., substratum transfer) but also borrowing transfer (i.e., the interference of the L2 on a previously acquired language).
6 See contrastive results by Birdsong (1992) who replicated Coppieters' (1987) study with methodological improvement.
7 Studies comparing different L1 groups are still scarce (Jarvis and Odlin, 2000) but those that have been conducted serve a critical role in language transfer research to demonstrate the effects of CLI (Odlin, 1989). Orr's (1987) dissertation research provides another case where both positive and negative language transfer were fully examined. By comparing speakers of Ngoni, a Bantu language, and Gujarati, an Indo-European language, in their acquisition of Chichewa (another Bantu language), he was able to show that both positive and negative transfer were at play in the acquisition of bound morphology in Chichewa.
8 Examples of direct (stem-sharing causatives), suppletive (lexical) causatives, and periphrastic causatives are as follows. Direct (stem-sharing causatives) can be found as in '*the vase broke*' and '*the vandal broke*'. Suppletive type has inherent causative meaning, such as *drop* in English and *tomeru* (*to stop*) in Japanese. Periphrastic causatives are verbs like *make, cause*, etc. as in '*I made the baby cry*'.
9 See Odlin (2002) where he focuses his discussion on relativism and universalism in its relation to language transfer.
10 It should be noted that Yanagimachi (2000) used more than one elicitation method, one of which was narration of a picture.
11 It should be noted that some studies demonstrate CLI in the production of zero anaphora. For instance, White (1985) showed that Spanish speakers allowed more pronoun omissions in the grammaticality judgment tests, as compared to French L1 learners of English. Since, like English, French does not allow subject pronoun omissions, this can be regarded as evidence of CLI in the production of zero anaphora.
12 For instance, a stative verb, *wakaru* (understand), takes *ga*, as an object marker, instead of *o*. See the following sentence.
    1. *John wa nihongo ga wakaru.*
       John TOP Japanese ACC understand.
   *2. *John wa nihongo o wakaru.*
       John TOP Japanese ACC understand.
13 See the following example to illustrate the case in which the object of a verb is marked by the topic marker when the speaker intended to make comparisons of two objects (*sushi* and *steak* in this example).
   John wa susi wa tabenakatta ga steeki wa tabeta.
   John TOP sushi TOP eat-NEG-PAST but steak TOP eat-PAST.

14 It should also be mentioned that the subjects were asked to fill in the blanks with either *wa* or *ga*. Because they were provided with only two choices, i.e., no distractors, the task involved a 50/50 guessing probability.
15 Chaudron and Parker (1990) note that a left-dislocated definite noun is used to refer to an already introduced referent in conversational English, citing Givón (1983). Thus this particular form might not be directly pertinent to the current study, due to the fact that the conversation is dialogic as compared to the monologic nature of narratives.

Chapter 3

The Present Study

I will describe in this chapter the quasi-experiment conducted for investigating how learners' L1 backgrounds and task complexity have an impact on the ways in which learners develop referent marking skills in L2 Japanese narratives. This chapter presents an overview of the study by describing the demographic and proficiency information of the participants, as well as the research design including data collection, and coding schemes.

3.1 Method

3.1.1 Participants

In order to answer the research questions and test the hypotheses formulated in this study, a quasi-experimental study was conducted. The participants consisted of 21 intermediate level learners of Japanese (10 Korean L1 and 11 English L1), 20 advanced level learners (10 Korean L1 and 10 English L1), 10 NSs of Japanese, 10 NSs of English (for English narratives) and 10 NSs of Korean (for Korean narratives), totaling 71 participants in total. The learners' proficiency levels were determined according to the ACTFL guidelines, the details of which will be explained in Section 3.1.3. Japanese, Korean, and English NS will henceforth be referred to as JNS, KNS, and ENS, respectively. Learner data will be referred to as follows: intermediate- and advanced-level Korean speakers as KOR-Mid, KOR-High, and intermediate- and advanced-level English speakers as ENG-Mid, ENG-High.

Instead of asking the same speakers who narrated the L2 Japanese narratives to perform the task a second time in their native languages (i.e., Korean and

English), 20 different Korean and English speakers were enlisted to narrate the story in their native languages in order to avoid language transfer (both forward and reverse transfer between L1 and L2). Moreover, this method was employed to prevent the situation in which a speaker might inadvertently introduce a new character as a 'known' character, using a definiteness marker, because the speaker had prior experience of the character, having talked about him/her in their initial L2 narrative.

The performances of novice level learners were not considered as viable candidates for this research, since they would likely have considerable, or even insurmountable difficulty with the requisite vocabulary and syntax. This would interfere with the production of appropriate narrative structures, and make the analysis of data problematic, if not impossible. The exclusion of the novice level learners for this task was also informed by the guidelines of the ACTFL, which suggest that novice level learners are likely to be incapable of narrating events successfully.[16] In addition, within my experience as a certified rater of the SOPI, I found that almost all the students who received the novice level rating were unable to produce connected discourse.[17]

Since the purpose of the current study was to fill a gap in prior research by investigating the relationship between proficiency level and CLI under different task conditions, it was imperative that considerable thought and care be given to choosing levels. As mentioned earlier, the inclusion of the intermediate proficiency level responds to the concern that many CLI studies have limited their investigations to learners with only high proficiency levels, and consequently limited the generalisability of their findings (see Kellerman, 1995; Odlin, 1990). Having already eliminated novice learners, intermediate, advanced and superior were then considered. Prior to this study, I conducted a small-scale study which informed my decision to eliminate the superior level, and settle upon the intermediate and advanced level students as the best informants for this study. In that earlier research, a single task type of low complexity, (a storytelling task) involving context-supported references to the shared information between the speaker and the listener, was employed. The study involved two intermediate, two advanced and two superior level learners, and it was found that the superior level learners' oral narrative production was very much like that of the NSs, in terms of marking topic continuity, including the production of the passive form. Inclusion of such a high proficiency level did not seem to offer many insights into L2 acquisition or pedagogy, other than to demonstrate that these discourse patterns can eventually be learned by L2 speakers. Thus, the present study excluded the superior level. Since 1999, ACTFL has further divided the Advanced level into Advanced-low, Advanced-Mid and Advanced-High, but the differences between the two lower divisions (Low and Mid) are quite minor, so for the purposes of this study, they were collapsed in a single Advanced group. There were two learners who were closer to Advanced-High level than Advanced-Mid level. The Korean and English speaker groups both had one of these types of learner and because of this balance it was decided that it did not create unfair comparison between the groups, and these learners were included in the study. Similarly, two intermediate levels (Intermediate-Mid and Intermediate-High) were grouped together and regarded 'intermediate level' in the study. Ten sets of narratives in English and Korean were collected in order to pinpoint CLI (positive and negative transfer) phenomena from the learners' L1, and 10 Japanese narratives were collected to serve as baseline data.

All 41 L2 Japanese learners were either graduate or undergraduate students studying in Japan. The speakers of Korean who provided L1 Korean data were all college students in Korea, whereas eight L1 English data were collected from college students in the U.S. and two remaining data came from businessmen in the U.S. None of these L1 Korean and English speakers had knowledge of the Japanese language. L1 Japanese data were collected from undergraduate students in Japan. Of the 21 English learners of Japanese, 19 were Americans and two were British, and all were either undergraduate or graduate students. Most of the undergraduate students were taking Japanese courses with other foreign students, as well as studying other subjects in either Japanese or English, whereas the graduate students were all studying in the language education field. Korean learners of Japanese were drawn from either of the following categories: students preparing to enter Japanese undergraduate programs, undergraduate students in Japan, and graduate students in Japan. The graduate level students were also students in the language education program.

Demographic information about the participants is summarised in the table below.

Table 3.1 Demographic Information of Participants

	N	Sex (M/F)	Age (mean)	Japanese Study (mean of months)	Stay in Japan (mean of months)
KOR-Mid	10	6/4	23.0	18.9	9.5
ENG-Mid	11	6/5	21.9	50.9	9.5
KOR-High	10	3/7	24.2	57.3	14.8
ENG-High	10	6/4	24.3	63.0	28.1
JNS	10	5/5	20.3	N/A	N/A
KNS	10	5/5	23.2	N/A	N/A
ENS	10	5/5	22.7	N/A	N/A

As Table 3.1 shows, the differences in the average length of study of L2 Japanese in the Korean and English groups are rather striking at the intermediate level, with native English speakers studying Japanese for a considerably longer time than their native Korean speaking counterparts. An independent t-test was conducted to compare the mean length of time studying L2 Japanese for the two L1 groups at each proficiency level. The result from the t-test indicated that the differences were statistically significant between KOR-Mid and ENG-Mid (t (19) = 2.93, p = .009). With regards to the advanced level learners, although the average length was longer in ENG-High (63 months) than for KOR-High (57.3 months), the difference was not found to be significant (t (18) = 0.56, p = .580). That it took the English speaking learners a significantly longer time to reach the intermediate level than the Korean speakers is consistent with the fact that Korean and Japanese are typologically close to each other, and supports the hypothesis that the proximity of languages likely expedites the language acquisition process. However, based on the result of the present study, it could be the case that once the learners reached a certain proficiency level, the amount of time they required to reach higher levels might not be greatly influenced by the learners' L1.

The general guidelines for maximum lengths of intensive language courses offered at the Foreign Service Institute of the U.S. State Department (1985) also seems to support this notion of greater language distance between Japanese and English. These guidelines list the number of weeks of intensive language study expected to achieve a high level of proficiency for a range of languages.

Japanese is one of the languages that requires as long as 44 weeks of intensive language study for English speakers to achieve respectable levels. Korean also belongs to this category, which suggests that it is also structurally distant from the English language. The list does not show the proximity between Korean and Japanese, but the current study evidenced how quickly Korean learners of Japanese achieve the intermediate proficiency level, as compared to their English L1 counterparts.

An independent t-test was also used to compare the mean length of stay in Japan, for both L1 groups at the advanced proficiency level.[18] The result showed that the difference between KOR-High and ENG-High groups was not significant, in terms of length of stay in Japan (t (18) = 1.55, p = .14).

Considering this result and the significant difference found in the length of Japanese studies between the Korean and English L1 speakers at the intermediate proficiency level, it could be said that the English L1 speakers spent much more time studying Japanese in their native countries than the Korean L1 speakers did, in order to achieve the same level. With regard to the learners' age, the results of the one-way ANOVA showed that the differences in average age among the different L1 groups at both proficiency levels were not statistically significant (F (3, 37) = 1.074, p = .372).

3.1.2 Interlocutor

There were 14 sets of narratives in the study. There were four clusters of L2 Japanese oral narratives (H/N and T/T narratives) performed by the Korean and English L1 speakers at two different proficiency levels for both groups. The remaining six sets of narratives consisted of L1 oral narratives in Japanese, Korean and English. Two Japanese research assistants and I served as the interlocutors with the L2 learner participants, whereas a Korean NS served as the interlocutor for the Korean L1 narratives, and I served as the sole interlocutor for both the English L1 and Japanese L1 narratives. A manual for being an interlocutor was created and interlocutor training was conducted face-to-face with the two Japanese assistants, and in writing with the Korean speaking interlocutor. A native speaker of English would have been a better choice to serve as an interlocutor for English L1 data, in order to obtain conventional oral narrative data in each language. However, due to the picture and film-elicited narrative telling tasks being monologic, rather than dialogic, it was determined that this shortcoming should not have a substantial influence on the participants' telling of the stories. In fact, I attempted to maintain uniformity by consistently suppressing active interaction, limiting participants to simple backchanelling, in all the narratives told. In addition, during a casual conversation after the data collection, some NS of English revealed that they thought of me as not only a NS of Japanese but also of English. Thus, I felt assured that this shortcoming in design would not have negative effect on the results.

3.1.3 Learners' proficiency levels

In order to determine learners' proficiency levels, the use of a standardised test was essential, especially because the participants were drawn from several different institutions. Moreover, as discussed in the literature review section, the relationship between CLI and proficiency level has not been established, in part due to the fact that measurements of learners' proficiency vary across studies.

The learners in the present study were given some parts of the SOPI in Japanese and later rated by certified SOPI raters, applying ACTFL guidelines. SOPI is similar to the OPI in that it is a performance-based speaking test. However, while OPI is a face-to-face interview with a NS interviewer present, SOPI is a tape-mediated speaking test. The learners read a test booklet, listen to prerecorded instructions and record their responses into cassette tapes. It is possible that OPI might present a closer approximation of real life language use, as compared to SOPI; however, since the investigator of the study was a certified rater of SOPI, but not of OPI, the former test was employed. Some research shows that these two different tests have high correlations (see e.g., Kenyon and Malabonga (2001) for high rank-order correlations ($r = .94$) of examinees found between OPI and SOPI). Thus, the tasks were used with confidence. The tasks used from SOPI included picture description tasks and role-playing tasks, and the pictures and instructions were provided to all the learners either by me or the two Japanese research assistants.

As discussed previously, there were 41 learners whose data was analysed in the study. Originally, there were 44 data altogether; however, three of them were pulled out because their proficiency levels, language backgrounds, and ages would not fit well with the rest of the participants. All 41 data were scored by the investigator and those who were rated intermediate-mid and intermediate-high were grouped together and regarded intermediate level, and those who were rated advanced-low, mid, and high were grouped together and considered advanced level for the current study. In order to ensure the reliability of the scores, three sets of interviews from each initially rated proficiency group were randomly selected and later rated by a different certified SOPI rater to ensure inter-rater reliability. Cohen's Kappa was applied to determine inter-rater reliability systematically, and it was found that the agreement rate was 0.86. The agreement rate 0.86 means that, if the chance agreement is taken away, 86 percent of the rating is the same between the raters, and "almost perfect" agreement between the raters is shown (Landis and Koch, 1977).

3.1.4 Tasks (H/N and T/T tasks)

Narration of a picture storybook and silent film story retelling were chosen as the quasi-experimental tasks. As discussed above, the former was considered an H/N condition task, as the speakers were relating the events while currently looking at the pictures, whereas the latter was considered a T/T condition task, as storytelling was done after watching the film and the speakers had to gather pieces of information from memory and reconstruct the story verbally afterwards.

The H/N task allowed a high degree of comparability among the narratives produced by the participants, since the appearance of references to the same entities, as well as similar temporal and locative relations, would reasonably be expected, since the structure of the narrative was controlled, at least to some extent, by the pictures in this type of task. As discussed in the literature review section, the present study employed the picture story book, *Frog, Where Are You?* (Mayer, 1969) which is comprised of 24 consecutive pictures (see Appendix). This picture storybook elicitation method was originally developed by Bamberg (1987); its use was later followed by a large-scale cross-linguistic study conducted by Berman and Slobin (1994). The story plot involves main characters (a little boy, his dog and his pet frog) as well as various peripheral characters that interfere with the protagonists' actions. The characters move from place to place through time, resulting in the production of very rich connected discourse.

As discussed earlier, Nakamura (1993) and Yoshioka (2005) analysed how references are introduced and maintained in narratives produced by L1 Japanese speakers (both adults and children) and L2 Japanese speakers, respectively. Therefore, a comparison will be attempted between the developmental patterns found in Nakamura's data on L1 acquisition by children and Yoshioka's on L2 acquisition, and the current study. Kajiwara and Minami (2008) investigated narrative constructions by bilingual children adapting Nakamura's (1993) and Nakahama's (2004) framework of referent marking. They compared the frequencies of the full NPs and zero anaphora, rather than calculating each particle use such as NP+*ga* and NP+*ni*. Therefore, comparison of the results of the current study with theirs will be limited to the context of the topic switch in the current study, where all the referent markings with postparticle markings were collapsed into one 'full NP' and compared with the percentage use of zero anaphora.

For the T/T condition task, a segment of an old puppet animation film, *Winter Carousel*, was used. The film was compiled, along with other films, in the DVD *The Cameraman's Revenge and Other Fantastic Tales*, written and directed by Wladyslaw Starewicz. Out of several films in this compilation, *Winter Carousel* was chosen because the story was the simplest and less quirky compared to the other films created by Starewicz. The story has three main characters (a rabbit, a bear and a sheep) gather around on a frozen pond; they play together on the ice and on a carousel, and then go on looking for things to pass time with. The story also involves peripheral characters, as well as the change of season from winter to spring. There is no specific goal in this story unlike *Frog, Where Are You?*, the tale chosen for the H/N condition. In that story the main characters embark on an adventure in a forest looking for their missing frog, which they finally find.

Other stories had been originally considered for the T/T condition task, such as Charlie Chaplin's silent film, *Modern Times*, which many researchers including the present investigator, have previously used; however, the plot was not only too complicated for the learners to retell, but also too different from the H/N equivalent. *Winter Carousel* was chosen due to the fact that at least the actions and character types in the story resemble those in the story chosen for the H/N condition. The whole film is 11 minutes long and as such a long film would challenge the learners' memory capacity, the first 5 minutes or so of the film was shown to the participants for retelling of the story.[19]

3.1.5 Design

After the learners were given the SOPI, they were asked to perform the narrative tasks. Their oral narratives were audiotaped as they performed the picture storybook telling and silent film retelling. The storytelling took place in two steps. First of all, the participants were given up to three minutes to prepare the narrative silently to organise their thought about the story.[20] After the preparation phase ended, the participants were asked to tell the story. They were given up to 30 minutes to explain the story in as much detail as possible, and were encouraged to look at the pictures while so doing. For the silent film retelling task, the participants watched the film without taking notes and after watching the film, they were allowed the same amount of time as they did in the H/N task to prepare the narrative in their head and then they started narrating the story. Further, they were given the same amount of time to tell the story as the picture storybook telling. The NSs of Japanese, English and Korean were given the same instructions to narrate the picture story and silent film in their respective languages. Previous studies such as Robinson (2001) revealed that the order of tasks might have an effect on the performance, thus, half of the participants in all the groups did the H/N task first and followed by the T/T task, while the other half carried out the tasks in the opposite order, in order to avoid a task order influence.

Follow-up interviews were given to all the Japanese NS participants as well as two KOR-Mid level, three ENG-Mid level, three KOR-High level and three KOR-High level speakers by the investigator a few days later. The recorded narratives were played and the participants were asked about the use of *ga*, *wa*, zero anaphora, passive forms, etc. as markers of topic continuity and discontinuity.

3.2 Analysis

3.2.1 Coding

The main concern of this study was to investigate how each animate referent was introduced into the discourse and subsequently maintained as a topic throughout the extended oral discourse. I partially adapted Nakamura's (1993) coding systems for depicting how speakers managed introducing and tracking referents in the discourse in order to provide increased comparability with her investigation of referent management in L1 (child and adult) Japanese oral narratives that used the same picture book. Her coding scheme included initial, second, and subsequent mentions of referents. Nakamura provided examples of these categories; however, there was no explicit description of these variables in her study. Therefore, it was difficult to determine the coding scheme, especially for the subsequent mentions. After a careful interpretation of her examples, and the other relevant studies to which she referred, I determined that the 'subsequent mention of a referent' in her study could be understood as the subsequent mention after the second mention, and/or as any subsequent mention of a referent occurring in the subject position.

In the present study, the referents were assigned to the following categories and coded accordingly: the introduction, the re-introduction (topic switch), and the continuous mention following the re-introduction of referents. Prior to the current study and Nakahama (2009), coding of the 'second mention referents' were considered. However, there were no discernible developmental patterns found in either the Korean L1 group or the English L1 group; thus, markings of the 'second mentions of the referents' were ruled out to be studied in the current research.

Referent introduction denotes the referents that were initially introduced into the discourse in any position in the sentence. The re-introduction of referent is defined as "the referent that is re-introduced into discourse in the subject position, which has previously been introduced but has lost its topicality, i.e., another referent has appeared in the subject position prior to re-introduction." Thus, the re-introduction of referent operates as a topic switch, since this referent takes over the topic of discourse by re-appearing in the discourse in the subject position.[21] Throughout the text, the terms, topic switch and re-introduction of the referent are interchangeably used. Lastly, the continuous mention of referents following their reintroduction can be defined as a referent that continues to be the topic of discourse (appearing in the subject position) until the topicality is taken over by another referent in the subject position. Example 3.1 illustrates the coding of referent introduction.

Example 3.1 Coding of Referent Introduction[22]

Otoko no	*ko*	*ga*	*kaeru*	*o*	*tsukamaetekite*
Male GEN	child	NOM	frog	ACC	catch and

sore	*o*	*bin*	*ni*	*iremashita.*
that	ACC	bottle	into	put-PAST

'A boy caught a frog and (he) put it in the bottle'.

This was taken from a Japanese NS narrative in the H/N task condition. In this example, the introduction of the boy was coded by *ga*, while the frog was introduced with the object marker, *o*. The following sample excerpt depicts how re-introduction of referents (topic switch) and their continuous mentions were coded.

Example 3.2 Re-introduction of Referents (Topic Switch) and Continuous Mentions

Inu	*ga*	*mado*	*kara*	*tobiorite*	*shimaimashita.*
Dog	NOM	window	from	jump	completely-PAST

Otoko	*no*	*ko*	*wa*	*okotte imasu.*
Male	GEN	child	TOP	angry-being

Ø	*mori*	*no*	*naka*	*e*	*itte*	Ø	*ana*	*o*
(boy)	forest	GEN	inside	to	go and	(boy)	hole	ACC

sagashitemimashita.
look-PAST

'The dog jumped from the window. The boy is angry. He went inside the forest and looked inside a hole'.

This excerpt appears several sentences into the H/N condition narrative. The boy has been introduced into the discourse prior to this mention. At this point, the speaker places the dog in the subject position and thus places focus on the dog's actions. At this point, the dog is the topic of the discourse. Then the topic of the discourse switches and the boy is promoted to the subject position and coded by the full noun form followed by *wa*. In this manner, the already known (previously introduced) referent (i.e., the boy) regains topicality by appearing in the subject position. This boy with *wa* marking (*otoko no ko wa*) in the second sentence is coded as topic switch (i.e., referent re-introduction). Once the boy is re-established as the 'on-going' topic of the discourse (topic switch), he continues as the topic for several clauses, marked with zero anaphora. Both first and second anaphoras in this example were coded as continuous mention of referent and until the topic (the boy) was interrupted by another referent (i.e., topic switch), these mentions would continue to be coded as continuous mention of referent.

These continuous mention of referent can be said to be the most continual topic of discourse since they regained the status of being a topic after a previous introduction followed by an interruption by other referents. It should be noted here that coding of the continuous mention of referent following their second mentions was initially attempted, however, these cases were rare, especially in the H/N context, possibly due to the fact several characters were involved in the story. This pattern is consistent with Clancy and Downing's (1987) findings; indeed, Clancy and Downing found so few instances of uninterrupted mention that they limited their investigation of the patterns of referent progression in narratives to the initial and second mention of the referent. In the current study as well, coding of the third (continuous) mention of referents was not considered.

Besides postpositional markings, the passive structure was also examined as a means to investigate how topic continuity and discontinuity is managed in oral narrative discourse. As discussed in Chapter 2, a claim was made by some researchers that the agent in the passive structure serves a non-topical role (e.g., Cooreman, 1987; Shibatani, 1985; Shotter, 1989), and the patient is more topical than the agent. L1 and L2 Japanese narrative studies (Nakahama, 2003, 2009 and Yanagimachi, 1997, 2000) also have shown that the passive structure was used to demote the agent or continue the topicality of the patient. Therefore, the passive structure was also coded. The passivisation of verbs normally occurs in conjunction with the by-phrase (NP+*ni/kara* in Japanese), thus the findings of the passive structure will be discussed along with the production of NP+*ni/kara*. In addition to these coding criteria, I followed the method of previous researchers (Clancy, 1980; Clancy and Downing, 1987; Yanagimachi, 1997, 2000) in that direct quotations were excluded from analysis.

Three sets of L2 Japanese narratives were randomly chosen from each proficiency level in the L1 Korean and English speaking L2 Japanese data (thus totaling 12 narratives), and they were coded by another native speaker of Japanese. The results reached inter-rater reliability with Cohen's Kappa = 0.99, indicating "almost perfect" agreement between the raters.

Notes

16 According to the ACTFL guidelines (1989), the description of the novice learners is as follows: "The [n]ovice [l]evel is characterised by the ability to communicate minimally with learned material. The speaker reacts to conversational initiatives of the conversational partner, primarily with formulaic or rote utterances in words and phrases, such as greetings and often-heard expressions, and lists vocabulary items that may have been learned in groups, such as colors, numbers, days of the week, months, articles of clothing, etc."
17 The SOPI will be explained further in 3.1.3 when I discuss the learners' proficiency levels.
18 The mean length of stay in Japan was the same between KOR-Mid and ENG-Mid groups, therefore a statistical test was only applied to the advanced level groups.
19 Due to its rather free flowing nature (not linear storytelling), cutting the story encountered no real loss or confusion for the viewer.
20 The time restriction was required since it has been found that planning of speech influences the learners' performance (see Williams, 1992).
21 It should be noted here that reintroduction of referents can be done in nonsubject positions in Japanese; however, they are not coded as a reintroduction/topic switch as they are not considered powerful enough to switch the topic of discourse.
22 Abbreviations used in the manuscript are: NOM - nominative, GEN - genitive, TOP - topic, ACC - accusative, PAST - past tense, DEC - declarative, PASS - passive.

Chapter 4

Results

This chapter presents the results of the analyses of all NS data (Japanese, Korean and English) as well as L2 Japanese data. The chapter consists of the following two main sections: 1) referent introduction and tracking in Japanese, Korean and English NS narratives, and 2) developmental patterns in referent introduction and tracking in L2 Japanese by Korean and English L1 speakers at two different proficiency levels. Given that many similarities are expected between Japanese and Korean, the results of the KNS narratives will be explained in comparison with the JNS data when relevant. I will show the results of the ENS data more comprehensively than the KNS, as marking of the referents is expected to be vastly different from that of the JNS narrative. After some tendencies of referent marking in Japanese, Korean and English are introduced, the NNS results will be presented in conjunction with the JNS data in order to regard the forms chosen by the JNS as the target forms. Although the current chapter will contain some analytical discussion, an in-depth interpretation of the key results will be presented in the Discussion section in Chapter 5.

4.1 NS narratives

To answer the first research question, "What kinds of referential devices are used by NS of Japanese, Korean and English for introducing and tracking referents in oral narratives?" the total number of occurrences of the forms used for referent introduction and its maintenance as topics were examined. To test Hypotheses 1(a), 1(b) and 1(c), corresponding to NS production, chi-square tests were conducted on the total number of occurrences for various referent markings. In order to claim CLI from the learners' L1 (Korean and English) in their acquisition of referent markings in L2 Japanese, it is critical to thoroughly investigate how NSs of the respective L1s perform referent marking in their native language.

This section will attempt to show how such strategies in English and Korean differ from and resemble those of Japanese, respectively. Further, Repeated Measure ANOVA tests were used to find out if task complexity triggered differing referent marking schemes between the H/N and T/T conditions for all three groups. The results of L1 Japanese, Korean and English data will be presented in that order. Since L1 Japanese will serve as the baseline data for the results of the L2 Japanese, the weight of discussion will be placed more heavily on the L1 Japanese data than the L1 Korean and English data.

4.1.1 L1 Japanese Narratives
4.1.1.1 Referent introduction
Quantitative Findings

Table 4.1 illustrates the forms used for encoding referent introduction by the NSs of Japanese. Although chi-square tests were conducted on the raw frequency of use in each category, average percentages of the proportional use of the forms for referent introduction are also presented in the table for reference purposes.[23]

Table 4.1 Referent Introduction by JNS

NP+	*ga* (NOM)	*wa* (TOP)	*o* (ACC)	*ni/kara* (by)	*mo* (also)	particle drop	others[24]
H/N	34	0	12	6	3	0	9
	52.9	0	19.7	9.8	4.5	0	13.3
T/T	33	0	0	5	3	0	12
	63.0	0	0	9.9	5.2	0	24.5

Total number of occurrences and average percentages are shown in the first and second lines, respectively. H/N: here-and-now task condition, T/T: there-and-then task condition.

Table 4.1 shows that in both the H/N and T/T tasks Japanese NSs followed the conventional pattern found in previous studies (Hinds, 1983, 1984, 1987; Nakahama, 2003, 2009; Nakamura, 1993; Yoshioka, 2005) in that the full NP with *ga* was the most frequently used device to introduce a new referent into discourse. Close to half of all the new referents were marked with *ga*. Recall *ga* is a particle which indicates that the referent, which appears in subject position, is assumed by the speaker to be new information for the listener. NP+*o* and NP+*ni/kara* together constituted about 1/3 of the marking of the first mentions of referents in the H/N narratives. NP+*o* is used for marking a direct object, while NP+*ni/kara* means 'by' and is used for marking the agent in the passive structure. In the T/T narratives, the usage of '*ga*' weighed 63% of all the particle uses, and NP+*o* was not used at all. The uses of *ga*, *o*, and *ni* were also analysed qualitatively and will be presented in the subsequent section.

A chi-square test was carried out to compare the number of total occurrences for all the forms used for encoding referent introductions for both the H/N and T/T. The result with χ^2 (4) = 47.4, p < .01 (in H/N) and χ^2 (3) = 43.6, p < .001 (in T/T) indicated that at least one item exhibits significantly more frequent occurrence than the others. In order to find out which item had significantly more occurrences than the others, a post-hoc test (pair-wise chi-square comparison) was conducted on the most frequently occurring form, NP+*ga* (34), and the second most frequently occurring form, NP+*o* (12) in the H/N narrative and NP+*ga* (33) and NP+*ni/kara* (5) in the T/T. The difference in occurrence between NP+*ga* and NP+*o* (χ^2 (1) = 10.52, p = .001), as well as the difference between NP+*ga* and NP+*ni/kara* (χ^2 (1) = 20.63, p < .001) were both significant. These results indicate that NP+*ga* was the most prevalent form used to encode referent introduction in both types of narrative, and thereby supports a part of Hypothesis 1 (a) which deals with referent introduction: 'the most conventional form used for encoding referent introduction (most discontinuous context) by Japanese NSs will be the full NP with indefinite marking (i.e., NP+*ga*)'.

While both types of task triggered high usage of NP+*ga*, higher percentage use of the form was observed in the T/T task (63.0% for the T/T and 52.9% for the H/N task). Although the percentage use of NP+*ga* increased with the increased task demands placed on the speakers, the results of Repeated Measure ANOVA within subject for the use of NP+*ga* between the H/N and T/T tasks revealed that the difference was not significant (F (1, 9) =1.17, p = .308), and this result supports Hypothesis 6 which states, 'L1 Japanese speakers' narrative discourse will not be affected drastically by task complexity.' The following section reports on the qualitative analysis; it focuses on the functional motivations for the use of the forms of referent introduction.

Qualitative Findings

I will provide qualitative analysis to explain the form choice to mark referent introductions by the JNS. I will first analyse the H/N narratives and then the T/T narratives.

H/N Narratives

A detailed qualitative analysis of the data revealed that there was systematicity among the NSs in introducing referents into discourse both in the H/N and T/T narratives. Overall, there seemed to be a predisposition for the Japanese NSs to use different types of postpositional markers depending on the status of the characters in the story. The canonical form for encoding the introduction of the main characters (the boy and the dog) was NP+*ga* in the H/N narratives. All the Japanese NSs (N=10) used NP+*ga* to introduce the most important character (i.e., the boy) into the story in the H/N setting. Of these speakers, three speakers combined the two main protagonists (i.e., the boy and the dog) and marked them with *ga*, while the other two speakers combined not only the boy and the dog but also the frog — another major character — and marked them with *ga*. Excerpt 4.1 and 4.2 demonstrate examples of referent introduction using the prototypical particle to refer to a new referent, i.e., NP+*ga*, in the H/N setting.

Example 4.1 Marking of the Main Characters with *ga* by JNS

Unn to	*mazu*	*otoko*	*no*	*ko*	*to*	*..inu*	*ga*	*ite*
Umm..	firstly	male	GEN	child	and	dog	NOM	exist

etto	*futari*	*wa*	*kaeru*	*o*	*tsukamaete*	*bin*	*no*	*naka ni*
umm.	two	TOP	frog	ACC	catch and	a jar	GEN	inside

iretokimashita
put-PAST

'Umm, firstly, there were a boy and a dog, umm..these two caught a frog and put it in a jar'.

As some other speakers did (three cases altogether), this speaker combined the boy and dog as one subject and marked them both as new information by placing *ga* after the NP *to* NP construction.

Example 4.2 Marking of the Boy with *ga* and the Frog with *o* by JNS

<u>Otoko</u>	no	<u>ko</u>	ga	<u>kaeru</u>	o	kattete	soshitara
Male	GEN	child	NOM	frog	ACC	keep	and then

yoru	nete	okitara	kaeru	ga	inakunatteta
night	sleep and	get up	frog	NOM	is-NEG-PAST

kara	<u>inu</u>	<u>to</u>	issho ni	sagashiniiku	nda	kedo
because	dog	with	together	go look for		but

'A boy had a frog and when (he) went to bed at night and got up, the frog was gone, so (he) goes looking for (the frog) with a dog, but…'

Unlike the speaker in Example 4.1, this speaker focused the importance on the boy by placing him in the topical (subject) position alone. Careful examination of his entire narrative reveals that he focused the journey of finding the frog entirely from the boy's perspective, instead of considering the search for the frog as the dog's intention as well. Interestingly, as a result, he used *ga* only for introducing the boy but after that he referred to the boy using zero anaphora throughout the narrative. He referred to the dog's actions once, but he switched the topic back to the boy immediately after that using the attenuated form (i.e., zero anaphora). It was evident that he maximised the role of the boy as a main character in this way. This perspective was established from the very beginning of his narrative by regarding the dog as the boy's companion for his escapade to the forest in search of the frog (linguistically marking the dog with '*to*', meaning 'with').

In previous studies (Nakahama, 2003; Nakamura, 1993; Yoshioka, 2005) which used the same picture storybook as was used for the H/N task in the current study, NP+*wa* was used to mark a referent introduction for the most important character, i.e., the boy, by a small number of speakers. However, the speakers in the current study opted for using the canonical form for marking new referents (i.e., NP+*ga*) and chose not to use NP+*wa* in either the H/N or

T/T narratives.

As far as the introduction of the frog is concerned, eight NSs used the direct object particle, *o* as in the following example.

Example 4.3 Marking of the Frog with *o* by JNS (#5)

Ee..	*ikutsu gurai*		*daroo*	*maa*	*chiisai*	*otoko*	*no*	*ko*
Hm..	how old approximately		wonder	well	small	male	GEN	child

ga	*bin*	*no*	*naka*	*ni*	*kaeru*	*o*	*irete*	*kattete,*
NOM	jar	GEN	inside	in	frog	ACC	put in	keep and

'Hm..I wonder how old he is but anyway, a small boy put a frog in a jar and kept it there…'

As this speaker did, all the eight speakers who used *o* to mark the frog regarded it as the boy's pet and made clear the hierarchical relationship between these two protagonists, though they both played important roles in the story. The distinct choices of how speakers encoded the boy, the dog, and the frog here might well be related to the relationship between animacy hierarchy and referential marking (see e.g., Comrie, 1989 for animacy scale). The notion of an animacy hierarchy and its relationship to topic provides that the topicality of the nominal referent in discourse is determined by animacy. The higher the animacy of a referent is (e.g., human referents being higher on the scale than non-human referents), the greater its likelihood of being the topic or focus of discourse (see Yamamoto, 1996 for a detailed explanation of animacy hierarchy). The results of Kim's (1989) study investigating Korean L1 narratives supported this animacy hierarchy hypothesis for Korean speakers in that 94% of human referents being introduced for the first time received *ka/i* marking in the subject position, displaying high topicality and focus of discourse. Non-human referents in her study, on the other hand, were brought into a story in less topical positions in a sentence. The same finding was also reported in Clancy (1980) in her Japanese narratives. The importance of the animacy hierarchy in human conceptualisation might explain why all the NSs of Japanese in the current study introduced the boy in the topical position and some speakers differentiated its topicality from the dog and the frog.

However, the animacy hierarchy itself cannot explain the subjects' choices concerning the introduction of non-human characters with NP+*ga*. When the frog was found with his wife and children toward the end of the course of search, these new characters (i.e., the frog's wife and the children) were mainly introduced in the form of NP+*ga* in the topical position. Furthermore, many of the peripheral characters (protagonists) tended to be introduced in less topical positions with *ni, o* or copula. Thus, an additional hierarchy might be proposed to supplement the animacy hierarchy in the present study. This additional hierarchy may tentatively be called "the significance hierarchy" and provides the basis for the hypothesis that the more significant role the referent plays in a story, the higher the topicality marking it warrants. Although the frog is a very important character in the narrative, it was represented as a pet of the boy (and the dog in some narratives) and played a less topical role, particularly in the opening of the narrative. This less topical role was coded grammatically by placing the frog in the object position.

Interestingly, however, when the boy and the dog finally found the frog and his family toward the end of the narrative, not only the introduction of the frog's family but also the re-introduction of the frog himself was marked with the particle, *ga*, with the exception of one speaker. The introduction of the frog's family seems to raise the status of the frog, redefining him from mere pet to a more human-like creature with family ties and emotions as was reflected in the particle use when he was reintroduced into the story.

In addition, the discovery of the frog was so important from the standpoint of the story plot, as the whole narrative was centred on the boy's search for the pet frog. Therefore, it could be said that the marking of the discovery of the frog with *ga* after the long search can be explained by the interface of 1) the animacy hierarchy (personified status of the frog) and 2) the significance hierarchy (the importance of the discovery of the frog). This predominant episode (nine out of ten NSs) of *ga*-marking of the re-introduction of the frog is consistent with what was found in Nakamura's (1993) study in that all re-introductions of the frog in her adult narratives were marked with *ga*. The re-introduction of the frog by the Japanese NS will be compared to that of the Korean and English NSs in the subsequent sections.

While NP+*o* was frequently used to introduce the frog into the story, it was also occasionally used to introduce peripheral characters, such as the bees, into narratives. Example 4.4 demonstrates a typical way in which the NSs of Japanese introduced some peripheral characters.

Example 4.4 Marking of the Bees with *o* by JNS (#10)

Inu	*ga*	*hachi*	*o*	*okorasete*	*shimatte*	
Dog	NOM	bees	ACC	angry-CAU	inadvertently	and

ee...maa..	*inu*	*ga*	*hachi*	*ni*	*oikakerareteiru*	*yoko*	*de*
um..well..	dog	NOM	bees	by	chase-PASS-ING	beside	at

otoko	*no*	*ko*	*ga*	*mada*	*ironna*	*tokoro*	*sagashiteite*	*ma*
male	GEN	child	NOM	still	various	place	look-ing	well

fukuroo	*o*	*okorasete*	*shimatte*	
owl	ACC	angry-CAU	inadvertently	and

'The dog inadvertently made bees angry and um..well, the dog gets chased by the bees, and next to the dog, the boy was looking for (the frog) at various places and well..inadvertently made an owl angry and..'

As is seen in Example 4.4, the speaker introduced *hachi* (bees) and *fukuroo* (owl) in the object position, which is not a topical position in a sentence, and this circumstance provides evidence that the speakers wished to assign minor status to these characters.

Once the initial introduction of the bees was made, the speaker used the marker *ni* (by), along with the passive structure, *oikakerareteiru* (is being chased), to explain that the dog was chased by the bees after he made the bees angry. This speaker did not continue to discuss the owl or its actions, which would indicate a perceived lack of importance to the story. As this speaker referred to the bees, some speakers introduced peripheral characters into their narrative discourse as objects or some other non-topical positions and then later referred to them as the agents in the passive structures, while others introduced the peripheral characters in the agentive position in the passive structures. Example 4.5 illustrates the latter case.

Example 4.5 Marking of the Owl with *ni* by JNS (#2)

Ee..	*shoonen*	*wa*	*sono*	*hachi*	*kara*	*ee..*
Um..	boy	TOP	those	bees	from	um..

nogaremashita	*ga*	*fukuroo*	*ni*	*osowaremasu*
escape-PAST	but	owl	by	attack-PASS

'Um..the boy escaped from the bees but gets attacked by an owl.'

In this example, the speaker begins the sentence with a full noun, *shoonen* (boy) followed by the definite marker, *wa*. Although this is not the first mention of the boy, the speaker seems to have used the full noun because in the immediately preceding clauses the dog was in the subject position and thus was the focus of that stretch of discourse. In other words, the topic of this stretch of narrative switches from the dog to the boy. The shift was accomplished by using the full noun with *wa* to avoid ambiguity. In fact, topic shift with the use of NP+*wa* was very common in the present study. The details of topic switch will be discussed in Section 4.1.1.2.

Moreover, once the new topic was established, the speaker in Example 4.5 used zero anaphora in the following reference to the boy. Maintaining the boy as the topic of the discourse, he introduced a peripheral character, the owl, as an agent in a less topical position. This exemplifies how a peripheral character gets introduced as the demoted agent of the passive structure, while the main characters remained in the topical (subject) position but in the semantic role of the patient. There were six occurrences of NP+*ni/kara* for referent introduction in the native Japanese speaker data, and all the instances of NP+*ni/kara* were used to introduce peripheral characters such as the owl and the bees.

In Nakamura's (1993) study, the use of some particles such as "NP+other particles" (29.4%), were combined and thus it is plausible that the NS in her study chose NP+*ni/kara* or NP+*o* for peripheral characters. However, direct comparison of such forms was not made possible since the researcher did not separately list these linguistic features. On the other hand, the proportional use of NP+*ni/kara* (9.8%) by the NSs of Japanese is quite similar to the percentage reported in Nakahama (2003a) and Yoshioka's (2005) NS narratives (11% and 10%, respectively), thereby confirming the common referent introduction patterns among NS of Japanese across studies.

In terms of passive expressions, 27 of them were found and every native Japanese speaker produced at least two passive expressions/constructions in his/her narrative. The only referents that were patients of the passive structure were the boy or the dog. This shows that the native Japanese speakers were keeping their topical focus on these two characters and suggests that these two characters were considered to be the main protagonists. Referents that appear to have been considered the antagonists of the story were demoted, even when they were the agents, by placing them in a non-topical position (see e.g., Bamberg, 1994; Cooreman, 1983; Shibatani, 1985 for this argument for the passive voice). Therefore, Hypothesis 2 that states 'topic continuity will also be expressed via voice alternation (active and passive voices) in Japanese, Korean and English NS narratives" was supported in terms of the JNS narratives.

Though it is not a marker to encode referent introduction *per se*, one particular adjective, *aru*, was frequently used in the beginning of NS narrative discourse to indicate the opening of the story. See Example 4.6.

Example 4.6 Beginning of Storytelling by JNS (#4)

Eeto	aru	tokoro	ni	otoko no		ko	ga	imashita.
Um..	certain	place	at	male	GEN	child	NOM	exist-PAST

Sono	otoko	no	ko	wa	uuto	inu	to	kaeru	o
That	male	GEN	child	TOP	um	dog	and	frog	ACC

petto	to shite	katteimashita.
pet	as	keep-ing-PAST

'Um..at a certain place there was a boy. That boy had a dog and a frog as his pets'

Aru means "a certain" and this phrase is typically used to start a story in Japanese. For instance, a well-known folk tale called *Momotaro* starts as follows.

Example 4.7 Typical Beginning of a Folk Tale in Japanese

Mukashi mukashi	aru	tokoro	ni	ojiisan	to	obaasan
Long long ago	certain	place	at	old man	and	old woman

ga	sundeimashita.
NOM	live-ing-PAST

'A long long time ago, an old man and an old woman were living in a certain place'

The phrase *aru* was used in a variety of ways in the Japanese NS discourse in the current study. *Aru* ("certain") was combined with "place" by one speaker, "day" by three speakers, and one speaker used the phrase with "the boy." All these phrases were used to show novelty of "place," "time" and "the character" to the listener. This characteristic of newness and specificity is in accordance with the particle, *ga*, which is used to describe "new" information in a discourse. Those speakers who used *aru* with "the boy" also used *ga* to mark this previously unshared character to the listener.

In sum, NP+*ga* was the predominant form used for bringing a new referent into the Japanese NS participants' narrative discourse. However, qualitative analysis showed that the NSs of Japanese used not only NP+*ga* but also other forms (such as NP+*ni/kara*) in the passive construction to introduce referents into discourse. The selection of the forms seemed to be motivated by the discourse status the speaker wished to assign to the characters, depending on their perceived importance in the story. For instance, two main characters in the story (i.e., the boy and the dog) were primarily marked with NP+*ga*, which is known as a prototypical marker for bringing a new referent into a discourse (Clancy, 1980; Nakamura, 1993).

More peripheral characters, on the other hand, were marked not only with NP+*ga* but also with various other postpositional markers in less topical positions in a sentence. For instance, these markers included NP+*ni/kara*, a marker which is used to denote agents for the passive construction in Japanese. The NSs of Japanese seemed to choose these grammatical positionings in order to keep the focus on the main character in the topical position even when that character was a patient in the event being discussed. These results indicate that the Japanese NSs used particular morphological and syntactic forms in order to accomplish specific discoursal functions in their L1 Japanese oral narratives. What follows next is the qualitative analysis of referent introduction in T/T narratives, and while similar trends between H/N and T/T are discussed, the centre of discussion will be focused on the differing findings between the two task conditions.

T/T Narratives
In the T/T setting, the Japanese NSs showed a similar pattern to what was

found in the H/N narratives, in that the sheep — one of the major characters in the story — was marked with *ga* by all the Japanese NSs.[25] There were two other main characters in the story, a bear and a rabbit, however, only six speakers marked them with *ga* and the remaining four speakers marked them with *ni* (with) in the following structure: *kuma to usagi ni aimashita* (met with a bear and a rabbit). Therefore, the speakers gave up the subject position to what they tentatively decided was the main topic of discourse (i.e., the sheep). While the sheep disappears from the plot when the season changes from winter to spring, this character seemed to be recognised as the most important in the storyline, at the time of the utterance, due to the fact that she appeared in the very beginning scene, and was the centre of attention between the two other major male characters. Example 4.8 illustrates an example of *ga* marking for all three major characters, and Example 4.9 shows *ga* marking for the sheep and *ni* marking for the rabbit and the bear.

Example 4.8 Marking of the Main Characters with *ga* by JNS (#10)

Mazu...	*usagi*	*to*	*kuma*	*to*	*shirokuma*	*mitaina*	*no*	*ga*
First	rabbit	and	bear	and	white bear	like	one	NOM

ite..	*de..*	*usagi*	*no*	*sukaafu*	*ga*	*kuma*	*ni*
exists	and..	rabbit	GEN	scarf	NOM	bear	by

torarete
take-PASS and

'First, there were a rabbit and a bear and a white bear-like thing and the rabbit's scarf was taken by the bear and'

Though the scene starts with the sheep (or white bear-like thing) making an appearance on the sleigh, the speaker grouped this character together with the other two major characters, and introduced them all at once.

Example 4.9 Marking of the Main Characters with *ga* and *ni* by JNS (#7)

Nanka	*yoku*	*wakannai*	*shiroi*	*doobutsu*	*ga*	*sori*	*ni*
Well...	really	know-NEG	white	animal	NOM	sleigh	on

notte	*sono*	*usagi*	*to*	*mooippiki*	*no*	*chairo*	*no*	*doobutsu*
ride	that	rabbit	with	one more	GEN	brown	GEN	animal

no	*tokoro*	*ni*	*asobini*	*itte*
GEN	place	to	go in order to play and

'A not really unrecognisable white animal got on the sleigh with a rabbit and a brown animal in order to play and…'

The speaker in Example 4.9 introduced the sheep independently and combined the rabbit and the bear together as characters with whom the sheep was interested in playing. There were no discernible differences in the ways in which these two types of speakers (those who introduced the sheep separately and those who introduced it together with the other two animals) developed the story throughout the narratives. In other words, the six speakers who started out their narratives placing importance on the sheep did not continue to tell the story from the sheep's perspectives probably because she disappears halfway into the story.

While close to 20% of the markings of referent introduction were done with *o*, the object marker, in the H/N setting, the form was not used at all in the T/T setting. This could be caused by the fact that the significance of the three major characters was somewhat equal in the T/T, whereas in the H/N the leading character was the boy and the two other characters were considered either his friends or pets, thus being relegated to the object position. Other miscellaneous markers such as copula were also used, but their occurrences were not so frequent as to warrant inclusion as a category of interest, and thus were counted simply as 'other'. Although different percentage use of NP+*ga* was observed between the two task types, the degree to which it was caused by the differing complexity of the task types or by the different storylines, will be discussed in detail when I present the results and discussion of the L2 learner data.

The use of NP+*ni/kara* was also found in the T/T narratives. Though there were six occurrences of *ni/kara* under the H/N narrative condition, there were five of them found in the T/T. Example 4.10 demonstrates an instance of the particle *ni*.

Example 4.10 Marking of a Peripheral Character with *ni* by JNS (#10)

Sono	*chiizu..*	*o*	*eta*	*yorokobi*	*de*	*odotteita*
That	cheese	ACC	get-PAST	joy	with	dance-ing-PAST

toki	*ni*	*yudanshite shimatte*	*<u>tori</u>*	*<u>ni</u>*	*torarete*
when	at	neglect inadvertently	bird	by	take-PASS and

'When (the rabbit and the bear) were dancing with joy for winning the cheese, they were careless and had their cheese taken away by a bird and..'

This was the last scene of the story. In this scene, the bear and the rabbit were gambling with mice, won the bet and got the cheese, but carelessly had the cheese taken away by a mother bird to feed her baby birds. The topic of the discourse had been the bear and the rabbit for four clauses prior to this utterance, and the speaker maintained the topic by allocating the agentive role (in the passive construction) to the bird, for its initial appearance in the discourse.

There were 27 passive expressions found in the T/T narratives, exactly the same amount found in the H/N narratives. There are some scenes in which passive forms can be produced, such as when one of the major characters was being teased by another character, or when the main characters had their food taken away by the bird. However, the scene does not provide as obvious an opportunity as the H/N narrative counterpart in terms of creating passive constructions. However, the JNS produced the same amount of passive expressions in both types of narratives. As was the case with the use of *ni/kara* under the H/N condition, the form was also used to introduce peripheral characters (four participants were to mark the mother bird, and one a snowman) as the agent in the passive constructions in the T/T narrative setting. A more detailed discussion on the formation of the passive forms will be discussed in the NNSs section, along with the results from all the NNS groups, the JNS, the KNS, and the ENS groups.

Lastly, as compared to the H/N setting, the T/T narratives did not generate many uses of '*aru*' (certain). Recall five speakers utilised '*aru*' in the H/N narratives; however, only two speakers used '*aru*' in the T/T narratives. Interestingly, seven speakers used '*mazu*' (first) to begin the T/T narratives. The remaining one speaker used '*nanka*' ('well'), instead of *aru* or *mazu*. The usage of '*mazu*' was rather rare in the H/N setting in that only two speakers used it. It appears that '*aru*' is used when the speaker is ready to set the background of the story, whereas '*mazu*' is used by the speaker to warm up not only the listener but also the speaker him/herself. By taking a close look at both the H/N and T/T narratives, in the H/N setting, with the context-embedded pictorial support, the speakers are ready to narrate a story as a typical Japanese folk tale, which would normally start with *aru* (see Example 4.7). In the T/T setting, on the other hand, the speaker does not have the leisure to make a fairy tale type story as he/she was trying to remember what happened in the film, and tell it as precisely as possible. Though the usage of *aru* did not directly relate to referent markings, this noticeable difference between the tasks should be noted.

A follow-up interview was given to all Japanese NS participants as mentioned in Chapter 3. It was found that none of them realised the distinction between NP+*ga* and NP+*wa*. When asked what the functions of *ga* and *wa*, were, they said these two particles mark the subject of a sentence, and there is no real difference. Further, they did not have metalinguistic knowledge of many of the particles, such as *ni* as an agentive marker, yet they were managing the appropriate form-function mapping in the story development. The results of the interviews with the learners will be discussed in the later sections.

In summary, in both the H/N and T/T narratives, NP+*ga* was the form used for marking referent introduction, therefore, a part of Hypothesis 1(a) was borne out. Qualitative analysis showed that the Japanese NSs allocated suitable forms based on the importance of the characters in the story, and that this was the case in both the H/N and T/T settings. To be specific, they tended to assign the topical position in the sentence to the leading character(s) marking them with *ga*, and less topical positions to the peripheral characters marking them with *ni*, *o* or other particles. They maintained the major characters in the topical position as a patient in the passive construction by introducing the peripheral characters as an agent in the less topical position in both the H/N and T/T narratives. Therefore, frequent occurrences of passive forms were observed, and this result verifies Hypothesis 2.

Though there was no statistical difference in the production of NP+*ga* between the H/N and T/T narratives, the T/T setting generated a little higher percentage use of *ga* than its H/N counterpart. Further, there were different ways that the JNSs started narratives between the two narrative settings (i.e., the use of *aru* and *mazu*). With regard to the production of passive expressions, JNSs produced the same amount of passive forms across the H/N and T/T narratives. Thus, Hypothesis 6 was supported, regarding the production of passives by JNSs.

What follows next is how the Japanese NSs managed topic continuity/discontinuity once referents were introduced into narrative discourse. The results of topic switch (i.e., re-introduction of referents) and the continuous mention of referent in both the H/N and T/T tasks will be shown. First, I will show the results of topic switch in 4.1.1.2 below.

4.1.1.2 Topic switch (Re-introduction of referent)

In this section, the results of the H/N and T/T settings will be presented together. Both quantitative and qualitative findings will be provided. Table 4.2 shows that Japanese NSs used various forms to switch the discourse topic in their narratives in both the H/N and T/T tasks, but the highest percentage use across tasks were *ga*, *wa* and zero anaphora.

Table 4.2 Topic Switch (Re-introduction of Referent) by JNS

NP+	*ga*	*wa*	*mo*	particle drop	zero anaphora
H/N	26	40	3	0	43
	25.1	33.1	2.3	0	39.6
T/T	68	49	6	5	28
	40.0	30.5	2.9	2.1	24.1

Total number of occurrences and average percentages are shown in the first and second lines, respectively.

The previous literature indicates that topic switch is generally done with full NPs, as opposed to zero anaphora, and these previous studies treated all NP plus postpositional markers as full NPs without distinguishing specific postpositional markers (e.g., Clancy, 1992; Kajiwara and Minami, 2008; Yanagimachi, 2000). Thus in order to compare the result of the current study with those that preceded it, NP+*wa*, NP+*ga*, and NP+*mo* were collapsed into the single category of full NP. As expected, when the difference in the total occurrences of full NPs and zero anaphora was compared with a chi-square test the result was significant for both the H/N setting ($\chi^2 (1) = 6.04, p = .014$ and the T/T setting (χ^2 (1) = 73.01, $p < .001$. This result indicates a predominant use of full NPs (over zero anaphora) for marking a topic switch in Japanese narratives, thereby supporting Hypothesis 1(a), which states 'topic switch will be achieved with full NP, rather than zero anaphora'.

While the total number of occurrences of full NPs outweigh those of zero anaphora, the percentage use of zero anaphora was significantly higher in the H/N versus the T/T type narrative (F (1, 9) = 6.73, p = .029). Switching topics possibly involves altering the direction of a story, and therefore requires a great deal of attention from both speakers and the listeners. Under the H/N condition, both speakers and listeners share information because they have the pictorial support in front of them, so the listeners could infer who the speaker was referring to without the speaker having to explicitly mention the subject. Under the T/T condition, on the other hand, the speaker would have to make sure that the listener follows the narrative without visual support, thus triggering the speaker to use more coding to explicitly mark the referent, especially when the topic of discourse was switched. Interestingly, it was found that the majority of cases of topic switch (over 90%) were done in order to bring back the main character as the topic of the story, and all the occurrences of topic switch with zero anaphora were found when switching the topic to the main characters, irrespective of task type. Table 4.3 illustrates this pattern in both the H/N and T/T settings.

Table 4.3 Subjects of Topic Switch

	H/N Main	H/N Peripheral	T/T Main	T/T Peripheral
JNS	105	6	143	15
	94.6	5.4	90.5	9.5

The total number of occurrences and average percentages are shown in the first and second lines, respectively.

To provide a specific example, in the H/N narrative, many instances of zero anaphora when switching topics were found between the frog, and the boy and the dog, especially from the beginning to the middle of the story. In the beginning of the story, the speakers first focused on the fact that the frog escaped from the jar and then switched to the boy's state (that the boy realised the frog was gone) and action (that he started to look for the frog). During the search for the frog in the forest, the topic shifted frequently between the frog and the boy/dog with the use of zero anaphora.

This restricted use of zero anaphora for the main characters (the boy, the dog, and the frog) may be explained by what Clancy (1992) called 'ellipsis for hero' strategy. Clancy claims that a hero of a story tends to receive an attenuated form (i.e., ellipsis) and that the 'ellipsis for hero' strategy was particularly more evident when topic switching took place, compared to when the same character was referred to as a topic continuously. In other words, when the participants in her study switched topics, they tended to use zero anaphora for the main characters, but not for peripheral characters. However, when the speakers continuously referred to characters, they tended to use zero anaphora regardless of the 'hero' versus peripheral status of the characters. The same pattern was also observed in Yoshioka's (2005) study.

In the current study, when the NSs of Japanese switched topics, they tended to differentiate markings for the main characters and the peripheral characters as well. The speakers not only used full NPs but also zero anaphora in order to switch the topic to the main characters, while they adhered to the use of full NPs to encode a topic switch to peripheral characters. Even when two or three important characters interfered with one another's actions or state, some speakers stuck to the 'ellipsis for hero' strategy. With the help of the context (i.e., the pictures in the book) and the saliency of the characters (and their roles), their discourse was never confusing to the listener in the H/N setting.

In the context of topic switch, another tendency was found. Particle drop was observed only for the T/T setting but not for the H/N, although the percentage of particle drop was low (2.1%) in the T/T. In conversations, particle drop is commonly practised, but in monologues, it can be considered rather uncharacteristic. In reintroducing a known referent back into a discourse via topic switch, the speakers delve into their memory in terms of what the character did, and how the story line should continue from then on. Unlike the introduction of a new character, the relationship between the current topic and the reintroduction of a known topic is intricate, and requires careful deliberation. It seemed that after the struggle of attempting to retrieve the information from their memory, the speakers ended up dropping the particles. In the H/N setting, on the other hand, the speakers — with the visible contextual support — knew clearly and unambiguously to whom or what they were switching the topic, and what action the referent would take, and this certainty led to no confusion of particle selection. With the findings from the context of topic switch, Hypothesis 1(a) was supported but Hypothesis 6 was not supported, as the percentage use of zero anaphora was significantly higher in the H/N versus the T/T type narrative in the JNS data.

Thus far, it was found that there are systematic ways in which the NSs of Japanese show topic continuity/discontinuity by way of referent introduction and topic switch (re-introductions of referent). I will now turn to the remaining aspect of investigating referent markings in this study, namely how the NSs of Japanese encoded the referents in the most continuous contexts.

4.1.1.3 Continuous mention of referent

The findings of referent markings in the context of continuous mention of referent in both the H/N and T/T settings, will be provided below. The data will be analysed quantitatively and qualitatively.

Table 4.4 Continuous Mention of Referent by JNS

NP+	*ga*	*wa*	*mo*	particle drop	zero anaphora
H/N	1	6	0	0	126
	0.7	4.1	0	0	95.1
T/T	10	16	2	2	125
	7.2	8.9	1.1	1.8	80.9

Total number of occurrences and average percentages are shown in the first and second lines, respectively.

As Table 4.4 shows, the form most frequently used for marking the highest topic continuity (i.e., in the context of continuous mention of a referent) was zero anaphora for both the H/N and T/T, and this result was expected from previous studies and Givón's (1983) 'iconicity principle'. Since it was obvious that the use of zero anaphora was much higher than the other forms, especially for the H/N setting, statistical testing was not conducted this time. As in the topic switch context, a higher use of zero anaphora was observed in the H/N than in the T/T context, and the difference was significant ($F(1,9) = 16.2, p = .003$). The follow-up interviews revealed that although no speaker intentionally manoeuvred the use and non use of zero anaphora depending on the task type, they all said that they paid greater attention to making their narration easy to follow for the listeners in the T/T context. In contrast, making a story with pictorial support (which allows visuals to be shared between the speaker and the listener) reduced the burden such that they could just tell the story naturally, and without particular effort. With this interview result, it is argued that for topic switch and topic continuation, speakers attempt to avoid ambiguity by using full NPs when referents are not in sight in order to be more explicit, though it might not be a conscious choice by the speakers (see comparable argument in Clancy's (1997) analysis of Korean children's L1 data).

Hypothesis 1 (a) which states that 'the most continuous topic will be coded most frequently with zero anaphora' was supported. However, the H/N narrative triggered less complex marking of referents (i.e., zero anaphora) than the T/T narrative; therefore, Hypothesis 6 was not supported.

A qualitative analysis of the data for the continuous mention of referent indicated that, in some cases, topic continuity via zero anaphora persisted for several clauses. Interestingly, most of the occurrences of zero anaphora were for the main protagonists in the H/N task (94%) and T/T task (98%), showing the high topicality of these characters in the discourse, compared to the peripheral characters that were rarely treated as continuous topics. Therefore, the investigation of the distribution of the use of zero anaphora for the continuous mention of the topical referent illustrates that the NSs tended to distinguish topicality of characters by using zero anaphora in the most continuous context.

In summary, judging from the results of the qualitative and quantitative analyses of the data, it seems apparent that forms were selected for their functions by the Japanese NSs in their discourse. This functional use of language resulted in the production of various forms besides the canonical one (NP+*ga*), for referent introduction in L1 Japanese oral narratives, across both types of task. It also generated the frequent use of zero anaphora for the characters which were deemed to deserve the highest topicality in the story. Task types had effects on how JNSs narrated the story in the context of referent introduction, topic switch, and continuous mention of referent, and the interviews revealed that the speakers attempted to enhance their listener's understanding via higher usage of full NPs in the T/T narratives.

4.1.2 L1 Korean narratives

This section presents referent markings by KNSs in the context of referent introduction, topic switch, and continuous mention of referent in both the H/N and T/T narratives. The KNS data will be compared to that of the JNSs wherever relevant.

4.1.2.1 Referent introduction

Table 4.5 shows the referent introductions in the L1 Korean discourse in both the H/N and T/T narratives. As with the JNS data, the average percentages of the proportional use of the forms are also presented in the table for reference purposes, although the statistical analysis using chi-square tests was conducted based on the number of occurrences.

Table 4.5 Referent Introduction by KNS

NP+	*ka/i* (NOM)	*(n)un* (TOP)	*(l)ul* (ACC)	*eykey, hanthey* (by)	*doo* (also)	particle drop	others
H/N	41	1	18	2	2	0	16
	56.6	0.9	21.1	2.3	1.8	0	17.2
T/T	48	3	7	1	1	2	16
	62.6	3.4	9.9	1.0	1.1	3.0	19.0

Total number of occurrences and average percentages are shown in the first and second lines, respectively.

As shown in Table 4.5, NP+*ka/i* was used with the greatest frequency (41 times in H/N and 48 times in T/T, 56.6% and 62.6% respectively) to encode a new referent in the oral narratives. As explained in Chapter 2, NP+*ka/i* is the Korean equivalent of NP+*ga* in Japanese and as such denotes the indefiniteness of a referent. This high percentage of use of NP+*ka/i* replicates the results of Kim (1989) for referent introduction in her Korean NS oral narrative study. As was done for the Japanese data, a chi-square test was carried out to compare the number of total occurrences for all the forms used for encoding referent introduction. The differences were significant (χ^2 (4) = 62.38, $p < .001$ for H/N, and χ^2 (5) = 157.48, $p < .001$ for T/T). A post-hoc test (pair-wise chi-square comparison) conducted on the most frequently occurring item NP+*ka/i* and the second most frequently occurring item NP+*(l)ul* (the object marker in Korean) revealed that differences in the total occurrence of these forms were statistically significant (χ^2 (1) = 13.64, $p < 0.001$ for H/N, and χ^2 (1) = 30.56, $p < .001$ for T/T). This result supports Hypothesis 1 (b) regarding the production of NSs of

Korean, predicting that 'the marking for referents in the most discontinuous context will be done with NP+*ka/i*'.

In order to make a direct comparison between Korean and Japanese, the following table delineates Korean postpositional markers and the approximately equivalent forms in Japanese (with English grammatical definitions).

Table 4.6 Korean and Japanese Referent Markings

Korean	NP*ka/i*	NP*(n)un*	NP*(l)ul*	NP*eykey, hanthey*	NP*doo*	Zero anaphora
Japanese	NP+*ga*	NP+*wa*	NP+*o*	NP+*ni/kara*	NP+*mo*	Zero anaphora
Classification	NOM	TOP	ACC	agentive	also	subject drop

As can be seen above, there is an equivalent form in Japanese for each post-participle marker in the Korean language. Recall that the JNSs used a variety of markers, in addition to NP+*ga*, to introduce referents into the discourse. The main forms besides NP+*ga* used by the JNSs were NP+*o* (19.7%) and NP+*ni* (9.8%) for the H/N. In the T/T setting, no other forms were prominent. In the H/N narratives, NP+*o* was used mainly in introducing the frog, since at least at the beginning of the story, he was considered as a pet of the boy (and sometimes of the dog), and thus played the role of the object. As was found in the JNSs, most Korean speakers (8) regarded the frog as a pet of the boy, and thus introduced it in the object position with *(l)ul* (the equivalent of *o* in Japanese). In fact, NP+*(l)ul* was the second most frequently used particle (21.1%), following NP+*ka/i*, in the Korean H/N narratives. In the T/T narratives also, *(l)ul* was the second most frequently used item (9.9%), whereas JNS did not produce NP+*o* at all in the T/T condition.

Example 4.11 shows an introduction of the boy, the dog and the frog.

Example 4.11 Referent introduction of the Main Characters by KNS (#10)

Eo	*eonu*	*jagun*	*bang e*	<u>*han*</u>	<u>*sonyon*</u>	<u>*han*</u>	<u>*kgoma*</u>	<u>*wa*</u>
Hmm	certain	small	room in	one	boy	one	child	with

<u>*kangaji*</u>	<u>*wa*</u>	<u>*kaeguri*</u>	<u>*ka*</u>	*gachi*	*jagun*	*bang*	*e*
puppy	with	frog	NOM	together	small	room	in

sal	go	it-eot-eoyo.
live	and	ING-PAST-DEC(Polite)

'In a certain room.. a boy.. a child, a puppy and a frog lived together in a small room…'

This speaker combined the boy, the dog and the frog (in NP *wa* NP construction) and marked them with *ka* (the prototypical new referent marker), giving all three major characters an equally important role. See Example 4.12.

Example 4.12 Referent introduction of the Main Characters by KNS (#8)

Kgoma	*hago*	*kangaji*	*ka*	*yuri*	*byong*	*an*	*e*
Child	with	puppy	NOM	glass	bottle	inside	in

keguri	*lul*	*bo*	*go*	*it-umnida*
frog	ACC	see	and	ING-DEC(polite)

'A child and a puppy were looking at a frog which was inside a jar.'

The speaker introduced the boy and the dog marking them with *ka*, whereas she assigned the object marker *lul* to the frog. This pattern represented the most canonical marking of these three characters in the story. Recall that the JNS used different forms depending on the level of topicality for the referent being introduced. For instance, most of the speakers used NP+*ga* for the main protagonists, while the peripheral characters tended to be introduced with different types of markers presumably due to their tangential distinctiveness in the story. All JNSs marked the most important character, the boy, with NP+*ga*. Interestingly, in the Korean narratives, too, all KNSs used NP+*ka*, the Korean equivalent of NP+*ga*, for the introduction of the boy.

While JNSs did not use *wa* to mark referent introduction, irrespective of narrative type, NP+*(n)un* was used once (0.9%) in the Korean L1 H/N narratives, and three times (3.4%) in the T/T narratives. In the H/N setting, since the picture was directly in front of the speaker and the listener, the speaker might have presumed that the listener shared information concerning the existence of the boy, and thus it is possible that the speaker subconsciously opted for NP+*(n)un* (as it was not technically new information). It was rather puzzling that the T/T task triggered more use of the topic marker than the H/N in the current study. Recall that *(n)un* was never used for referring to newly introduced referents by NSs in Kim's (1989) study. Participants in Kim's study engaged in the retelling of a silent film (Pear Story), so there was no picture in front of them as they narrated the story. Thus, the speaker did not use the topic marker, *(n)un*, to mark a new referent. There was no accounting for this divergent result in the current study, except that the frequency was so low that the occurrences might be considered one-off incidents.

Although many similarities were found between KNS and JNS narratives due to the typological resemblance in their post participle marking system of both languages, some notable differences were evidenced in the way in which some peripheral characters (such as the owl) in the H/N case were introduced. Whereas some auxiliary characters were introduced into discourse as agents in the passive construction in the Japanese narratives, they tended to be introduced in the topical position with *ka/i* (and *nun* by one speaker) in the Korean narratives. In fact, eight out of ten KNSs chose to mark the owl in the topical position, mainly with *ka/i*. This result seems to have some connection to the fact that fewer occurrences of passive construction were found in the KNS narratives than in the JNS narratives. In the KNS narratives in the H/N setting, 17 passive morphemes/expressions were found, and eight out of 10 speakers produced them. Recall that 27 passive constructions were found in the H/N narratives of the JNS participants.

A greater difference was found in the T/T narratives with regard to the frequency of passive expressions between JNSs and KNSs. While JNS speakers produced the same amount of passive expressions between the two tasks (27 instances in both tasks), the KNS speakers produced passive forms/expressions only twice under the T/T condition (two speakers produced a passive expression once each). The lesser frequency of the production of passive forms/expressions could be attributable to the different frequencies of NP+*ni* and NP+ *eykey, hanthey* in the JNS and KNS data respectively.

The difference in the total number of occurrences of passive structures between the JNS and the KNS narratives might be explained by the fact that the two languages have slightly different ways in which concepts are articulated, as was suggested by Kim (2001) and Jung (2002). According to those researchers, as was discussed in Section 2.4.2, Korean speakers tend to place focus more on the actions of each scene rather than on the main characters. In contrast, Japanese speakers tend to fix viewpoints on limited key referents by keeping them in the subject position, and placing the peripheral characters in less topical positions, as agents in passive constructions. In Slobin's terms, this may be an instance of thinking for speaking.

Out of 17 occurrences of passive expressions in the H/N narratives, nine of them were conveyed via derivational suffixes, whereas eight were expressed through lexically passive verbs that have inherent passive meanings. In the T/T narratives, where two passive expressions were found, one was a passive form with derivational suffix, and the other one was a lexically passive verb. Example 4.13 shows how a passive expression was used by a KNS.

Example 4.13 Passive Expression Produced by a KNS (#4)

Ø	beol	dul	hanthey	jjyoki	m	ul	bat-gguyo
	bee	plural	by	go	after	ACC	receive polite

'Lit: (the dog) received 'following' by the bees'

This KNS speaker did not use a passivised verb, but instead an expression that depicts passivisation. Many of the KNS passive expressions were found to be lexicalised passives like this one. As was the case in this example, the patients of the passives were protagonists in both types of task. To be specific, the dog was the patient of ten passive structures (as seen in Example 4.13), and the boy of seven passive structures in the H/N, whereas the rabbit was the patient of one passive structure, and all three major characters were the patients of the other passive structures in the T/T condition.

Obvious actions that interrupt the boy and his dog's search for the frog, in the plot of the H/N narratives, prompted some passive expressions. However, when the story did not have a specific goal for the main characters to achieve, and thus no clear case of interference in the story, such as was found in the plot in the T/T narratives, the KNS participants did not attempt to keep their viewpoint on the major characters. As was shown in 4.1.1.1, the JNS speakers adhered to the same strategy of storytelling in both instances, in that they related the events from the perspective of the main characters, throughout their narratives.

With the above findings, it could be said that Hypothesis 2, which states that '…topic continuity will also be expressed via voice alternation (active and passive voices) in Japanese, Korean and English NS narratives...' was supported in terms of the H/N KNS narratives. The remainder of Hypothesis 2, which states 'but the degree of passive form usage varies among the three languages; Japanese narratives are expected to show the highest occurrences of passive forms' will be discussed once ENS data is revealed in the following section.

What follows next is a summary of the forms used for marking a topic switch in KNS narratives in both the H/N and T/T settings.

4.1.2.2 Topic switch (Re-introduction of referent)

Table 4.7 Topic switch (Re-introduction of referent) by KNS

NP+	*ka/i*	*(n)un*	*doo*	particle drop	zero anaphora
H/N	60	90	13	1	51
	29.1	39.6	5.3	0.6	25.4
T/T	147	71	11	13	28
	53.5	25.8	4.5	5.2	11.0

Total number of occurrences and average percentages are shown in the first and second lines, respectively.

The form most frequently used to mark a topic switch was *(n)un* in the H/N setting and *ka/i* in the T/T setting. Repeated Measure ANOVA was conducted on the percentage use of *ka/i* and *(n)un* in both narrative types, and it was found that the difference was significant at p< .01 level for the use of *ka/i* ($F(1,9) = 25.9, p = .001$) and at $p < .05$ level for *(n)un* ($F(1,9) = 5.6, p = .042$).

Besides the different percentage use of *ka/i* between the two task types, there were two noteworthy tendencies in the context of topic switch. First, particle drop was more frequently observed in the T/T than H/N condition. Although the percentage of particle drop was rather low compared to other forms, nine out of ten KNSs dropped particles at least once in the T/T setting. Recall that the same tendency was found in the JNS narrative. While no particle drop was found in the H/N narrative, 2.1 % of topic switches were marked with particle drop in the JNS data. Although the differences between the two tasks were so small that no definite conclusion can be made, this shared pattern between the two languages suggests a task effect regarding the speakers' particle drop in the T/T narrative.

Higher use of zero anaphora in the H/N as compared to their T/T narrative counterpart in the topic switch context was also found in the KNS data. As argued in explaining the same phenomenon in the JNS data, referring to the elements in the displaced context (the T/T condition) forced the speakers to be more explicit in order to avoid possible confusion or misunderstandings. The differences of percentage use of zero anaphora within subject between the two different tasks were found to be significant ($F(1, 9) = 8.25, p = .018$).

Finally, in addition to these results, the total occurrences of the collapsed full pronouns (NP+*(n)un*, NP+*ka/i* and NP+*doo*) were also compared to zero anaphora, and the differences were significant ($\chi^2 (1) = 30.45, p < .001$). This shows that Korean NSs tend to use full NPs to mark a topic switch in a similar way as was seen in the Japanese NS data, and this result supports Hypothesis 1(b) regarding topic switch.

Qualitative analysis was attempted to find out if there is any discernible pattern in the way the NSs of Korean marked a topic switch in their narrative discourse in the H/N and T/T settings. It was found that the majority of the instances of topic switch involved marking the main characters (the boy, the dog, and the frog for the H/N condition, and the rabbit, the sheep, and the bear for the T/T condition), which was the same situation as was found in the NS Japanese discourse. Furthermore, as was the case with the Japanese NS data, all the instances of zero anaphora for encoding a topic switch were used with the main characters. Therefore, what Clancy (1992) called 'ellipsis for hero strategy' was found to be applicable to Korean L1 narratives as well.

Re-introduction of the frog
In the H/N narratives, regarding the re-introduction of the frog toward the end of the story, a parallel pattern was found between the JNS and KNS narratives. That is, even though the pet frog was already a part of the common knowledge between the speaker and the listener, it was re-introduced with NP+*ga* and NP+*ka/i* in the existential sentence structure, a common pattern that is used to introduce a new referent into narratives in Japanese and Korean respectively. It is arguable that this result, as well as the other wide-ranging similarities in the ways in which referent introduction was encoded in the two languages, indicate that the Japanese and Korean speakers had similar notions of the roles these characters played in the narratives. Consequently, this similar mindset regarding the roles of the characters was reflected in the results of the narrative discourse. In other words, the Japanese and Korean speakers similarly position

morphological and syntactic forms in order to achieve particular discoursal functions in their narratives.

The following section will discuss how the KNS speakers coded continuous mention of referents.

4.1.2.3 Continuous mention of referent

Table 4.8 shows how continuous mention of referent was encoded in the KNS narratives.

Table 4.8 Continuous Mention of Referent by KNS

NP+	ka/i	(n)un	doo	particle drop	zero anaphora
H/N	16	15	2	0	203
	9.1	7.6	1.4	0	81.9
T/T	40	13	17	2	269
	11.9	3.8	7.4	0.6	76.2

Total number of occurrences and average percentages are shown in the first and second lines, respectively.

As was observed in the context of topic switch, the uses of NP+*ka/i*, NP+*(n)un*, NP+*doo*, particle drop, and zero anaphora were found in the context of continuous mention of topics. As Table 4.8 shows, zero anaphora was the key device used (81.9% and 76.2% of markings were done by zero anaphora, in the H/N and T/T cases respectively). Again, a chi-square test was conducted to find out whether the differences in the occurrences of all items were significant, and the differences were significant (χ^2 (3) = 470.68, p < .001 for H/N, and χ^2 (4) = 750.25, p < .001 for T/T). A post-hoc test (pair-wise chi-square comparison) was conducted on the most frequently occurring item, zero anaphora, and the second most frequently occurring item, NP+*ka/i* in both H/N and T/T narratives, and the results indicated that the use of zero anaphora was significantly higher than that of NP+*ka/i* in both the H/N (χ^2 (1) = 169.68, p < .001) and T/T (χ^2 (1) = 169.72, p < .001) narratives. Therefore, Hypothesis 1(b), which predicted that the most continuous topic would be encoded by zero anaphora in Korean, was supported by this result. The use of zero anaphora was higher in the H/N than the T/T condition; however, the difference was not statistically significant (F (1, 9) = 0.26, p = .622) unlike what was found in the context of topic switch.

A qualitative analysis of the data indicated that as was the case with the JNS group, most of the occurrences of zero anaphora were used for the main protagonists (i.e., the boy and the dog for the H/N, and the rabbit, the sheep and the bear for the T/T), showing the high topicality of these characters in the discourse compared to the peripheral characters that were rarely treated as continuous topics. When comparing all the contexts (i.e., referent introduction, topic switch, and continuous mention), it appears that speakers of Japanese and Korean display a similar pattern in managing referential topics in their oral narrative discourse in both the H/N and T/T narratives. However, a big difference was found in the production of passive expressions; JNSs produced many passive structures irrespective of task type, whereas KNSs produced passives only when the story obviously triggers the production of passives, i.e., in the H/N narratives. Qualitative and quantitative analyses of the data revealed that forms were selected by their functions in the Japanese and Korean oral discourse. The form-function mapping resulted in the production of the various forms besides the canonical ones (NP+*ga* for Japanese and NP+*ka/i* for Korean) for referent introduction in oral narratives; they tended to use NP+*ga* (Japanese) and NP+*ka/i* (Korean) for marking major characters, whereas tangential characters received various markings besides the canonical ones. Furthermore, the frequent use of zero anaphora was found for marking the characters that warranted the highest topicality in the story. In other words, the NSs of Japanese and Korean managed to fix their viewpoints on the main characters, with the use of various linguistic devices, throughout their narrative discourse. Different complexity of task triggered differing referent markings in both JNS and KNS data. The percentage use of zero anaphora was significantly higher in the H/N narrative than the T/T narrative in the context of topic switch in both languages. In the context of referent introduction, the T/T condition narrative triggered slightly higher use of NP+*ga* in JNS and NP+*ka/i* in KNS narratives, however, the differences were not found significant. The following section discusses the results of referent markings in English L1 narratives.

4.1.3 L1 English narratives

As was the case with the JNS and KNS narratives, the ways in which referents were introduced, re-introduced and maintained as topics in L1 English have been analysed. The forms that the speakers used can be broken down into three major production types: full NPs, pronouns, and zero anaphora. Full NPs can be further classified into categories such as NPs with definite and indefinite articles. Many researchers (e.g., Clancy 1980) coded referents in English into only two types, full NPs and pronouns, when they investigate topic continuity in narratives. However, in the present study, a more comprehensive coding scheme was applied since the information status (e.g., new, known, and current) of referents is an important key to the investigation of topic continuity.

4.1.3.1 Referent introduction

Table 4.9 shows how the referents were introduced into the English narratives.

Table 4.9 Referent Introduction by ENS

	Indefinite Markers[26]	Quantifiers	Possessive Pronouns	Definite Article	Proper Nouns
H/N	61	15	9	5	2
	66.3	15.6	10.3	5.6	2.2
T/T	53	13	4	7	0
	69.5	15.7	5.6	9.2	0

Total number of occurrences and average percentages are shown in the first and second lines, respectively.

As is presented in Table 4.9, indefinite markers, quantifiers, possessive pronouns, definite article, and proper nouns were used to mark referent introduction. The majority of the referent introductions were encoded with indefinite markers (66.3% in H/N narratives, 69.5% in T/T narratives), and this usage is substantially higher than that of the next most frequently occurring item, quantifier+NP (15.6% in H/N and 15.7% in T/T).

A chi-square test was carried out to compare the total number of occurrences for all the forms used for marking referent introduction, and it was found that the differences were significant in the H/N narrative (χ^2 (4) = 128.4, p < .01) and the T/T narrative (χ^2 (3) = 81.01, p < .01). A post-hoc test (pair-wise chi-square comparison) was conducted for indefinite article+NP and quantifier+NP for both narrative types. The significant results for H/N narrative (χ^2 (1) = 27.84, p < .01) and T/T narrative (χ^2 (1) = 24.24, p < .01) indicate that the number of occurrences of indefinite article+NP is significantly higher than that of any other forms used for encoding referent introduction in the ENS narratives under both the H/N and the T/T narrative conditions. Therefore, Hypothesis 1(c), regarding the production of NSs of English, predicting that "the most conventional form used for encoding referent introduction by NSs would be the full NP with indefinite article", was supported.

Analysis of ENS Narratives: The H/N Condition
Five speakers (50% of the ENS) chose to begin the story either by explicitly making a remark regarding what the story is about, or how the story starts in the H/N narrative. Examples 4.14 and 4.15 depict the pattern of how the story was introduced.

Example 4.14 Referent Introduction by ENS (#3)
Okay, the next story is about <u>a little boy</u> and <u>his dog</u> and <u>their pet frog</u>.

In Example 4.14, the speaker gave a brief explanation of what the story is about- what Labov (1972) in his structural framework of narratives can be regarded as, the 'abstract' phase of a storytelling exercise. He introduced the leading character, the boy, with the indefinite article, *a*, and his dog and frog with possessive pronouns, '*his*' and '*their*', correspondingly. Note that he regards the dog as the boy's pet and the frog as both the boy's and the dog's pet. Therefore, it seems that among the three major characters, the speaker designates the highest hierarchical status to the boy, then to the dog, and finally the frog, in that order. A similar tendency was observed in another speaker. See Example 4.15.

Example 4.15 Referent Introduction by ENS (#4)
The story starts off with <u>a boy</u> and <u>his dog</u>. And it looks like the boy has caught <u>a frog</u>, and so he's put him in a jar in his bed room.

The speaker introduced the boy with the indefinite article and the dog with a possessive pronoun to indicate that the dog belonged to the boy. He further introduced the frog as an object of the verb, *caught*, portraying a possible hierarchy of the three characters, in the same order as the speaker in Example 4.14 did. Two speakers used a conventional referent introduction style found in old folk tale by using the existential structure. See Examples 4.16 and 4.17.

Example 4.16 Referent Introduction of the Main Characters by ENS (#5)

Um there's *a little boy* in his room with *his puppy*, and he caught *a frog* and put it in a jar.

Example 4.17 Referent Introduction of the Main Characters by ENS (#8)

Once upon a time, there was a boy and his dog. They were in the boy's room. And they had a jar with a frog in it.

In these existential constructions, too, the boy was marked with the indefinite article, the dog with a possessive pronoun (indicated status as the boy's pet). The frog was the direct object of the verb, *caught*, in Example 4.16 and a compliment in Example 4.17. It seems that there is a shared pattern in NSs of English in marking the main characters in the H/N narrative. The linguistic forms used to mark the referent introduction of the three main characters in the H/N are presented in Table 4.10 below.

Table 4.10 Marking of the Main Characters for Referent Introduction in the H/N

	Indefinite Article	Possessive Pronouns	Definite Article	Total
Boy	9	0	1	10
Dog	3	7	0	10
Frog	8	2	0	10
Total	24	9	1	30

The numbers displayed in the table are frequencies, not percentages.

There was one speaker who used the definite article, *the*, in marking the boy's introduction, but all the other speakers used the indefinite marker, *a*, for introducing him. Seventy percent of the marking of the dog was done with possessive pronoun, *his*, indicating the ownership of the dog by the boy. The rest of the marking of the dog was done with the indefinite article, *a*. However, two of these three speakers used the phrase, *a pet dog*, indicating that the dog was the boy's pet, without using a possessive pronoun. The frog was mainly introduced with the indefinite marker, *a*, and the rest were done with the possessive pronouns, *his* and *their*. The former refers to 'the boy' and the latter 'the boy and the dog' collectively. Fifty percent of the introductions of the frog were done as the direct object of the verbs, *catch* (2), *get* (2), and *find* (1), indicating that the frog had a less significant role, at least in the beginning of the story.

As presented in Table 4.10, the total occurrences of possessive pronouns was nine, and it was found that all of the instances were used to mark either the dog or the frog, and not any of the more peripheral characters. There were 15 instances of quantifiers, and it was found that all of them were used for introducing the frog's family, or his wife. They were not used for marking the main characters. Besides the use of the quantifiers and possessive pronouns, there were no vast differences in the ways in which main characters and peripheral characters were introduced into the narratives. Further, I argue that the choices of these forms were motivated not by the roles the speakers intend to assign, but by the content of the storyline itself.

The formation of the passive constructions was examined in the H/N narratives. Although all the passive constructions were counted in the narratives, not only those occurring in the context of referent introduction, the results will be shown and discussed in the current section, in order to be consistent with how results were reported for the JNS and the KNS narratives. Recall that there were 27 passive constructions/expressions in the H/N narratives in the JNS group. The NSs of English produced 21 passive constructions displaying similar results to the JNS narratives. This part of the findings was somewhat unexpected, as previous studies (Nakahama, 2009; Yanagimachi, 2000) reported that their English NSs did not produce many passive forms in their L1 storytelling.

As was the case with the JNS H/N narratives, the patients of the passive structures, with one exception, were either the boy, the dog, or the boy and the dog. With this result, it can be argued that the speakers used the passive construction to keep the main characters in the topical position, and that this helped their narrative discourse flow well, as Bamberg (1994) rightly claimed.

In summary, as predicted from the previous literature, a prototypical pattern of introducing new referents with indefinite markings (indefinite articles or bare NP for plural nouns) + NP was found in the H/N narratives. Henceforth, the results of the referent introduction in the T/T narrative will be presented.

Analysis of ENS Narratives: The T/T Condition
As was done in the H/N narrative, the ways in which the major characters were introduced into discourse were examined quantitatively and qualitatively. Table

4.11 presents the results.

Table 4.11 Marking of the Main Characters for Referent Introduction in the T/T

	Indefinite Article	Possessive Pronouns	Quantifiers	Definite Article	Total
Sheep	9	0	0	1	10
Bear	7	2	1	0	10
Rabbit	7	2	1	0	10
Total	23	4	2	1	30

The numbers displayed in the table are occurrences, not percentages.

As the ENS speakers acknowledged that the boy played the most important role in the H/N narrative by marking it with the indefinite article, *a*, the role of the female sheep was regarded as the most influential character in the T/T narrative, being marked in a similar way. The other two major characters, the male bear and the male rabbit were also mostly coded with the indefinite article; however, three speakers grouped them together and marked them with a quantifier (one case) or with possessive pronouns (two cases). The quantifier used to mark the two male characters was 'two' as in 'two other animals' and the possessive pronoun chosen was 'her', as in 'her friends'. Example 4.18 illustrates how the possessive pronoun was used.

Example 4.18 Use of the Possessive Pronoun (ENG #4)
So the story starts out with sort of like <u>a dog or wolflike looking animal</u> riding on a sled um..and it's a wintery scene and the dog is riding to um an ice-skating rink to meet his friends? Um <u>her friends</u>?

The speaker introduced the sheep (described as *a dog* or *a wolflike animal* here) with the indefinite article and then continued to describe her actions. The speaker described the sheep's encounter with the two other major characters on the icy pond, using the possessive pronoun, *her*. The use of *her* in this speaker's narrative was quite similar to how most speakers introduced the dog into their H/N narrative discourse, in that the male bear and the rabbit played (at least in the beginning of the story) subsidiary role to the leading character. The story develops in such a way as these two characters attempt to receive her attention by competing with each other, thus it is postulated that the speakers attempted to differentiate the types of roles portrayed by the female sheep and the two male characters. Another speaker grouped the two leading male characters as one pair and referred to them as 'her friends' just, as the speaker in example 4.18 did. Besides the uses of personal pronouns and quantifiers by these three speakers, all the other speakers in the ENS group used the same marking, i.e., the indefinite marking for all three major characters. However, all but one speaker emphasised the significance of the female character by referring to her and the bear/rabbit separately.

Recall that there were no major differences in the ways in which the main characters and the peripheral characters were introduced into the discourse in the H/N narrative, except for the quantifiers and possessive pronouns. After the careful examination of all the occurrences of the referent introduction in the T/T narratives, it was found that a similar pattern was observed. That is, whereas personal pronouns were not used at all in introducing the peripheral characters, many instances of quantifiers were located in the marking of the peripheral characters. Two such instances are presented in Examples 4.19 and 4.20 below.

Example 4.19 Introduction of Peripheral Characters with a Quantifier (ENG #8)
There were <u>a couple of mice</u>.. They started playing a little dice game.

Example 4.20 Introduction of Peripheral Characters with a Quantifier (ENG #2)
Then we look at the snowman and he starts melting and <u>what's left is</u> <u>some strange creature</u> with flowers for eyes and sticks for legs

Speaker #8 in Example 4.19 was referring to the mice that appeared toward the end of the video segment. The storyline was that the two major male characters joined two mice to roll the dice and ended up winning some cheese. In fact, only one mouse rolled the dice and played against the male character and his introduction was grouped together with that of the other mouse. The role that the two mice played was rather insignificant as the camera's focus was on the two major characters. It appeared that the insignificance of the peripheral characters' part was suitably reflected in the form choice made by the speaker. The same speculation can be posited in Example 4.20. Speaker #2 made some vague introduction of the scarecrow that came out of the snowman. Furthermore, the fact that it was introduced in a Wh-cleft sentence would explain the lesser information status of the scarecrow, as the clefted constituent in a Wh-cleft sentence always displays the topic of the sentence, with the following clause serving as a comment to identify the topic (see Hedberg and Fadden (2007) on information status in the Wh-cleft sentences).

Again the narrative was thoroughly investigated regarding the occurrences of passive constructions all through the T/T narratives. Whereas the H/N narratives generated a total of 21 passive structures (all the speakers except for one produced at least one passive structure), the T/T narratives produced only six passive constructions. The qualitative examination of these six cases of passives revealed that there was only one passive construction with the main character as the patient of the sentence. With regard to the five remaining cases of passive construction, the patients were the peripheral characters or inanimate entities. Recall that the speakers in the KNS group also produced a much higher number of passive structures/expressions in the H/N in comparison to the T/T narratives. Comparing the uses of the passive structures in the T/T narratives among the JNSs, the KNSs, and the ENSs narratives, I argue that these results derived from differing ways of viewing and constructing events, and twists and turns in a story, among Japanese, Korean and English native speakers. The usage of passive structures in the NNSs narratives will be examined both quantitatively and qualitatively in a later section, and their results will be compared to those of the ENSs and the KNSs in regards to possible CLI.

In summary, the form used most frequently to mark the introduction of referents was indefinite marking (indefinite articles and bare nouns) in both types of narrative with the ENS group. Therefore, Hypothesis 1 (c) was supported, with regard to the context of referent introduction. In the production of passive forms, the Japanese NSs produced the highest number of passive constructions/expressions among the JNSs, the KNSs, and the ENSs. However, the difference was not very big in the H/N narratives. In contrast, the T/T condition narrative had a significantly higher number of passive constructions in the JNS group, as compared to the ENS and the KNS groups, and therefore, Hypothesis 2 was supported in the T/T narrative. The next section will present the results of how topic switch (i.e., re-introduction of referents) was encoded by the English NS participants.

4.1.3.2 Topic switch (Re-introduction of referent)

In this section, the results for the H/N narrative and the T/T narrative will be presented together to be consistent with the JNS and the KNS sections. Table 4.12 shows how the participants in the ENS group encoded the topic switch of referents.

Table 4.12 Topic Switch (Re-introduction of Referent) by ENS

NP+	Definite Article	Pronouns	Possessive Pronouns	Zero Anaphora
H/N	148	80	11	2
	57.3	36.1	5.8	0.7
T/T	111	80	0	0
	50.5	49.5	0	0

The total number of occurrences and average percentages are shown in the first and second lines, respectively.

Definite article with NP was the most frequently used form for encoding topic switch in both the H/N and T/T narrative discourse (148 times (57.3%) and 111 times (50.5%), respectively). A chi-square test was conducted to determine whether the differences among the four forms were significant in the H/N narrative, and the differences were found to be significant (χ^2 (3) = 230.85, $p < .001$). The post hoc test conducted between definite article plus NP (148 times) and pronoun (80 times) was also significant (χ^2 (1) = 5.01, $p = .025$), therefore, it can be said that the speakers used definite articles most frequently to mark topic switch in the H/N condition. In the T/T narrative, on the other hand, only the definite articles and pronouns were used (111 times and 80 times), therefore a chi-square test was only conducted on these two items, and the differences in the occurrences between these forms were found to be significant (χ^2 (1) = 5.01, $p = .025$) at $p < .05$ level. Thus, consistent with the results of previous studies, it was found that NSs of English used full NPs in preference to pronouns for denoting a switch of the topics (e.g., Clancy, 1980) and this result supports Hypothesis 1(c) concerning topic switch.

Recall that both the JNSs and the KNSs both produced much higher numbers of full NPs than the attenuated form (i.e., zero anaphora) in both narrative types. Thus, the almost 50% use of pronouns in the T/T narratives by the ENSs was rather unexpected. The T/T narratives were examined qualitatively. First, recall that over 90% of topic switches were done by the main characters irrespective of narrative type, both in the JNS and the KNS groups.

The ratio of main and peripheral characters of the referents that were used for topic switches are illustrated in the following table.

Table 4.13 Subjects of Topic Switch by ENS

ENS	H/N Main	H/N Peripheral	T/T Main	T/T Peripheral
	211	32	168	23
	86.8	13.2	88.0	12.0

As Table 4.13 shows, the majority of the subjects of topic switching was done with the main characters under both the H/N and the T/T narrative conditions (86.8% and 88%, respectively), therefore, this pattern seems to be consistent across the three languages, (i.e., Japanese, Korean and English).

Table 4.14 Ratio of Main and Peripheral Characters in the Use of Definite Article and Pronouns in Topic Switch

	H/N Main	H/N Peripheral	T/T Main	T/T Peripheral
Definite Article	136	25	97	16
	84.5	15.5	85.8	14.2
Pronouns	73	7	71	7
	91.3	8.8	91.0	9.0

In order to grasp the higher usage of pronouns in the topic switch context in the T/T condition, the data were further examined quantitatively. Within the marking of the definite article and pronouns, the ratio of main/peripheral roles was counted and it is shown in Table 4.14. As is illustrated here, most of the topic switching was done by re-introducing the main characters in both task types. More importantly, the pattern found in the JNSs and the KNSs was also found here in that the use of pronouns tended to be restricted to a topic switch of major characters (91.3% for the H/N narrative and 91% for the T/T narrative).

Since there is no vast difference between the two narrative types, with the percentage of the major characters being the object of the topic switch, the T/T narrative underwent qualitative analysis. It was found that some of the occurrences of pronouns were to mark the combination of all the three main characters (*they*) and they were used to switch topics from one of the individual main characters, to the collective group of main characters. Some other cases were found wherein the two main male characters were grouped together as *'they'*, and the topicality goes back and forth among the three characters (routinely between the female sheep and the male bear & rabbit). Therefore, with the contextual help, deciphering the topic of discourse was not impossible when topic switch was done with pronouns. When the speakers chose the third person singular pronouns, referring to the major characters, the competing topic was marked either with a definite article or the opposite gender, therefore, the use of pronouns did not lead to confusion. However, the reason that the T/T condition triggered a higher use of pronouns compared to the H/N narrative remains to be identified. Verbal reports were not collected from the ENS group to deconstruct with the speakers the rationales behind their T/T narrative productions; therefore, this unpredictable task effect by the English speakers needs to be explored in a future research investigation.

Re-introduction of the Frog

While similarities were identified in the way in which topic switch was encoded in the H/N narratives among the three language groups as shown above, a striking difference was also found between Japanese and Korean NS narratives and English NS narratives in terms of the re-introducing the frog. The JNSs and the KNSs used indefinite markers (NP+*ga* and NP+*ka/i*) in an existential sentence, whereas the ENSs employed various markers (e.g., definite and indefinite marking) mainly in the less topical position. To be specific, in 60% of the cases, the frog was marked as the object of the verbs, *find* and *see*. See Example 4.21.

Example 4.21 Re-introduction of the Frog by ENS (#2)
and when they come on the other side of the log they see <u>the frog</u>

This speaker, as many others did, used definiteness marking, as the frog has already become shared information, despite the fact that it only appeared in the pictures at the beginning of the narrative, before it was finally found at the end of the story. Following Chafe (1994) this pattern suggests that the speaker assumed that the frog remained in the consciousness of the listener, and this activation level of consciousness was signaled via definiteness marking, in the case of English NS narratives.

One would assume that the frog must also have been in the consciousness of the both the Japanese and Korean narrators. However, different markings were preferred by users of those languages, perhaps because the speakers wished to place emphasis on the discovery of the frog by using the new information markers, NP+*ga* and NP+*ka/i*, which also may on occasion be used to denote emphasis. The different ways in which the event of the finding of the frog was encoded between the English and Japanese/Korean speakers provides a clear example of how differently various languages act as a "filter" with respect to how people talk about events (see Berman and Slobin, 1994). This premise will be investigated further with the L2 learners' H/N narratives in a later section, as it would of interest for us to learn how these differing ways of filtering might influence the choice of encoding grammar in L2 story narrations.

4.1.3.3 Continuous mention of referent

Table 4.15 Continuous Mention of Referent by ENS

NP+	Pronouns	Zero anaphora	Definite Article
H/N	104	56	10
	61.0	32.3	6.7
T/T	149	64	8
	72.2	24.6	3.2

Total number of occurrences and average percentages are shown in the first and second lines, respectively.

As is shown in Table 4.15, the use of pronouns received the highest percentage in marking the most continuous referent in both types of narratives. The total number of the occurrences of all the linguistic items (pronouns, zero anaphora, and definite article) was compared with a chi-square test and the differences were significant (the H/N setting: χ^2 (2) = 136.84 , $p < .001$, the T/T setting: χ^2 (2) = 77.98, $p < .001$). A post-hoc test was conducted to compare the occurrences of the most frequently occurring items (i.e., pronouns (104) and zero anaphora (56) for the H/N and pronoun (149) and zero anaphora (64) for the T/T narratives), and the result was significant (H/N setting: χ^2 (1) = 14.4, $p < .001$., T/T setting χ^2 (1) = 33.92, $p < .001$), confirming that pronouns were the most prevalent linguistic form used to mark continuous mention of referent in the English NS narratives. Therefore a part of Hypothesis 1 (c), predicting 'that pronouns would encode the most continuous topic in English NS discourse, was supported.

Interestingly, the use of zero anaphora was also found in marking the most continuous referents. A thorough examination of the data revealed that all the occurrences of zero anaphora, except for two, were found in cases where clauses were conjoinable. Li and Thompson (1979) referred to this notion as topic-chaining. They argue that topic-chaining represents a state in which two clauses can be conjoined if the speaker wants to portray them as a single grammatical unit, instead of two independent units. In English, topic-chaining is restricted syntactically (Li and Thompson, 1979) and thus zero anaphora was found where omission of the NP was syntactically permissible. Similarly, Yoshioka (2005) reported that close to 80% of the occurrences of zero anaphora were found in overtly coordinated structures (which would be equivalent to Li and Thompson's syntactically motivated topic-chaining) in her Dutch speaking participants' L1 Dutch narratives. Example 4.22 depicts this pattern found in the current narrative data.

Example 4.22 Zero Anaphora in Continuous Mention in the T/T by ENS (#5)
And then um then both the poodle and the rabbit um.. teamed up and (Ø) started teasing the bear

As shown in Example 4.22, zero anaphora was used by the English speakers where it is allowed syntactically. Thus, they should be able to produce such a form in the equivalent positions in Japanese (i.e., conjoinable clauses). In fact, in some previous studies, zero anaphora was successfully used by the NNSs of English where the form was motivated syntactically rather than pragmatically (see e.g., Muñoz, 1995 and Williams, 1998). However, there were two cases of zero anaphora that were not syntactically motivated. One example is shown below.

Example 4.23 Zero Anaphora in Continuous Mention in the T/T by ENS (#9)
And and so, the, the fox went skating and then the other animals joined joined him except the, the um, the uh, the rabbit was uh, he was not a very good skater. And. um and (Ø) fell over almost immediately.

In the second line of Example 4.23, the speaker was talking about the rabbit, one of the main male characters, and then he paused and hesitated uttering, 'um', before continuing. He omitted the subject, but from the context, it was obvious that the subject was the rabbit. However, because of the pause, the hesitation marker, and the fact that the clauses before and after were not syntactically conjoinable, the use of zero anaphora is not commonly practised in such cases in English. Pragmatically inspired zero anaphora in English like this are rather unique in monologues, and this example represents one of only two instances found in the ENS narratives.

With regard to the differing ways of marking referents in the context of continuous mention of referent between the two task conditions, as Table 4.15 above shows, the percentage use of pronoun was higher in the T/T as compared to the H/N narratives (72.2% and 61.0%, respectively), and Repeated Measure ANOVA test revealed that the difference was significant ($F(1, 9) = 6.68, p = .029$). This result could have been caused by the higher use of zero anaphora in the H/N narrative. Although the Repeated Measure ANOVA showed that the difference of the percentage use of zero anaphora did not reach the level of significance ($p = .11$), the descriptive statistics show a difference (32.3% in the H/N and 24.6% in the T/T condition). The higher usage of the attenuated form (i.e., zero anaphora) in the H/N narrative was evidenced in the JNS and the KNS data; therefore, the study showed that the speakers used more attenuated form in the H/N narrative, regardless of language.

The next section will present how the NNSs in the study demonstrated referential topic management.

4.2 NNS Narratives

This section presents how learners performed referent marking of topic continuity/discontinuity (introduction and tracking of referents) in L2 Japanese narratives under the two task conditions (H/N and T/T). L2 data from all four learner groups (KOR-Mid, KOR-High, ENG-Mid, ENG-High) will be compared to their NS baseline data (i.e., JNS data). Their results will then be compared to the two task types: H/N and T/T. Differing patterns of development (from the intermediate to the advanced level) found between the Korean and the English groups will be examined in the context of referent introduction, topic switch, and continuous mention of referent.

In order to test Hypotheses 3 and 4 which claim increased performance with proficiency, as well as superior presentation of referent marking by Korean speakers over their English speaker counterparts (due to the typological similarities shared between Korean and Japanese), average percentages of the proportional use of the forms, instead of the number of occurrences, were used as dependent variables. This was done to ensure fair comparisons. This choice was made due to the fact that some of the participants' utterances were much longer than others, thus comparison of the total frequency of the dependent variables would not accurately reflect the general patterns.

One-way ANOVAs were then conducted across five groups (four L2 groups plus the JNS group) to test if the use of the forms for marking referents differed significantly. It should be noted that for some forms (e.g., NP+ particle drop) that occurred infrequently, the percentages could be zero for a number of participants; this circumstance may cause a violation of the normality assumption for ANOVA. However, some published simulation studies (e.g., Harwell, Rubinstein, Hayes, and Olds, 1992; Martin and Games, 1977) indicated that ANOVA was quite robust with respect to normality assumption violations, which means that even if the data were not normally distributed, the ANOVA results would still be valid.

The results are presented in a fashion similar to that found in the NS results section. First, quantitative findings are presented in tables and features that are either unique to each language group or common between the two L1 groups are explained in detail. In order to capture the discoursal or functional motivations for language use, if there are any, the learners' narrative data were analysed in a detailed qualitative manner. The findings from KNSs and ENSs might be discussed if needed, with the aim of claiming CLI. In each context (i.e., referent introduction, topic switch, continuous mention of referent), the results from H/N and T/T narratives will be presented first, and then notable tendencies will be pointed out and explained.

4.2.1 Referent introduction

The mean percentages of the linguistic devices used for referent introduction are illustrated by the two L1 groups at two different proficiency levels for the H/N and T/T narrative conditions in Table 4.16 and 4.17, respectively. The total number of their occurrences is also provided for reference purposes, and the JNS data is also presented in the table for comparison purposes. As explained in Section 4.1.1.1, infrequently occurred items were collapsed into a single category called 'others' and displayed in the table. They were NP+copula, *ni* (at, to, with), *to* (with), *no* (possessive), and errors.

Table 4.16 Referent Introduction by NNSs and JNS: H/N Narratives

NP+	ga	wa	o	ni/kara	mo	particle drop	others
ENG-Mid (N=11)	21 28.5	7 12.3	11 13.8	0 0	7 9.5	12 16.5	9 19.4
KOR-Mid (N=10)	37 63.1	0 0	9 14.6	2 3.9	2 2.9	0 0	9 15.5
ENG-High (N=10)	39 47.6	7 10.9	9 11.0	1 1.1	2 2.5	0 0	19 26.8
KOR-High (N=10)	12 50.5	3 4.5	9 12.0	7 9.7	1 2.0	0 0	12 21.4
JNS (N=10)	34 52.9	0 0	12 19.7	6 9.8	3 4.5	0 0	9 13.2
Total	164 48.1	17 5.7	50 14.1	16 4.8	15 4.4	12 3.6	58 19.3

Total number of occurrences and average percentages are shown in the first and second lines, respectively.

Table 4.17 Referent Introduction by NNSs and JNS: T/T Narratives

NP+	ga	wa	o	ni/kara	mo	particle drop	others
ENG-Mid (N=11)	26 41.5	16 28.6	2 3.0	0 0	4 7.1	2 3.8	9 16.8
KOR-Mid (N=10)	37 71.8	2 3.1	2 5.0	0 0	4 6.4	0 0	7 13.7
ENG-High (N=10)	32 64.4	1 2.0	1 1.7	2 3.3	8 13.0	0 0	9 15.7
KOR-High (N=10)	25 65.2	1 1.7	0 0	0 0	2 4.5	1 5.0	11 23.7
JNS (N=10)	33 63.0	0 0	0 0	5 9.9	3 5.2	0 0	12 22.0
Total	153 60.8	20 7.5	5 2.0	7 2.6	21 7.2	7 1.8	48 18.3

Total number of occurrences and average percentages are shown in the first and second lines, respectively.

Some developmental patterns were found in NNS productions of encoding of referent introductions and the patterns differ between the two NNS groups. The most discernible differences found were in the use of NP+*ga*, NP+*wa*, NP+ni/*kara* and NP+particle drops. Further, the use of NP+*o* and NP+*ni/kara* differed between the two narrative conditions (H/N and T/T).

As Table 4.16 and Table 4.17 show, NP+*ga* is the most prominent particle for encoding new referents in most of the L2 oral narratives, irrespective of narrative type, which was the pattern also found in the JNS narrative. However, there are some variations in the performances across the proficiency levels, especially for the English L1 speakers. I will first compare the performance of NP+*ga*, between the four NNS groups and the JNSs in the H/N and T/T narratives separately, and will then reveal the effects of CLI and task complexity on how the learners develop referent marking skills. Other noteworthy patterns found in the use of NP+*wa*, NP+*o*, NP+*ni/kara* and NP+ particle drop across proficiency levels, L1 backgrounds, and task types will also be presented.

4.2.1.1 NP+*ga* for referent introduction in H/N narratives

Before I discuss the production of NP+*ga* for a marker of referent introduction, I will present its percentage use in H/N and T/T narratives in Figure 4.1, to graphically illustrate different patterns found between the task types, L1 backgrounds, and the learners' proficiency levels.

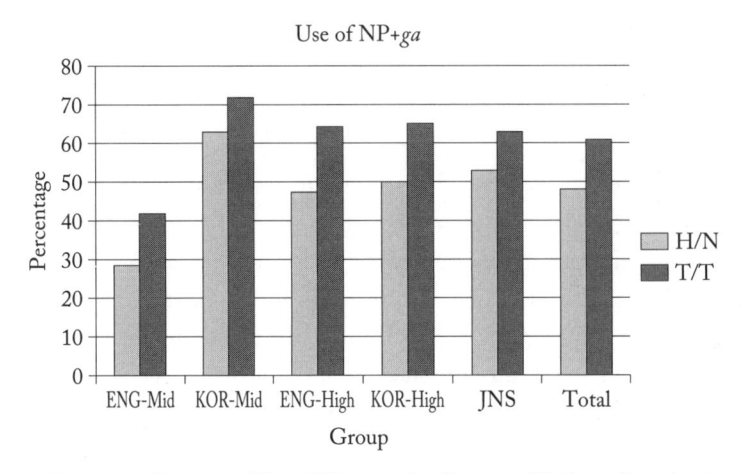

Figure 4.1 Percentage Use of NP+*ga* in the Context of Referent Introduction

As Table 4.16 illustrates, irrespective of the learners' L1 and proficiency level, NP+*ga* scored the highest percentage use among all the forms used in marking referent introduction in the H/N narratives. Likewise, in the JNS narratives, over 50% of referent markings were done with NP+*ga* in the context of referent introduction. Figure 4.1 illustrates that there was a great rise in the production of NP+*ga* with increased proficiency in the English L1 group (28.5% for Intermediate level and 47.6% for the Advanced level). Notice that the Korean group produced NP+*ga* quite differently compared to their English L1 group counterpart. There were no substantial differences in the production of NP+*ga* between the two proficiency levels among the Korean learners of Japanese. In fact, the percentage use of NP+*ga* was higher among the lower proficiency level learners than with the higher proficiency learners in the Korean L1 group. 63.1% of all new referents were marked with NP+*ga* at the intermediate proficiency level and its percentage use of the form decreased to 50.5% at their higher proficiency level counterpart. One-way ANOVA was conducted on all five groups (i.e., JNS, KOR-Mid, KOR-High, ENG-Mid, ENG-High), and it was found that there was a significant differences among the groups (F (4, 46) =3.81, p=.009).

Scheffe's multiple comparison tests were applied to determine where the significance lay, and it was revealed that the difference was found between the KOR-Mid and the ENG-Mid (p < .05) groups. While the percentage use of NP+*ga* in the ENG-Mid group seemed very low compared to the other four groups, it did not achieve statistical significance, possibly due to the small sample size. The data was analysed from a different angle; ANOVA was again conducted on the KOR-Mid, the ENG-Mid and the JNS group, and the difference was found to be significant (F (2, 28) = 8.9, p =.01). Scheffe's multiple comparison tests revealed that the difference was found between the ENG-Mid and the other two groups (i.e., JNS and KOR-Mid). Furthermore, there was no significant difference between the upper proficiency groups and the JNSs. Therefore, it is argued that, in terms of the English L1 group, the learners have not acquired the ability to properly mark referent introduction with the use of NP+*ga* at the intermediate level; however, its percentage use increases with proficiency.

Given that there is no significant difference between the KOR-Mid and the JNSs in terms of the performance of NP+*ga* suggests that the Korean L1 speakers have achieved the appropriate form-function mapping ability at as early a stage as the intermediate proficiency level. Therefore, Hypothesis 3, stating that "the target-like performance of referent introduction and tracking will increase with proficiency" was supported in terms of referent introduction (with the use of NP+*ga*) for English L1 speakers but not for Korean L1 speakers in H/N narratives.

With the result of the ANOVA tests, it can be postulated that the acquisition rate of NP+*ga* might be different for learners whose L1s are English and Korean. A previous study by Hanada (1993) revealed that it takes longer for English L1 speakers to acquire NP+*ga* (for subject/topic marking) than for Korean L1 speakers. Recall that Hanada's small-scale study used a cloze test, while the current study used oral narratives as the data elicitation method. Therefore, the results of the present study, with larger samples, were able to confirm the existing finding of an accelerated rate of acquisition of NP+*ga* by the Korean over the English L1 speakers, using the different data elicitation method. This part of the result supports Hypothesis 4 claiming differing developmental patterns between the two L2 groups (regarding the production of NP+*ga* for referent introduction). The data was carefully analysed where NP+*ga* was produced in order to depict any characteristics discernible for each L1 group in the H/N condition. The analysis is presented below.

Qualitative Findings
A qualitative analysis of NP+*ga* revealed that the ways in which intermediate level English L1 speakers used *ga* seems to differ from those of the other four groups under the H/N narrative condition. Recall that the JNSs had the propensity to use the prototypical marker *ga* to introduce the main characters (the boy and/or the dog) and other forms such as NP+*ni* and *o* to refer to characters of less significance. Narratives by the KOR-Mid, the KOR-High, and the ENG-High groups revealed a similar pattern, with regard to the use of NP+*ga*. The ENG-Mid group, in contrast, used various markers to mark the most important character, i.e., the boy. Specifically, four speakers used NP+*ga*, five speakers used NP+*wa*, and two speakers dropped the particle. Peripheral characters, too, were introduced with various forms, including NP+*ga*. Example 4.24 is from a speaker in the ENG-Mid level.

Example 4.24 Referent Introduction of the Boy, the Dog and the Frog by ENG-Mid Level (# 9)

Aru	*otoko*	*no*	*otoko*	*no*	*ko*	*wa*	*kaeru*	*o*
Certain	male	GEN	male	GEN	child	TOP	frog	ACC

katte…imashita	*un..*	*sorede*	*aru*	*hi..*	*u..a..a.. i.*
keep…ING-PAST	um..	then	certain	day	u..a..a..d..

inu	*mo*	*katteimashita*
dog	also	keep-ING-PAST

(literal translation) 'The certain boy had a frog and um..then on a certain day, he also had a dog.'

This speaker marked the boy with *wa*, the topic marker and the frog with *o*, the object marker, whereas she placed the dog also as an object of the verb, *kau* (Japanese equivalent of *to keep*). The object marker was replaced with '*mo*', as she wanted to convey the meaning that the dog was 'also' the boy's pet. The fact that she did not use *ga*, the canonical marker for referent introduction could possibly mean she has not acquired the form yet in her L2 system. However, consider Example 4.25, which was also taken from the narrative told by the same speaker, halfway into the narrative.

Example 4.25 Referent Introduction of the Peripheral Characters by ENG-Mid Level (#9)

nezumi	*ga*	*detekite…*	*etto..*	*ryoohootomo*	*wa..*	*chotto*
mouse	NOM	come out and	um..	both also	TOP	little

okotteruyoona	*bi.bikkurishite*	*okotteruyoona*	*kao*	*o*
angry-like	s..surprised and	angry-like	face	ACC

shiteimasu	*yo*	*ne.*	*aa..sorede* …… (several utterances in between)
do-ING P	P	P	um..then..

eeto..	*ookina*	*tori*	*ga*	*detekite..*	*un…*
um…	big	bird	NOM	come out	um…

(literal translation) 'a mouse came out and um..they both also seem angry s.. looked surprised and angry un…then..(several utterances later) um…a big bird came out um…'

The same speaker who introduced the boy with *wa* in Example 4.25 above introduced peripheral characters such as a gopher and an owl with an appropriate marker for referent introduction, i.e., *ga*. Therefore, this speaker apparently knew how to use NP+*ga* for referent introduction and thus, it was not the case that she had not acquired the use of the form. She might have attempted to differentiate the statuses of characters by allocating different markers. Another ENG-Mid speaker used the same pattern for introducing the boy and the peripheral characters, that is, *wa* for the most important character and *ga* for the peripheral characters. The motivation of the usage of NP+*wa* will be discussed in the subsequent section after the discussion of NP+*ga* in T/T narratives.

Whereas these two speakers appear to display systematic differentiation of *wa* and *ga* in their L2 Japanese discourse, the other ENG-Mid speakers tended to use the same markings for the boy and the rest of the characters. Those who dropped particles for marking the boy or marking it with *wa* also did so for the peripheral characters and those who successfully marked the boy with *ga* also marked his antagonists with *ga*. In other words, it appeared that, in general, the English L1 speakers at the intermediate proficiency level showed a preference for using the same markers irrespective of the characters' status in the H/N narrative setting.

While the English L1 speakers at the lower proficiency level used *ga* quite randomly, in a majority of instances (70%) the most important character (i.e., the boy) was marked by *ga* among their advanced level English L1 counterparts. In other words, the ENG-High level learners seem to follow the same pattern of *ga* usage as found in the narratives of the JNSs as well in the L2 narratives produced by the Korean learners at both the intermediate and the advanced levels. This suggests that the advanced level English L1 speakers were generally able to distinguish the function of *ga* from that of other particles, and as a result displayed this form-function relationship quite skilfully. Thus, it could be argued that not only the number of instances of the form increased with proficiency, but also that the appropriate form-function mapping skills did as well. Three speakers from the ENG-High group used NP+*wa* for marking the boy.

Interestingly, their referent marking style resembled those two speakers in the ENG-Mid group who marked the boy with *wa*, in that the three speakers from ENG-High who used NP+*wa* tended to mark the boy's antagonists with NP+*ga* (and NP+*ni* in the passive sentences).

Similarly, 30% of the KOR-High group marked the boy with *wa*, and as was the pattern found in the ENG-High group, they used a variety of forms such as NP+*ga* and NP+*ni* (in a passive sentence) for introducing peripheral characters. The KOR-Mid group learners did not produce NP+*wa* for referent introduction throughout the narratives, which mirrored the performance of the JNS narratives.

In summary, qualitative analysis of NP+*ga* in H/N narratives revealed that the Korean speakers were able to produce somewhat native-like narrative discourse to introduce a new referent even at an intermediate level of proficiency. They seem to have a grip on the appropriate relationship between form and function in terms of the use of NP+*ga*. The English speakers' performance, on the other hand, improved immensely with proficiency in regards to referent introduction using this form.

4.2.1.2 NP+*ga* for referent introduction in T/T narratives

As was the case in the H/N narratives, NP+*ga* was the form most frequently used to mark referent introduction in the T/T narratives. As Table 4.17 shows, across five groups, including the JNS group, the average use of NP+*ga* was 60.8% which was a higher percentage use than that of their H/N counterpart (48.1%). Figure 4.1 clearly illustrates this increased use of NP+*ga* in T/T, even in the ENG-Mid group. Both Korean and English learner groups were compared with their native Japanese counterparts (JNSs), and it was found that there was no statistical difference between proficiency levels in either language group. Therefore, unlike under the H/N condition, the learners had already achieved target-like performance in the use of NP+*ga* at the intermediate level, irrespective of their L1 backgrounds. The performance of NP+*ga* across groups was compared with Repeated Measure ANOVA between the H/N and T/T tasks, and it was found that the difference was significant at $p < .05$ level ($F(4, 46) = 3.58$, $p = .013$). Therefore, Hypothesis 5 which claimed higher task complexity resulting in more accurate referent markings, was supported.

Qualitative Findings

The use of NP+*ga* in the T/T narratives was examined qualitatively. Recall that JNSs differentiated the ways in which main characters and peripheral characters were introduced into narratives in both the H/N and T/T settings. Even among the main characters, JNSs tried to single out the most important character (the boy for the H/N case and the sheep for the T/T case). These two important characters tended to be marked with *ga* by the speakers in the JNS group. Six ENG-Mid level learners marked the sheep with *ga*, whereas the other five speakers in the same group marked it with *wa*. The percentage uses of NP+*ga* for marking the sheep by the speakers in the other groups were as follows: 80% in ENG-High and KOR-Mid groups, and 90% in the KOR-High group. ENG-High level speakers did not use NP+*wa*, while two speakers from KOR-Mid and one speaker from KOR-High used it.

The vast majority of the marking for the other two important characters, the bear and the rabbit, was also done with *ga* in the ENG-High, KOR-Mid and KOR-High groups, whereas the ENG-Mid level speakers used various participles, including particle drops. In terms of marking the peripheral characters, too, the majority of marking was done with *ga*. In ENG-Mid level learners; however, various particles were again used for marking peripheral characters just as was done for marking the main characters. Recall that the majority of the ENG-Mid group did not differentiate between the markings of main and peripheral characters in the H/N setting. Thus, it can be concluded that linguistic distinction among characters based on the characters' significance in the story was not attempted within the lower level of English speakers included in this study, irrespective of task type.

As mentioned earlier, the follow-up interview data were collected from all the NSs of Japanese and some NNSs (three ENG-Mid level, three ENG-High level, two KOR-Mid level, three KOR-High level speakers) in the current study. The ENG-Mid level learners did not differentiate between NP+*ga* and NP+*wa* and they considered both particles as 'subject markers'. Two of the three ENG-High level learners who were interviewed, on the other hand, had the grammatical knowledge of the difference between the two particles. All five Korean participants who were interviewed stated that they have mastered the use of NP+*ga* and *wa* quite easily (or at least they 'feel' they had mastered them quite easily), since they have the exact equivalent forms in Korean.

The follow-up interview data confirms that the superior performance of the usage of NP+*ga* by the Koreans was not a fluke. The interview results verified that when the L1 and the L2 are very close to each other, the learners are aware of the similarities and make use of the knowledge when they construct narrative discourse. In contrast, as the English speakers experienced, when an L1 does not have grammatical features parallel to the L2, learners must start from zero, and with exposures to positive and negative evidence and self study, they eventually learn to properly use such forms (NP+*ga* in an extended narrative discourse, in this case). With regard to the narrative types and the use of NP+*ga*, the participants did not make specific comments, therefore, the interpretation of the higher use of NP+*ga* in the T/T narratives remains the researcher's supposition.

4.2.1.3 NP+*wa* for referent introduction in H/N narratives

The production of NP+*wa* (in percentages) by the NSs and NNSs in both the H/N and T/T narrative settings is shown in a graphic figure below.

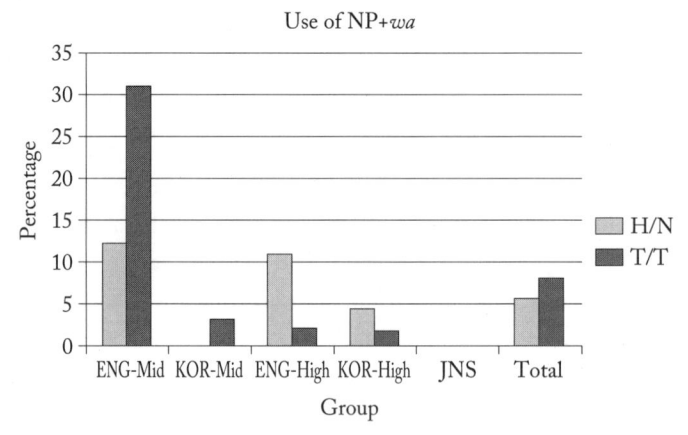

Figure 4.2 Percentage Use of NP+*wa* in the Context of Referent Introduction

As shown in Table 4.16 and Figure 4.2, the use of *wa* in H/N narratives was rare by both the Korean L1 speakers and the JNSs. The percentage uses of NP+*wa* by English L1 speakers were 12.3% (ENG-Mid Level) and 10.9% (ENG-High Level). One way ANOVA was applied to all five groups and it was found that there was a statistically significant difference across groups ($F(4, 46) = 2.86, p = .034$). However, Scheffe's multiple comparison tests did not show significant group difference probably because of relatively small sample sizes.

The slight decrease in the use of NP+*wa* with proficiency level by English L1 speakers could be the result of the increase in the use of NP+*ga* and NP+*ni* by ENG-High learners as compared to their Mid level counterparts. In Nakahama (2009), low-intermediate level learners' performances in marking referent introduction/tracking were also examined in a context-embedded type (i.e., H/N) narrative, and it was found that overgeneralisation of NP+*wa* persisted until English L1 learners reached an advanced proficiency level in Japanese. Korean speaking Japanese learners, on the other hand, hardly produced any NP+*wa* in that study, as well as in the current one. Yoshioka's (2005) study revealed a similar pattern of overgeneralisation of NP+*wa* by her Dutch speaking learners of Japanese at an intermediate level. Thus, it can be construed that Korean learners of Japanese are able to manage the appropriate use (or nonuse, in this case) of NP+*wa* irrespective of proficiency level. English speaking learners of Japanese gradually get a grip on appropriate use (and nonuse) of NP+*ga* and NP+*wa* as their proficiency levels increase. Moreover, given the results from Nakahama (2009, current) and Yoshioka (2005), researching appropriacy in the use of NP+*ga* and NP+*wa* might be made challenging due to the fact that postpositional marking systems do not exist in the learners' L1.

4.2.1.4 NP+*wa* for referent introduction in T/T narratives

The percentage use of NP+*wa* was much smaller in T/T narratives, as compared to H/N narratives, except for the frequent use of the form by ENG-Mid level speakers (28.6%). The difference of the percentage use of NP+*wa* between ENG-Mid and the other groups in the T/T narrative setting was to be found significant (F (4, 46) = 7.82, p = .000). It appears that this high use of NP+*wa* caused their lower percentage use of NP+*ga*.

As was mentioned in section 4.2.1.2 above, learners tend to use NP+*ga* for introducing characters into a story irrespective of the learners' L1 backgrounds in the T/T condition. ENG-Mid level learners were not an exception, in that the percentage use of *ga* increased from 28.5% in the H/N condition to 41.5% in the T/T condition. Taking a closer look at the ENG-Mid level learners' performance in the two different types of narratives, it was also found that narrating the events in the H/N condition triggered the learners to use NP+*o* and particle drop more frequently than in the T/T setting. Further, incorrect uses of other particles (that was collapsed into the category of 'others' in the table) weighed up 6.1% of referent introduction in the H/N, whereas the learners did not use particles incorrectly in the context of referent introduction in the T/T narratives. Therefore, it can be argued that relating events in different conditions might have contributed to differing marking of referents in the context of referent introduction.

The high percentage use of NP+*wa* by the low level learners replicates the results of Nakahama (2003). The study showed that the proportional use of NP+*wa* for referent introduction decreased greatly from the intermediate level (39.7%) to the advanced level (7.0%), and since the proportional use of NP+*wa* by the NSs was 7.3%, it seems that the performance of *wa* moved toward that of the NSs' discourse as proficiency increased. This overuse of NP+*wa* (in contexts where *ga* is normally expected) found in both the current study and the previous one might have resulted from the fact that NP+*ga* cannot be properly acquired until certain proficiency levels are reached (Doi and Yoshioka, 1990; Sakamoto, 1993).

Qualitative Findings
The learner narratives were examined qualitatively in order to identify characteristic distributions of NP+*wa* that might have been influenced by their proficiency and L1 backgrounds, as well as by the differing complexity of the tasks. Given that the majority of production of NP+*wa* was by ENG-Mid level learners in the T/T narratives, and by ENG-Mid and ENG-High level learners in the H/N narratives, their utterances were the foci of analysis.

Recall that in the H/N narratives, while the majority of the ENG-Mid level learners randomly used NP+*ga* and other forms irrespective of the status of referent, two ENG-Mid level learners attempted to differentiate the main characters from peripheral ones by using NP+*wa* for marking the former, and NP+*ga* for the latter. Interestingly, in T/T narratives, too, the same speaker displayed the same pattern (*wa* for the most important character, i.e., sheep) and *ga* for the peripheral characters. The other speaker used *ga* for the sheep, and *ga* and *kara* (from) for the peripheral characters. Both speakers used NP+*ni* (with) for marking the other two major characters besides the sheep, and this might indicate that both speakers attempted to raise the sheep character's status higher than those of the other two major characters in the story. In the other ENG-Mid learners' narratives, however, the use of NP+*wa* was ubiquitous irrespective of the characters' roles in the story or the narrative types.

As mentioned previously, three ENG-High level learners marked the main characters with NP+*wa*, and the peripheral ones with NP+*ga* in H/N narratives. The same speakers' narratives in the T/T settings were examined, and it was found that none of them used NP+*wa* to mark any referent in their T/T narratives. Rather, two of these speakers differentiated the major characters from the peripheral ones by marking the former with *ga* and the latter with other forms such as *ni* (by), *mo* (with) and *o* (ACC). It is suspected that these three speakers used NP+*wa* to mark the main character in H/N setting because they assumed that the listeners were aware of which character they were referring to due to the fact that there were pictures right in front of them. Therefore, they used the definite marking, i.e., *wa*, in marking the main character.

The same premise can be used to explain higher usage of NP+*wa* in H/N narratives across the groups as compared to their T/T narrative counterpart, except for ENG-Mid level. The higher usage of NP+*wa* by ENG-Mid level speakers in the T/T versus the H/N narratives might be indicative of their inability to linguistically differentiate the information status of the characters with or without the graphic support in front of them. Alternatively, higher percentage use of NP+*wa* could have been an artefact of lower percentage use of the forms including particle drops.

In summary, with few exceptions, there was no discernible pattern to the use of NP+*wa* among most of the ENG-Mid level learners. In contrast, ENG-High, KOR-Mid, and KOR-High level learners managed to differentiate the ways in which they marked the characters based on their importance within a story, as well as the condition of narrative elicitation (i.e., H/N and T/T settings). This systematic shift in the use of NP+*wa* from ENG-Mid to ENG-High demonstrates that the learners acquire the appropriacy of form-function mapping as they gain in overall proficiency. The performance of the use (or non-use) of NP+*wa* increases with proficiency in terms of English groups, as Hypothesis 3 predicted. Moreover, the native like performance of NP+*wa* by the intermediate level Korean speakers confirmed Hypothesis 4, which states that 'the Korean and English L1 speakers will display differing acquisition patterns in referent markings. Specifically, Korean speakers will achieve target-like performance earlier than English speakers due to the typological similarities shared between Korean and Japanese.' With regard to Hypothesis 5, task complexity did not have a positive effect on the 'non-use' of NP+*wa* for the English intermediate level learner discourse, whereas it helped increase the appropriate 'use' of NP+*ga*, the prototypical particle to mark indefiniteness of referents.

4.2.1.5 NP+*o* for referent introduction in H/N and T/T narratives

While NP+*o* weighed only 2% of the average percentage use of the entire markings of referent introductions in the T/T narrative condition, as much as 14.1 % of referent markings were done with *o* in the H/N narratives. The NNSs seemed to be able to use this direct object (case) particle, NP+*o*, without difficulty across proficiency levels under the H/N narrative condition.

Figure 4.3 below illustrates this difference in the use of NP+*o* between the two narrative conditions.

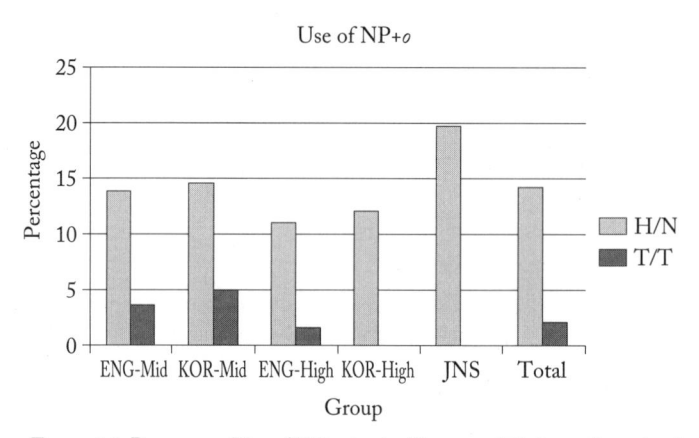

Figure 4.3 Percentage Use of NP+*o* in the Context of Referent Introduction

As can be seen in Figure 4.3, there is no vast difference in the average percentage use of NP+*o* across groups in the H/N setting. In other words, even lower proficiency level learners were able to use NP+*o*, regardless of their L1 background. One-way ANOVA was used to compare the intergroup differences among the five groups, and the test confirmed that the intergroup difference was insignificant (F (4, 46) = 0.60, p = .663). Given that there is hardly any use of NP+*o* in the narratives under the T/T condition, qualitative analysis was conducted only on the H/N narratives.

Qualitative Findings

Recall that eight JNSs used *o* to mark the frog which was one of the main characters in the story, and it was referred to as the boy's pet in those eight narratives in the beginning of the story. All the NNSs' narratives were examined, and it was found that about half of the marking of the frog were also done with *o* by the NNSs of Japanese (45% in ENG-Mid, 40% in KOR-Mid, 40% in ENG-High, 50% in KOR-High). Interestingly, the verbs the NNSs used display language specific tendencies. Three English L1 speakers (two from ENG-Mid level, one from ENG-High level) used the word, *motteiru* (to have). Given that the same use of the verb was found in English L1 narratives, this could be explained by CLI from English. The same verb was not used by KOR-Mid, KOR-High or JNSs, as the word, *motteiru* and its Korean equivalent is used only for inanimate objects, thereby not a proper expression for referring to the frog. Other verbs that were used with the particle *o* included *kau* (to have a pet), *miru* (look at), *tsukamaeru* (catch) and *mitsukeru* (find).

JNS data was revisited to compare the verbs used by the NSs and the NNSs of Japanese for marking the introduction of the frog. It was found that out of eight who used *o* for marking the frog, five NS Japanese speakers used the verb, *kau* (to have), while two used the verb *tsukamaeru* (catch) and one *ireru* (put in). Only three learners (one from ENG-Mid, ENG-High, and KOR-High each) used *katteiru*. Whereas Korean speaking learners of Japanese displayed quite similar patterns as JNSs in marking particles, the verb choice was rather different from the NSs of Japanese. Korean L1 (KNS) narratives were again examined, and it was found that nine out of ten speakers marked the frog with *lul*, a Korean equivalent of *o*. Out of these nine speakers who used *lul*, only two speakers used a Korean equivalent of *kau*. Three speakers used a Korean equivalent of *ireru* (put in), two *hirou* (pick up), and two *miru* (look at) in various tenses/aspects. Analysis of English L1 narratives revealed that three speakers used 'has got' or 'has' to refer to the frog, and this might mean that the use of *motteiru* by L1 English speaking learners is a CLI from English. See the following example.

Example 4.26 Referent Introduction of the Dog and the Frog by ENG-High Level (#9)

Eeto..	ja..	ano..	kono	kodomo	wa..	ano..	a..	petto	no
Um..	well..	um..	this	child	TOP	um..	u..	pet	GEN

inu	*to*	*nanka*	*atarashii*	*petto*	*no*	*kaeru*	*o*	*nanka*
dog	and	well	new	pet	GEN	frog	ACC	well

motteimasu.
has

'Um..well, um..this child has a pet dog um..well..and a pet frog..'

This speaker used the word, *motteimasu* (to have) which is not appropriately used for referring to an animate object. It appears that he directly translated the concept, *to have*, into Japanese, and as a result made an inappropriate remark regarding the dog. In contrast, the following example displays the correct usage of NP+*o* in conjunction with the conjugated version of the verb *kau* (to keep) by one of the advanced level Korean learners of Japanese.

Example 4.27 Referent Introduction of the Frog by KOR-High Level (#6)

Aru	*aru*	*kodomo*	*ga*	*imashita*	*sono*	*kodomo*
Certain	certain	child	NOM	exist-PAST	that	child

wa	*kaeru*	*o*	*kaukoto ni shita.*
TOP	frog	ACC	keep decide-PAST

'There once was a certain child. That child decided to keep (have) a frog'

This speaker chose to use the word, *kau*, in a phrase, *koto ni shita* (decided to …), to make an eloquent introduction of the frog. After he conveyed the little boy's decision to keep the frog, he further explained the boy's actions in detail, such as putting the frog into a jar. This speaker hardly referred to the dog throughout the narrative and told the story from the boy's perspective and provided a detailed explanation about the frog and his family in the end. Thus, it can be said that he seemed to have placed his focus on the boy and his relationship with his frog, and that strong tie between the two characters was expressed from the beginning.

There are no discernible differences between L2 Japanese narratives by Korean and English speakers except for with the use of *motteiru* (have) by English L1 speakers. The fact that only three speakers from the entire NNSs pool, regardless of their L1 backgrounds, used the vocabulary most preferred by JNSs could mean that the learners tend to have different word choices, and these choices might make their L2 discourse somewhat inauthentic.

4.2.1.6 The use of NP+*ni/kara* and the passive construction/expressions in H/N and T/T narratives

NP+*ni/kara* is a noun phrase with agentive marker, roughly equivalent to "by NP" in English, and is mainly used in the passive structure in Japanese. As in English, the Japanese passive can also occur without mention of an agent. The use of NP+*ni/kara* in percentages is shown in Figure 4.4 to illustrate the differences among the five groups under the two narrative conditions (H/N and T/T).

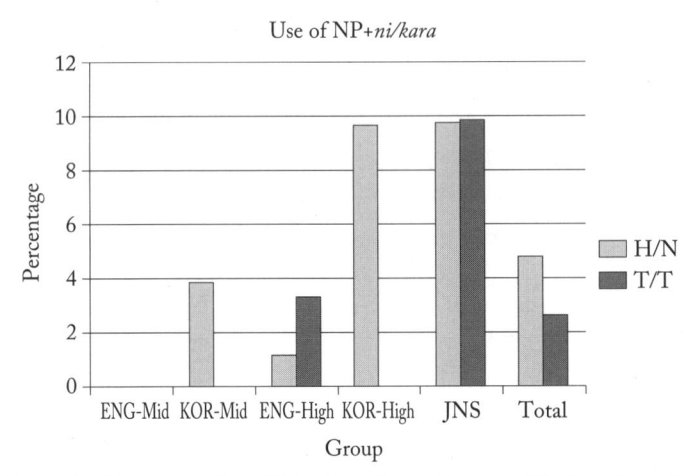

Figure 4.4 Percentage Use of NP+*ni/kara* in the Context of Referent Introduction

As Figure 4.4 shows, the NNSs did not produce *ni/kara* under the T/T condition except for in the ENG-High group. In the H/N narratives, on the other hand, all the groups except for ENG-Mid produced *ni/kara*, though the percentage varied across groups. One-way ANOVA was conducted for the H/N narratives, and it was found that the difference in the use of NP+*ni/kara* among groups was not significant in terms of the H/N narratives ($F(4, 46) = 2.35, p = .069$)[27]. Due to the fact that the use of *ni/kara* was produced by only two groups in the T/T setting, statistical testing was not applied. Although NP+*ni/kara* only made up to 9.8% of the total markers for introducing new referents, it was one of the most prevalent forms used to introduce more peripheral characters in the story (e.g., the owl, and the bees) by the NSs. As can be seen in Table 4.16, the use of NP+*ni/kara* was not produced in the narratives by ENG-Mid level speakers and only once by the ENG-High level speakers. In contrast, the use of *ni/kara* was observed in the narration of Korean speakers at both levels; moreover, its use increased with proficiency (3.9% to 9.7%). The increase between the two proficiency levels by the Korean speakers suggests a steady progression towards target-like use. The increase, though slight, in the use of NP+*ni/kara* with proficiency supports Hypothesis 3 in terms of the Korean group.

Comparing the H/N condition narratives and the T/T condition narratives, the percentage uses of *ni/kara* differed greatly within the NNSs data but there is not much difference within the NSs narrative data (9.8% in H/N and 9.9% in T/T). This similar percentage use of the form might have some relevance with equally high occurrences of passive expressions regardless of task type. The NNSs data will be carefully examined, in terms of the usage of NP+*ni/kara* in conjunction with passive expressions in both the H/N and T/T narratives. The total frequency of passive expressions will also be provided.

Qualitative Findings

There were 12 total occurrences of NP+*ni/kara* in the NNSs narratives. Seven of them were by KOR-High, two by KOR-Mid, and one by ENG-High in the H/N narratives, and two cases by ENG-High in the T/T narratives. All the cases were examined, and it was found that except for one case in the T/T narrative, NP+*ni/kara* was used for peripheral characters (such as the bees and the owl in the H/N and the mother bird in the T/T), while the main characters remained in the topical position (subject of the sentence) as patients in the passive construction. One exception was found in the T/T narrative by an ENG-High level speaker. He used the form to introduce the second most important character into the discourse, by putting him in the agentive position, while putting the most important character in the patient position. See the example below.

Example 4.28 Use of NP+*ni/kara* in the T/T by ENG-High Level (#9)

Aa..	*kuma*	*shiroi*	*kuma*	*ga*	*usagi*	*ni*	*aa..*
Um..	bear	white	bear	NOM	rabbit	by	um..

hippa	*hippararete*	*ano..*	*aisu sukeeto*	*ni*	*ikimashita.*	
pul..	pull-PASS-and	um..	ice skate	to	go-PAST	

'Um..a bear a white bear was pulled by a rabbit and went ice skating.'

Recall that although there were three major characters in the T/T story. One character (the female sheep) played the most important role in the beginning of the story, due to the fact that the two male animal characters did a play-fight in order to win her attention. This ENG-High speaker (#9) referred to the sheep as a white bear throughout the narrative and regarded it as the central character in the story until she decided to leave the two male animals toward the end. It is surmised that the speaker promoted the introduction of the female sheep by demoting the secondary character into a less topical role, in order not to have main characters compete with each other, with regard to gaining topicality.

As is found in this Example 4.28, all 12 occurrences of NP+*ni/kara* appeared in the passive constructions/expressions. Example 4.29 shows one successful formation of passives by one KOR-High level learner in the H/N narrative.

Example 4.29 Successful Construction of Passive Structure by KOR-High Level (#1)

Soko	*ni*	*shika*	*ga*	*ite...*	Ø	*sono*	*shika*	*no*	*atama...*
There	at	deer	NOM	exist	(boy)	that	deer	GEN	head...

no	*ue*	*ni*	*noserarechaimasu*
GEN	above	at	carry-PASS-unfortunately

'A deer was there and (the boy) got carried on the deer's head.'

This advanced level speaker introduced the deer in the topical position with *ga*; however, he switched the topic to the boy (marked with zero anaphora), accompanied by passivisation of the verb, *noseru*. Unlike this advance level speaker, a learner from the KOR-Mid level used NP+*ni/kara* in conjunction with passive construction with incorrect conjugation of the verb. See Example 4.30 below.

Example 4.30 Use of NP+*ni/kara* in the H/N by KOR-Mid Level (#10)

Doobutsu	*ni...*	*ano..*	*ee...*	*de..*	*bu..*	*a...*

Animal   by   um..   ah...   well..   b..   a...

<u>okorechatte</u>...   ano..   eeto..   ee..   ee..
scold-PASS- unfortunately   um..   well..   um..   well

maa   takai   tokoro   kara   ano..   ochichaimashita
um..   high   place   from   um...   fall-unfortunately-PAST

'Um..well..(he) got scolded by an animal unfortunately, and um…well…um… fell from a high place unfortunately.'

It is evident in this example that the speaker struggled with producing an appropriate lexical item, and as a result he uttered hesitation markers, such as *ano* and *eeto*. He could not produce the correct passive morpheme *okorare* (getting scolded) and ended up with the inaccurate conjugation *okore*. The following two examples also demonstrate other speakers' attempt to use passive construction with or without an agent (NP+*ni/kara*).

Example 4.31 Attempt of Passivisation of Verb in the H/N by KOR-High Level (#2)

...Ø   doobutsu   no   miki   ni   <u>kakerete</u>
...(boy)   animal   GEN   branch(antler)   on   stuck

chotto.. (inaudible)   toko   made   itte..
a little...   place   till   go and...

'(the boy) was stuck (hung) on the animal's antler and…um… (he) went to (inaudible) place and…'

It appeared that this speaker meant either *hikkakatte* (got stuck without the deer's intention) or *hikkakerarete* (was hung on the antlers by the deer). Either way, it was his intention to keep the main protagonist (i.e., the boy) as the topic of discourse. The conjugated part of the verb (*rete*) indicates that the speaker in all probability attempted to passivise the verb (*kakeru* or *hikkakeru*- 'hang'), and thus this was counted as a passive expression.

Example 4.32 Attempt of Passivisation of Verb in the T/T by KOR-High Level (#5)

Akai	kuma	wa...	ano..	yuki	o	<u>n</u>a<u>gurarete</u>...	yuki	ni
Red	bear	TOP...	um..	snow..	ACC	throw-PASS...	snow	by

<u>n</u>a<u>gurarete</u>..	tabun	attchi	kara	attchi	ni	anoo..	usage	ka
throw-PASS...	maybe	there	from	there	at	um...	rabbit	or

hitsuji	ka	maa	dare	ka	wakannai	kedo	tabun	attchi	ni
sheep	or	well	someone	or	know-NEG	but	maybe	there	in

iru	na	to	omotte...
exist	P	P	think and

'The red bear got snow thrown …thrown by snow…probably from there… thinking that there might be rabbit or sheep or someone there.'

The verb that Speaker #5 in this example used, *nagurarete*, is the passive form of *naguru* (meaning to 'batter'). As is apparent from the context, he meant to use *nagerarete* (the passive form of *nageru* meaning 'throw') but made the wrong word choice. Further, he used *ni* (by) to make an effort to mark an agent in the passive construction but incorrectly marked the object (snow) rather than the agent (the rabbit or the sheep). While Speaker #2 in Example 4.31 wrongly conjugated the correct verb, Speaker #5 in Example 4.32 conjugated the wrong verb correctly.

While speakers in above examples did make attempts to passivise the verbs, some speakers opted not to use the passive structures after some struggling. Example 4.33 illustrates this trend.

Example 4.33 Opting Out to Use Passive structures by KOR-Mid Level (# 3)[28]

Bii	tachi	<u>ni</u>...	bii	tachi	<u>ni</u>...	bii	tachi	ga...
Bee	plural	by	bee	plural	by	bee	plural	NOM

inu	o	tsuite..tsuite
dog	ACC	follow

(Bees by…bees by… bees follow the puppy)

The topic of the utterance before this was the dog, and the speaker had made an attempt to keep the dog as the topic by introducing the bees in the agent position, preceding *ni* (by). However, the speaker could not produce a proper conjugation of the verb, and thereby switched the topic from the dog to the bees with the subject marker, *ga*. All the H/N and T/T narratives were examined in terms of the frequencies of passive constructions/expressions throughout the narratives without having the examination restricted to the context of referent introductions. Table 4.18 and Figure 4.5 display the results.

Table 4.18 Number of the Occurrences of Passives by JNS and NNSs[29]

	H/N	T/T	Total
ENG-Mid[30] (N=11)	4	9	13
KOR-Mid (N=10)	7	5	12
ENG-High (N=10)	18	9	27
KOR-High (N=10)	18	7	25
JNS (N=10)	27	27	54

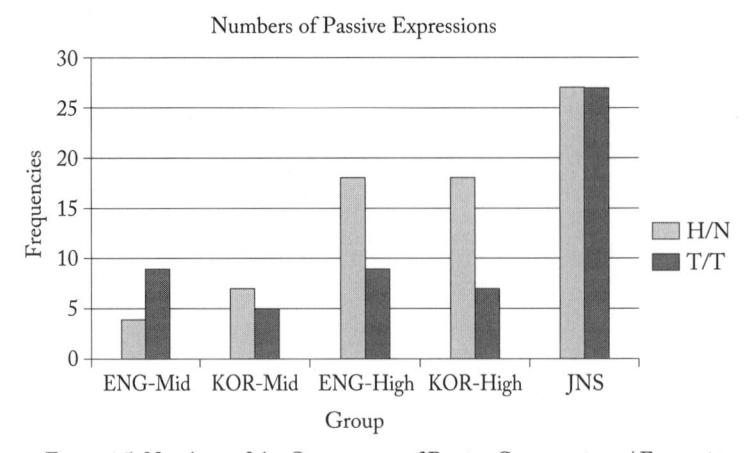

Figure 4.5 Numbers of the Occurrences of Passive Constructions / Expressions

Recall that in contrast to the NNSs narratives, nine NSs produced passive structures at least twice, irrespective of narrative type, and in total 54 occurrences of passivisation of verbs or passive expressions were found in the NS narratives.[31] As is shown in Table 4.18, there was a substantial difference among groups. The lower proficiency groups (both in the English and Korean speaker groups) produced much fewer passive expressions (ENG-Mid: 4, KOR-Mid: 7) than their advanced level counterparts (ENG-High: 18, KOR-High: 18) under the H/N narrative condition. Due to the fact that there were only two inaccurate conjugations of passivisation of verbs, it can be postulated that the learners produced passive constructions or expressions when they felt confident enough to accurately conjugate the verbs. The ability to conjugate verbs properly seems to increase with proficiency under the H/N narrative condition given the increased frequencies of passive structures in higher proficiency levels. However, the amount of total passive constructions in the ENG-High or KOR-High still did not reach the NS level. This part of the results might suggest that the learners have not fully achieved the native speaker level capacity to manage voice alternation in oral narratives even at the advanced level. Such a circumstance is not unreasonable to expect as the acquisition of passivisation is observed late in the developmental phase (Pienemann, 1998).

In the T/T setting, however, the data did not display big differences in the number of production of passive expressions/structures between the two different proficiency levels for both Korean and English groups. Both L1 groups did not produce many passive expressions/constructions irrespective of their proficiency levels. Given that the NNSs produced many more passive expressions at the higher proficiency level than their lower proficient counterparts in the H/N setting, it is clear that they had the ability to produce passive forms at the advanced levels but did not do so under the T/T condition.

The stories of the H/N and T/T narratives had some similarities in that they both had three main characters and miscellaneous peripheral characters with whom these central characters interacted. On the other hand, they had differences in that the H/N story had several scenes that would directly trigger passivisation of verbs whereas the T/T story did not. Despite this difference, as previously discussed, the JNSs produced almost an equal percentage use of NP+*ni/kara* and the same frequency of passive forms/expressions regardless of the narrative type. Thus, this segment of results can be interpreted in the following two ways. 1) The NSs told the story from the standpoints of the main characters using voice alteration strategies without being provided obvious reinforcement, whereas the NNSs needed an apparent tip-off to do so. 2) Task complexity did not affect the way in which the NSs narrated the events; however, the NNSs could not produce passives due to the high complexity of the T/T task itself.

Besides the premise that the learners lacked the ability to accurately produce passive constructions, in explaining lower frequencies of passives by the advanced level NNSs than the NSs in the H/N narratives, the differing tendencies in the formation of viewpoints in Korean and English versus Japanese discourse can be posited. Recall that Kim (2001) and Jung (2002) maintained that Korean speakers prefer to focus on actions, not the characters in a story. When they narrate events, they consequently change the subject of utterances quite frequently. Japanese speakers, in contrast, tend to keep the focus on a limited number of main characters by placing them in the subject position (Kim, 2001, Jung, 2002). This differing pattern between the two languages in realising story narration, might have influenced the Korean speakers' production of fewer passive structures, even in their L2 Japanese discourse.

In order to investigate the possibility of CLI from English and Korean, L1 narratives of English and Korean will now be revisited in terms of how many passive forms were used in the narratives. The results are presented again in conjunction with the results of JNSs in Figure 4.6.

Number of Passive Expressions

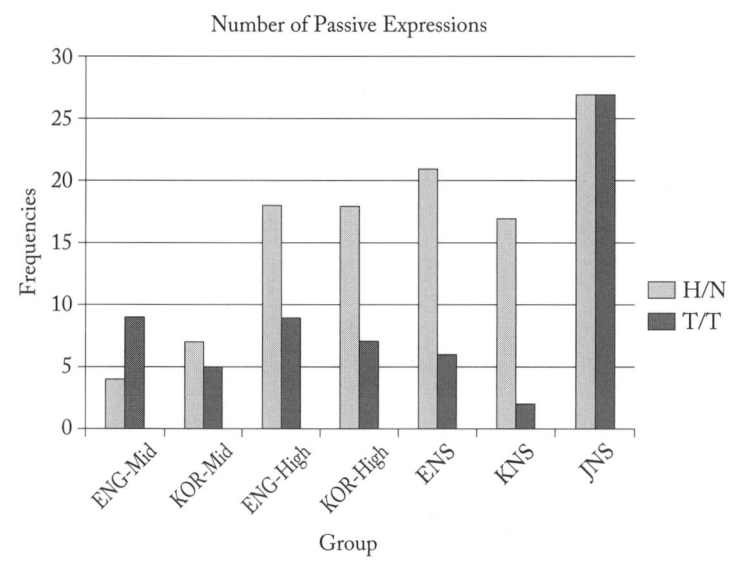

Figure 4.6 Numbers of Occurrences of Passive Constructions / Expressions by All Groups

As Figure 4.6 above illustrates, there is a clear case of CLI from Korean and English in the L2 learner data. That is, ENS and KNS participants produced far more passive constructions in the H/N than the T/T narratives, just as the learners of Japanese did in their L2 narratives, except for the ENG-Mid level. It should be noted again here that the speakers in the ENS and KNS groups are not the same participants as any of the L2 groups. Therefore, the similar pattern found in the L2 Japanese data and ENSs/KNSs reflects a general pattern, rather than an individual one.

The results of some previous studies of L2 Japanese (e.g., Tanaka, 1996) showed that learners were able to produce passive structures without major problems. However, these studies employed data elicitation methods that would directly elicit passive structures, such as cloze tests or a series of pictures in which the actions that would invite 'suffering passives' and the patient and agent of the actions are obvious. In contrast, Yanagimachi (1997, 2000) revealed that even his advanced level learners did not produce even a single passive construction in their narrations of a film. Considering the results of the current study and those of Yanagimachi's, it is possible that learners might avoid the use of passive constructions when they have freedom to state the story using different structures. In fact, only two errors were found in passive construction in the learner data in the current study. This might be an indication that the learners used passive voice structures only when they felt confident to do so. They might have chosen to use active forms without taking the risk of making an error. While we need more studies like the current one investigating passive forms in relatively uncontrolled discourse, more controlled tests to assess learners' grammatical knowledge might provide us more leverage to make a conclusive claim.

What follows next is a detailed analysis of the distribution of the occurrences of the passive structure. The patients of the passive structure in the H/N narrative and T/T narrative were summarised in Table 4.19 and Table 4.20 below.

Table 4.19 Patients of the Passive Structures in the H/N Narrative

	Boy	Dog	Boy & Dog	Others	Total
ENG-Mid	1	1	0	2 (bees)	4
KOR-Mid	4	2	0	1 (bees nest)	7
ENG-High	11	5	0	2 (deer, frog parents)	18
KOR-High	9	8	0	1 (frog couple)	18
ENS	8	9	3	1 (bees)	21
KNS	7	10	0	0	17
JNS	12	11	4	0	27

Table 4.20 Patients of the Passive Structures in the T/T Narrative[32]

	Bear	Rabbit	Sheep	B&R	B&R&S	Others	Total
ENG-Mid	7	1	0	0	0	1 (tree)	9
KOR-Mid	3	0	0	0	0	2(snowman)	5
ENG-High	6	2	1	0	0	0	9
KOR-High	5	2	0	0	0	0	7
ENS	1	0	0	0	0	5 (snowman(1) bird (1), sled (3))	6
KNS	0	1	0	0	1	0	2
JNS	16	1	1	7	2	0	27

As illustrated in Table 4.19, the JNSs and the KNSs only chose the main protagonists (the boy, the dog, or the boy and the dog combined) as the patients of the passive constructions. While speakers from the ENS groups also tend to assign the role of the patient to the protagonists of the story, some passive structures had an antagonist as the patient. Example 4.34 shows a passive construction that has a peripheral character as the patient and a main character as the agent.

Example 4.34 Bees as Patients in the Passive Construction by ENG-Mid Level (#6)

Kodomo	*ga*	*ki...*	*no*	*ue*	*kara*	*ochite*	*kimashita*
Child	NOM	tree	GEN	top	from	fall	come toward

ato	*wa*	*inu*	*ga*	*nanka*	*hachi?*	*hachi*	*ka*	*hachimitsu*
else	TOP	dog	NOM	well	bees?	bees	or	honey

no	*hachi*	*a...*	*ga*	*okosa..okosarete*		*a..*	*(Ø)*
GEN	bees	um...	NOM	wak...wake-PASS and		um..	(dog)

hashittemashita
run-ING-PAST

'The child fell from the top of the tree. What else (happened) was that the dog...well...bees were awaken (by the dog) and (the dog) was running.'

This speaker was explaining the two consecutive scenes in which the boy fell from the tree and the dog upset the beehive and therefore got chased by the bees. Instead of keeping the dog as a discourse topic, placing it as the patient in the passive structure as many of the JNS did, the speaker introduced the bees with *ga* and then kept them as the discourse topic by appointing them to be the patient of the passive construction. However, the speaker switched the discourse topic to the dog referring to the dog's action without explicitly mentioning the subject of the sentence.[33] Frequent subject switches like this not only disrupt the flow of the narrative but also make the story harder to follow. Other instances of passive constructions with the peripheral characters in the patient position revealed a similar pattern. Compared to the passive constructions with the peripheral characters in the patient position, it takes less effort to follow the story with the passive constructions with the main characters in the patient position (seen in Example 4.29 above).

While the actions or the storyline themselves would not inevitably guarantee passive constructions in the T/T narratives, as compared to the H/N narratives, the JNS participants told the story from the perspective of the main characters by placing them as patients in the passive constructions. In fact, as mentioned previously, there are not sizable differences in terms of the numbers of NP+*ni/ kara* and the passive constructions/expressions between the H/N and T/T conditions by the JNSs. The participants from the other groups also chose the main characters (the sheep, the bear, and the rabbit) as the patients of the passive constructions/expressions. However, there were eight cases where the participants chose peripheral entities to be the topic of passivisation. They were found in the narratives by the ENG-Mid, KOR-Mid and ENSs groups. As can be seen in Table 4.20 above, three passive forms were produced with the snowman in the passive structures. See Example 4.35.

Example 4.35 Passivisation to Modify the Snowman by KOR-Mid Level (#2)

Saisho	*ni*	*usagi*	*to*	*uun...*	*usagi*	*to*	*ookami*	*to*
Beginning	in	rabbit	and	um...	rabbit	and	wolf	and

aru	*shootai fumei*		*no*	*(laugh)*	*doobutsu*	*to..*
certain	identification unknown		GEN	(laugh)	animal	with..

mata..	*yuki..yukibito?*	*yuki..*	*de*	*tsukurareta*
further..	snow..snow person?	snow..	of	make-PASS-PAST

yoo na	*hito*	*ga*	*dete te...*
seems	person	NOM	appear and

'In the beginning, a rabbit and um..a rabbit, a wolf, a certain unknown animal and snow, snow person? a person that seems to be made of snow appear and...'

It seems that the speaker passivised the verb, *tsukuru*, not because she chose to place the focus on the snowman, *per se*, but because she was not aware of the word *yukidaruma* (snowman) and tried to substitute with '*yuki de tsukurareta yoona hito*' (a man who seemed to have been made of snow). Since all the passive forms/expressions were coded in the narrative data, cases like this one were included in the counts. In fact, two cases of passivisation to modify the snowman were found in the KOR-Mid level narratives, and the choice of passive voice has no bearing on the roles the speakers wanted the characters to play in the story.

With regard to the ENS narratives, there were twenty cases in which the speakers from the ENS groups allocated the patient role to the protagonists in the H/N narratives, but only one episode of passive construction that had the main character as the patient in the T/T narratives. In the ENS narratives, three speakers mentioned 'a sled being pulled' in the beginning of the story. The movie does starts with a female wolf-like sheep in a sled that is being pulled by a lot of small toy-like rabbits. She arrives at an icy pond, gets greeted by a snowman and then later meets the other two main characters, the bear and the rabbit. Though the sled itself does not have significance in the story plot itself, the speakers might have regarded this action as important because it was the very beginning of the movie, and one of the most important characters was in it. Further, the fact that she was being pulled by other animals might raise the importance of her role in the story as a whole.

Interestingly, the same scene was captured differently by the speakers of the other groups, including the ENG-Mid and the ENG-High groups. In the beginning of the scene, some speakers did mention the sled but it did not become the topic of the discourse; instead, their focus was kept on the animals themselves. Therefore, CLI was not evident in the way in which the English speaking learners of Japanese narrated the beginning of the story. The differing ways of depicting the first scene between the English L1 speakers (at least by three of the English L1 speakers) and the rest of the participants, illustrates what Slobin calls 'thinking for speaking' in that languages influence the ways in which the speakers form the way of thinking and relating events.

In summarising the production of NP+*ni/kara* and passive constructions, the most remarkable finding was how the learners' storytelling scheme in their L1 affected the way in which they constructive narratives. To be specific, as previous studies maintained, the English and the Korean speakers in the current study tended to take a more neutral stance on characters and focused rather on the actions or the happenings in the story, unless the passive forms were circumstantially (and intentionally) prompted. The JNSs, on the other hand, have a propensity for relating the events from the main characters' perspective throughout the narratives. In other words, the study also revealed that the contextual support affects the speakers' molding of their storytelling style. The pictures in the H/N narrative had various scenes that would naturally trigger the use of the passive voice; as expected, the ENSs, KNSs and advanced level L2 learners of Japanese produced many passive constructions/expressions, though the total frequency level did not reach the same level as found with the JNSs. It was the T/T narratives that display considerable difference between the JNSs and the rest of the groups; all the groups except for the JNSs produced much fewer occurrences of passive forms/expressions. This provides consistent evidence of differing storytelling constructs between the Japanese informants and their Korean/English L1 counterparts.

4.2.1.7 NP+particle drop in H/N narratives and T/T narratives

Figure 4.7 illustrates the average percentage of NP+particle drop graphically.

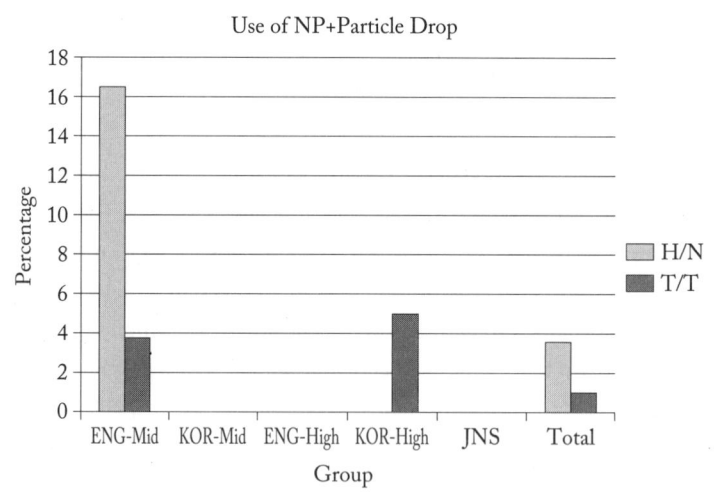

Figure 4.7 Percentage Use of NP+Particle Drop in the Context of Referent Introduction

As is shown in Table 4.16 and Table 4.17 in an earlier section, and in Figure 4.7 above, the majority of NP+particle drop was found in the H/N narrative except for two cases by ENG-Mid level learners and one case by a KOR-High level learner in the T/T narratives. Only ENG-Mid level learners dropped particles in marking referent introduction under the H/N condition, and the percentage use was 16.5%, and that was the second highest use after NP+*ga*

(28.5%) in marking of a new referent. This result supports my previous study (Nakahama, 2009) that employed the same picture storybook for data elicitation. In Nakahama (2009), the lowest proficiency level (intermediate-low by the ACTFL guidelines) English L1 learners of Japanese produced 19.7% particle drop and middle proficiency level (intermediate-high by the ACTFL guidelines) learners 9.7%. By the time learners reached advanced levels, the percentage use dropped down to only 3.3%.[34] With the result of my previous study as well as the current one in terms of the H/N context narrative, it can be postulated that particle drop for marking referent introduction decreases with proficiency by learners whose L1 is English.

When the data was looked at closely, it was found that particles were dropped when they were supposed to be marked with *ga* (subject marker), *o* (object marker) or *to* (with). I have been referring to all the markers in the study as postpositional markers or postpositional particles for the sake of simplicity since the main point was to indicate the differences in the location where the form appears (i.e., post NP in Japanese and Korean, as compared to 'pre'-positional marking in English). However, some brief explanation of the differences between case particles and postpositions might be pertinent here. Markers that are considered case particles (such as nominal or genitive) can be omitted and the sentence can remain grammatical. On the other hand, markers which do not mark a case are called postpositions, such as *de* (at), *e* (to), *to* (with), and these cannot be omitted due to the fact that they hold an inherent meaning such as *de* implying location (Tsujimura, 1996). Case particle omission is quite common in native Japanese language discourse, especially in casual speech (see Hasegawa, 1993 and Maruyama, 1996 for relevant discussions). In narratives, on the other hand, new information is typically marked with NP+*ga* (Hinds, 1984) and it hardly ever gets omitted. This difference might be influenced by the fact that the former discourse type is dialogical and the latter monological. Some studies have shown particle omissions in narratives (e.g., Nakamura, 1993); however, it is rather a rare episode, unless the speaker intended to involve the listener to co-construct a narrative together.

Example 4.36 illustrates a very rare episode of particle drop by a very proficient speaker of L2 Japanese from KOR-High level group.

Example 4.36 Episode of Particle Drop by KOR-High Level (#3)

Fuyu	*no*	*toki*	*wa*	*denakatta..*		*ano..*	*kaeru*	*san*
Winter	GEN	time	TOP	appear-NEG-PAST..		um..	frog	Mr.

toka	*hachi*	*san*	*toka..*	*(Ø)..*	*iroiro*	*deteimasu*	*ne.*
etc.	bee	Mr.	etc.	<u>(Ø)..</u>	various	appear-ING	P

'Various (living things such as) Mr. Frog, Mr. Bees and others appear, which did not show up during the winter time, <u>you know</u>.'

Where (Ø) is inserted in Example 4.36 above, *ga* is normally expected to mark the listing of creatures to indicate it is the subject of the sentence (topic of discourse). Notice that at the end of this utterance, he used the sentence final particle, *ne*, after the verb, *deteimasu* (to appear). This particle has the function of 'seeking agreement' and its meaning is explained as 'tag question' in many Japanese grammar books. Example 4.37 explains the simple usage of '*ne*' in casual Japanese conversation.

Example 4.37 Use of '*ne*' in Japanese

Speaker A: *Ano hito (Ø)   hontooni   ii   hito   desu ne*
                That person   really   good   person   COP P

Speaker B: *Ee,   hontooni soo desu yo ne*
                Right really   so COP P P

'A: That person is really nice isn't he? B: Yeah, he really is, isn't he?'

Although this example is a made up conversation by the author, it is a typical dialogic exchange between friends/acquaintances in Japanese. Note that Speaker A ends her utterance with *ne*, seeking an agreement from her interlocutor. Speaker B reciprocates by repeating the same content with the use of the same sentence final particle, *ne*. She also uses another sentence final particle, *yo*. When *yo* is used by itself, one of its main functions is to provide information to the listener (Kinsui, 1993); however, when used with *ne*, it denotes 'confirmation' or 'seeking an agreement' with the listener. Thus, Speaker B starts her utterance with *Ee*, agreeing with Speaker A's preceding utterance, and then reconfirms the fact with the combination of these two sentence final particles.

The narrative told by Speaker #3 from the KOR-High group was examined thoroughly. It was found that he produced *ne* four times and *yo* twice in his T/T narratives and his storytelling method was quite interactive from his end, whereas the listener limited her interaction to simple backchannels. Due to the speaker's interactive storytelling style, particle drop did not seem inappropriate, unlike all the other cases of particle drop found in lower proficiency level learners. See Example 4.38 for a typical example of particle drop from a lower proficiency level learner.

Example 4.38 Episode of Particle Drop by ENG-Mid Level (#7)

ano...	saisho	no	e	wa...	ano...	inu	to	aa..	kodomo
um...	first	GEN	picture	TOP...	um...	dog	and	um..	child

(Ø)	aa..	ima	issho	ni	aa..	kurooku.kurooku..		ano..
Ø	um..	now	together	with	un..	kurooku (frog?) frog...		um...

doobutsu..	*(Ø)*	aa..	mimasu
animal..	Ø	um..	look

'um..as for the first picture, um. (Ø) dog and boy look at (Ø) frog frog..um.. animal...'

The first particle this speaker dropped was supposed to be *ga*, as it marks the subject of the sentence (a boy and a dog) and it is new information. She dropped another particle, *o*, to mark the object of the sentence (a frog). Out of 11 participants in the ENG-Mid group, six speakers dropped particles at least once, and two speakers dropped more than two types of particles, as is shown in Example 4.38 above. These two speakers dropped particles regardless of the positions of the NP in the sentence or the roles the characters played in the story plot. In other words, particle drop appeared to be random.

In the case of Example 4.38, the speaker omitted a marker where it can be done in a grammatical manner (i.e., omission of 'case particles' rather than 'postpositions'). In fact, of all the particle drops found in the data (12 cases in H/N and 3 cases in T/T), 13 of them were case particle drops. Thus, the utterances were not, in theory, ungrammatical because of these omissions.

However, due to the monologic nature of the discourse, as well as the unsystematic way in which particle omission was performed as stated above, the omission of case particles made the discourse somewhat incoherent and non-target like. In similar situations in their narrative, the higher proficiency level counterparts and the Japanese NSs produced appropriate particles, depending on the context (e.g., *o* for marking an object, and *ga* for marking a topical new referent), which made the narrative more coherent and easy to follow.

To respond to Hypotheses posited in the study, Hypothesis 3 was supported with regard to particle drop by the English L1 speakers, as their performance did improve with proficiency. Hypothesis 4 which presupposed differing patterns of acquisition of referent markings between the two L1 groups, was also supported, as the Korean speakers performed target-like 'non-use' of particle drop already at the lower proficiency level. Hypothesis 5 that predicts higher accuracy of grammar marking in the T/T narrative was also supported, as the use of particle drop was lower in the T/T narrative by the English speakers.

To summarise the referent markings in the context of referent introduction, as was predicted by Hypothesis 3, the performance of the NSS's referent marking (in terms of marking new referents, i.e., least continuous topics) generally increased with proficiency. Further, developmental patterns were vastly different between the two different L1 groups in the L2 Japanese data with regard to referent introduction. The two different L1 groups demonstrated unique predispositions to mark referents, which would indicate a possible transfer from their L1. The English L1 group showed significant improvement between the Intermediate level and the Advanced level groups with regard to the use of NP+*ga*. The Korean group, on the other hand, demonstrated the target-like use of the form at the lower proficiency level. The use of NP+*ni/kara* which was used for introducing peripheral characters, increased with proficiency among the Korean group, while the English group did not produce such a form irrespective of proficiency.

The English group displayed distinctive developmental patterns in the production of NP+particle omission and NP+*wa*. The target-like production of the forms increased significantly with proficiency. A close investigation of the distributional patterns of NP+*wa* and NP+*ga* in the English L1 group revealed that the functional use of the form reached target-like behaviour at the higher levels of proficiency, indicating that the ability to map forms and functions developed with proficiency. In contrast, their Korean counterparts already displayed target-like form-function mapping skills at the intermediate proficiency level. With reference to the production of passive constructions, target-like performance developed with proficiency by both L1 groups in the H/N narratives. However, the number of total occurrences of passive structures in the advanced level groups did not reach the level of the JNSs. The ENS and the KNS groups also produced less passive structures as compared to the JNSs. To explicate this result, it was postulated that Japanese, Korean and English speakers have differing ways of conceptualising events. Task complexity affected the learner oral narrative production but not for the NS narratives, in the context of referent introduction. The cognitively more challenging task generally triggered more accurate referent markings in the English speakers' L2 Japanese narratives. Task complexity did not have a major effect on the Korean learners' L2 Japanese discourse, in terms of accuracy, largely because they already showed target-like proficiency in marking referents at the lower level of proficiency.

4.2.2 Topic switch (Re-introduction of referent)

As was identified in Chapter 1, referent marking was studied in three parts: 1) referent introduction, 2) referent re-introduction (topic switch), and 3) referential topic maintenance. How referents are introduced into narratives was examined in the context of 'referent introduction' above. In order to understand how participants in the story move in and out of the topical position (subject position in a sentence), the re-introduction of referents into the subject position after previously having lost their topicality to others was examined. Since this involves the current discourse topic's being taken over by another referent, the re-introduction of a referent is called 'topic switch' in the current study, interchangeably. Tables 4.21 and 4.22 show how referent re-introduction (i.e., how the current referential topic was switched to another referent) was linguistically marked by the NNSs of Japanese in the H/N and T/T settings, respectively. The JNS results will also be provided for the purpose of comparison with the NNSs data. The findings and their quantitative and qualitative analysis will be provided for the H/N and T/T narrative types separately.

Table 4.21 Topic Switch by NNSs and JNSs in the H/N Narratives

NP+	*ga*	*wa*	*mo*	particle drop	zero anaphora
ENG-Mid (N=11)	54 36.3	38 30.1	1 0.6	16 11.2	29 21.8
KOR-Mid (N=10)	60 33.5	79 43.4	3 1.6	0 0	33 21.5
ENG-High (N=10)	138 41.2	73 36.9	12 3.6	1 0.4	37 18
KOR-High (N=10)	61 29.7	100 44.8	6 1.8	0 0	49 23.7
JNS (N=10)	26 25.1	40 33.1	3 2.3	0 0	43 39.6
Total	339 33.2	330 37.5	191 1.9	17 2.5	25 24.8

Total number of occurrences and average percentages are shown in the first and second lines, respectively.

Table 4.22 Topic Switch by NNSs and JNSs in the T/T Narratives

NP+	*ga*	*wa*	*mo*	particle drop	zero anaphora
ENG-Mid (N=11)	59 36.7	61 42.4	4 2.2	16 11.9	10 6.7
KOR-Mid (N=10)	61 45.3	41 31.9	2 0.9	4 4.2	17 17.8
ENG-High (N=10)	124 52.1	37 25.5	10 7.7	6 4.1	22 10.6
KOR-High (N=10)	80 46.7	51 23.4	5 1.9	7 6.0	17 22.0
JNS (N=10)	68 40.0	49 30.5	6 2.9	5 2.1	28 24.1
Total	392 44.1	239 31.0	27 3.1	38 5.8	94 16.0

Total number of occurrences and average percentages are shown in the first and second lines, respectively.

In the context of topic switch, the uses of NP+*ga*, NP+*wa*. NP+*mo*, particle drop, and zero anaphora were found in both types of narratives. As can be seen from Tables 4.21 and 4.22, NP+*ga* and NP+*wa* dominated the percentage use in marking referents in this context in both the H/N and T/T conditions. Further, although the percentage use was somewhat lower than that of *ga* and *wa*, zero anaphora also had a fair share of use.[35] The differences in the percentage use of NP+*ga* and NP+*wa* among groups was found to be insignificant in both instances ($F_{(4,46)} = 0.73, p = .58$ for *ga* and $F_{(4,46)} = 0.63, p = .65$ for *wa* in the H/N narratives, and $F_{(4,46)} = 0.54, p = .71$ for *ga* and $F_{(4,46)} = 1.1, p = .37$ for *wa* in T/T). In investigating referent markings, previous studies grouped the NPs into full NP or zero anaphora and discussed the results (e.g., Clancy, 1985; Yanagimachi, 2000). Those studies revealed that speakers tend to use full NPs when switching topics, despite the fact that these referents have been previously introduced into the discourse and thus they are known to the speaker and the listener.

Herewith, in order to compare the results of the current study with those of previous studies, the total number of occurrences of full NPs (i.e., NP+*ga*, NP+*wa*, NP+*mo*) were collapsed into one and treated as one category. The recalculated frequencies and percentages are shown in Table 4.23 and Figure 4.8.

Table 4.23 Use of Full NP and Zero Anaphora in the H/N and the T/T Narratives[36]

	Full NP H/N	Zero anaphora H/N	Full NP T/T	Zero anaphora T/T
ENG-Mid (N=11)	93 67.4%	29 21.0%	124 82.7%	10 6.7%
KOR-Mid (N=10)	142 81.1%	33 18.9%	104 86.0%	17 14.0%
ENG-High (N=10)	223 85.4%	37 14.2%	171 88.1%	22 11.3%
KOR-High (N=10)	167 77.3%	49 22.7%	136 88.9%	17 11.1%
JNS (N=10)	69 61.6%	43 38.4%	123 81.5%	28 18.5%
Total (N=51)	694 81.5%	191 18.5%	658 85.6%	94 12.2%

Total number of occurrences and average percentages are shown in the first and second lines, respectively.

Percentage use of Full NP and Zero Anaphora

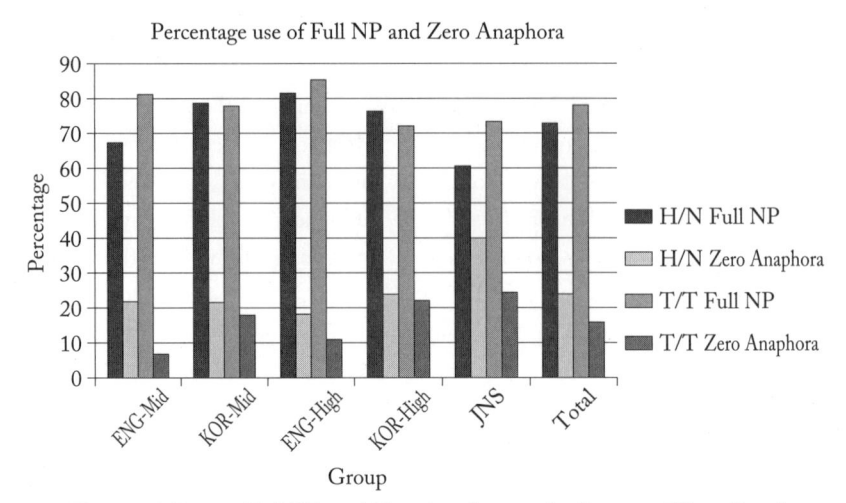

[Bar chart showing percentages for groups ENG-Mid, KOR-Mid, ENG-High, KOR-High, JNS, Total with series: H/N Full NP, H/N Zero Anaphora, T/T Full NP, T/T Zero Anaphora]

Figure 4.8 Ratio of Full NPs and Zero Anaphora in the Context of Topic Switch

Recall that the average percentage uses of forms have been used to compare the results among groups (besides the analysis of L1 narratives by JNSs, ENSs and KNSs) in order to make a fair assessment of the performances. However, given that the comparison is being made within subject, not within group this time; a chi-square test, instead of ANOVA, was used on the total frequencies, as the issue of fairness of speech length would not be a concern here. The results showed that the participants in the NS and the NNS groups produced significantly higher numbers of full NPs than zero anaphora in both types of narratives.[37]

In order to capture a pattern of topic switch and narrative formation, the referents that were coded in the context of topic switch underwent further coding; the roles the referents played in the story plot (whether they were the main characters or the peripheral ones) were further coded. Table 4.24 and Figure 4.9 illustrate the ratio of main and peripheral characters that were marked in the context of topic switch in percentile format.

Table 4.24 Ratio of Main and Peripheral Characters in Topic Switch

	Main Characters H/N	Peripheral Characters H/N	Main Characters T/T	Peripheral characters T/T
ENG-Mid	100 (91.7%)	9 (8.3%)	117 (88.0%)	16 (12.0%)
KOR-Mid	173 (94.0%)	11 (6.0%)	113 (94.2%)	7 (5.8%)
ENG-High	239 (89.2%)	29 (10.8%)	182 (87.5%)	26 (12.5%)
KOR-High	205 (94.5%)	12 (5.5%)	156 (90.2%)	17 (9.8%)
JNS	105 (94.6%)	6 (5.4%)	143 (90.5%)	15 (9.5%)
Total	822 (92.5%)	67 (7.5%)	711 (89.8%)	81 (10.2%)

Total number of occurrences and average percentages are shown in the first and second lines, respectively.

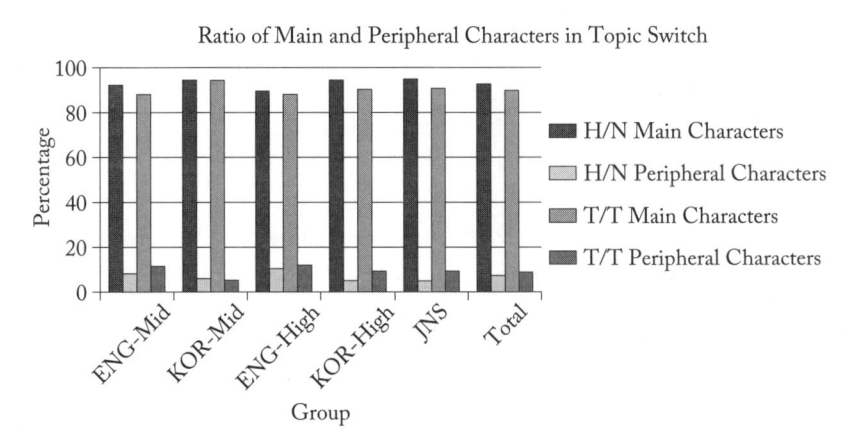

Figure 4.9 Ratio of Main and Peripheral Characters Marked in Topic Switch

As is evident in Figure 4.9 above, most of the referents that were coded in the context of topic switch were the main characters (92.5% in the H/N task and 89.8% in the T/T task), and this result supports the previous findings (Clancy, 1992; Nakahama, 2009; Yoshioka, 2005). It is speculated that because of the significant role the main characters play in the plot, they tend to become the central topic of discourse and even though they formerly lost topicality to other characters, the speakers bring the major characters back in the central stage of the story.

Now I will describe the analysis of the production of zero anaphora in the context of topic switch in the H/N and the T/T narrative types.

4.2.2.1 Zero anaphora in the context of topic switch

Figure 4.10 provides the percentage use of zero anaphora by the NNSs and the JNS in both H/N and T/T narratives.

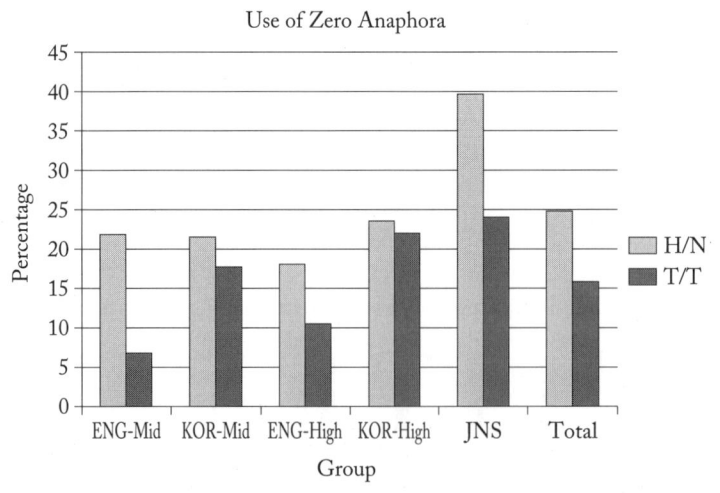

Figure 4.10 Percentage Use of Zero Anaphora in the Context of Topic Switch

With regard to the production of zero anaphora, there was no considerable difference among the L2 learners, irrespective of their proficiency levels, in either the H/N or the T/T narratives. One-way ANOVA was conducted to examine whether the differences among groups were significant for both task types. The results revealed that the differences within group were insignificant for both narrative types ($F(4, 46) = 1.78, p = .151$ for H/N; $F(4, 46) = 1.81, p = .144$). Repeated Measure ANOVA was conducted between the H/N and T/T tasks for all five groups in order to examine whether the performances were different between the two tasks. It was found that there was a significant difference between the two narrative tasks ($F(1, 46) = 8.04, p = .007$) and a multiple comparison test revealed that the significant difference (at $p < .05$ level) between tasks was found in the ENG-Mid ($p = .027$) and the JNS ($p = .030$) groups. Though the ENG-High, KOR-Mid and ENG-High groups did not show significant differences between the H/N and T/T tasks, descriptive statistics revealed that the former task generated a higher percentage use of zero anaphora across groups. The higher use of zero anaphora in the H/N narrative could have been caused by the fact that the speaker and the listener shared the picture book in front of them, and thus, non-mentioning of the new topic in topic switch would not cause misunderstandings in the H/N narratives. This premise, along with the low percentage uses of zero anaphora in the T/T task by the ENG-Mid level, will be discussed along with the results of continuous mentions of topics, in a later section.

As was discussed in section 4.2.2, most of the referents that were used for switching topics were the main characters, irrespective of task type. Interestingly, it was found that all the uses of zero anaphora for marking topic switch were the main characters, except for three cases by the KOR-High level learners. This part of the results may be explained by what Clancy (1992) called 'ellipsis for hero' strategy discussed previously. Recall that Clancy claims that the main character(s) of a story tends to receive an attenuated form (i.e., ellipsis) for topic switch. In marking a topic switch, the participants in her study were inclined to use zero anaphora for the main characters, but not for peripheral ones. The same pattern was found in the current study irrespective of the learners' L1 or proficiency level.

Furthermore, there were more topic switches between the main characters, than there were topic switches from peripheral characters to the main characters. In other words, it appears that the speakers tended to compare the actions of the main characters (the boy, the dog and the frog in the H/N; the sheep, the bear, and the rabbit in the T/T) and went back and forth between these characters while taking the listeners through the adventure of the narrative world. Example 4.39 illustrates this pattern. The speaker is describing a scene in which the boy and the dog were anxiously looking for the frog in their house.

Example 4.39 Use of Zero Anaphora in Topic Switch in the H/N by KOR-Mid Level (#1)

<u>Inu</u>	<u>to</u>	<u>shoonen</u>	<u>wa</u>	heya	no	naka	o	sagashite
Dog	and	boy	TOP	room	GEN	inside	ACC	search and

mimashita	*n da*	*kedo*	*Ø*	*dokodemo*	*inakatta desu.*	
attempt-PAST	COP	but	(frog)	anywhere	exist-NEG-PAST	

de..	*Ø*	*mado*	*o*	*akete..*	
then..	(boy)	window	ACC	open and…	

'The boy and the dog attempted to search inside the house, but (the frog) was not found anywhere. Then (the boy) opened the window and…'

Prior to this utterance, the topic of discourse was the boy. The speaker switched the topic from the boy to 'the boy and the dog' in the beginning of the utterance and then to the frog without mentioning the frog. He then switched the topic to the boy, again without explicitly mentioning the boy as can be seen in the third line in Example 4.39. The speaker continued with this method in that he switched the topic between the boy and the dog throughout the narrative until he found his pet frog.

What follows next is a discussion of particle drop. Although the occurrences of particle drop were rather low in both types of narrative, with the exception of with the ENG-Mid level learners, there seems to be a pattern that the T/T narrative task triggered slightly more occurrences of particle drop across groups. In the next section, I will compare the two narrative conditions, in terms of particle drop phenomenon.

4.2.2.2 Particle drop in the context of topic switch

Under the H/N condition, particle drop was found in ENG-Mid level learners' narratives.[38] One-way ANOVA test revealed that there was a significant difference among groups and Scheffe's multiple comparison tests showed that the significant difference lay in between the ENG-Mid level and all the other groups ($F(4, 46) = 8.31, p = .000$) in the H/N condition narratives. Given that particle drop was not observed in the NS narrative discourse at all, dropping particles is regarded as a divergence from the target form in marking referents in the context of topic switch. Compared to the H/N, the T/T condition narrative prompted higher use of particle drop. In fact, in the T/T narratives, particle drop was observed in every group, though the percentage use was low except for the ENG-Mid level group. Once again ANOVA was conducted and the test showed that the difference among group was not significant ($F(4, 46) =$

2.24, p = .079).

The percentage use of particle drop in the H/N and T/T was compared by Repeated Measure ANOVA, and it was found that the difference was significant (F (1, 46) = 0.47, p = .004). Scheffe's test revealed that the significant difference within subject was found in the KOR-High group (p = .018). Although statistical difference between tasks was found only in the KOR-High group, it appears that task complexity has some effect on the production of particle drop. Examples 4.40 and 4.41 illustrate typical examples of particle drop in the T/T narratives.

Example 4.40 Particle Drop in the T/T by KOR-High Level (#7)

Usagi	to	kitsune	ga	nanka..	kuma	o..	me	o	mienai
Rabbit	and	fox	NOM	um..	bear	ACC..	eyes	ACC	see-NEG

yooni	shite	*nanka*	kuma	*(Ø)*	hashitte..	koori	no	ue
way	make	well..	bear	(Ø)	run and..	ice	GEN	above

aruitarishite..	mata	yukidaruma…
walk and the like do	again	snowman…

'The rabbit and the fox um..made the bear..eyes..cannot see um..the bear ran and walk on the ice and the like, and the snowman again…'

This speaker had previously switched the topic to two of the main characters, the rabbit and the fox (sheep), and then again to the other main character, the bear. As is obvious from the discourse marker, *nanka*, as well as the pause afterwards, when she hesitated in her telling of the story. While she attempted to switch topics among the main characters, she was trying to remember who the next active character was, and to describe the actions performed, and as a result, she ended up dropping the particle. See Example 4.41 by another KOR-High level speaker.

Example 4.41 Particle Drop in the T/T by KOR-High Level (#3)

Sonna kanji	de..	koo	asondete..	*ano*..	sannin	*(Ø)*
Such way	P..	like	play-ING	um..	three people	(Ø)

ano..	_fuyu_	_no_	_naka_	_de_..	_issho ni_	_asobimasu_
um..	winter	GEN	inside	at..	together	play

'Like that, (the sheep) was playing um..three people (∅) um..play together during winter.'

The topic was the sheep in the beginning of this utterance, and it was coded as a continuous mention of 'the sheep'. And then the speaker switched to all three major characters, *sannin* (three people), without marking it with a particle. As the speaker in Example 4.40 used *nanka* when she was searching for what the next topic should be, this speaker used the hesitation marker, *ano*, before he switched the topic from the female sheep to all three of the major characters. Similar patterns were observed with the use of particle drop across groups, and thus it can be surmised that the complexity of the task influenced the way in which the speakers marked topic switch. More detailed interpretations of the task effects will be provided in the discussion section.

4.2.2.3 Re-introduction of the frog

The re-introduction of the frog was investigated in the JNS, KNS, and ENS narratives, though the marking of the frog did not always appear in the context of topic switch (re-introduction). As was discussed in earlier sections, the ways in which the English NSs re-introduced the frog differed from the methods employed in the Japanese and Korean NS narratives. Recall that to encode the re-introduction of the frog, the English NSs used the definiteness marking (*the*), pronouns (*his, their*), or indefinite marking, since it was introduced together with new information (e.g., frog's wife and children). The majority of the re-introduction (60%) was done as a direct object of a verb such as *'found'* and *'saw'*. In contrast, with very few exceptions, the speakers in the JNS and the KNS groups used indefiniteness markings (NP+*ga* and NP+k*a/i*) for marking the re-introduction of the frog, and in the vast majority of the cases, it was introduced in the existential sentence structure.

With these results, it was apparent that English and Japanese/Korean L1 background perspectives triggered different linguistic measures to recount the same event of encountering a long lost friend. Herewith, the NNSs narratives were examined regarding how the learners of Japanese encoded the re-introduction of the frog, in order to locate possible CLI from their L1s, English and Korean. Table 4.25 illustrates the linguistic forms used for marking the re-introduction of the frog by all four learner groups and the JNSs.

Table 4.25 Re-introduction of the Frog

	ga	o	ni	mo	drop	Ø	Total
ENG-Mid	2	5		1	2		10
KOR-Mid	7	2				1	10
ENG-High	7	2	1				10
KOR-High	9	1					10
JNS	9	1					10
Total	34	11	1	1	2	1	50

The numbers displayed in the table represent frequencies.

While the majority of markings for the re-introduction of the frog were done with *ga* in the KOR-Mid, ENG-High, KOR-High groups, the ENG-Mid group displayed a differing pattern. The form most frequently used was *o*, and this was because the speakers re-introduced the frog in the object position of the verbs, '*mita* (saw)' and '*mitsuketa* (found)'. There were two occurrences of particle drop, and the particle that was dropped was also the object marker, '*o*'. Therefore, if these two learners successfully marked the frog as they intended to, it would have been, *o*, making a total number of seven occurrences of *o*. This demonstrates a clear case of CLI (in this case, negative transfer) from English, as the frog was re-introduced as the object of verbs with English equivalents by the ENSs. However, the advanced level speakers showed a different pattern. The particle they most frequently used was *ga* and it was used in existential sentences, just as was the case with their Korean counterparts (both at the intermediate level and the advanced level), as well as with the JNSs. Therefore, it can be said that the target-like marking of the re-introduction of the frog increased with proficiency, for the English L1 speakers.

The Korean speakers, on the other hand, already showed target-like use of NP+*ga* for referring to the frog at intermediate level proficiency. This superior performance by the Korean learners might be a result of CLI (i.e., positive transfer) in that Korean and Japanese languages share a comparable way of referring to similar events in narratives. The differing results in the performance of re-introduction of the frog between the Korean L1 speakers and English L1 speakers provides a clear example of both positive and negative influence from the learners' L1, with respect to how a concept is transformed into language through choice of perspective (emphasis on the discovery of the frog), and through the options available in the target language (NP+*ga* and NP+*ka/i*). This conceptual transfer will be addressed further in Chapter 5.

To summarise the referent markings in the context of topic switch, while there were not many discernible differences among the groups, English speaking intermediate level learners showed fairly distinctive patterns, as compared to the rest of the groups. Most notable were the instances of particle drop, regardless of the task type. It appears that the English L1 learners of Japanese in the present study had not yet been able to appropriately switch topics in their L2 narrative discourse. This result is supported by the finding from the context of referent introduction in terms of the high use of particle drop in their H/N narratives. Furthermore, comparing two types of storytelling activity with different complexity revealed that task complexity might generate different types of linguistic markings in the topic switch context, just as was the case in introducing new referents into a narrative discourse. The study was able to show some developmental patterns and CLI by delving into both NS and NNS narratives of Japanese as well as English and Korean narratives in two different types of discourse context (i.e., referent introduction and topic switch). We also found that the task types have an influence on the ways in which speakers construct narratives. Further discussion of these three factors (i.e., learners' L1 backgrounds, proficiency levels, task types) and how they influence one another, will be provided in the discussion section, after examining referent markings in the context of continuous mention of referent, to which I now turn.

4.2.3 Continuous mention of referent

The definition of the "continuous mention of referent" is repeated here. Continuous mention of referents in the topical position following their re-introduction (topic switch) were coded and referred to as continuous mention of referent in the current study. While referents in the context of referent introduction were the least continuous referents in narratives, referents that were coded as continuous mention of referent are considered to be most continuous, as they remain to be the topic of discourse after re-promotion to subject position (i.e., re-introduction).

The total number of occurrences and percentage use of the forms that were used to mark continuous mention of referent in the H/N and T/T narratives will be presented in Tables 4.26 and 4.27, respectively.

Table 4.26 Continuous Mention of Referent in the H/N Narratives

	NP+ga	*NP+wa*	*NP+mo*	NP+particle drop	zero anaphora
ENG-Mid	9	11	0	3	133
(N=11)	4.9	6.4	0	1.7	87.1
KOR-Mid	4	16	0	0	143
(N=10)	3.0	11.4	0	0	85.6
ENG-High	17	15	0	0	215
(N=10)	4.8	7.1	0	0	88.1
KOR-High	5	7	0	0	196
(N=10)	1.6	3.6	0	0	94.8
JNS	1	6	0	0	126
(N=10)	0.7	4.1	0	0	95.1
Total	36	55	0	3	813
	3	6.5	0	0.4	90.1

Total number of occurrences and average percentages are shown in the first and second lines, respectively.

Table 4.27 Continuous Mention of Referent in the T/T Narratives

	NP+ga	NP+wa	NP+mo	NP+particle drop	zero anaphora
ENG-Mid (N=11)	25 20.7	11 13.0	2 1.0	5 3.6	78 61.7
KOR-Mid (N=10)	11 10.1	10 8.2	1 0.6	1 1.0	81 80.0
ENG-High (N=10)	32 10.1	16 9.5	1 0.2	2 1.6	202 78.5
KOR-High (N=10)	24 9.3	19 8.5	0 0	3 1.4	183 80.7
JNS (N=10)	10 7.2	16 8.9	2 1.1	2 1.8	125 80.9
Total	102 11.7	72 9.7	6 0.6	13 1.9	669 76.1

Total number of occurrences and average percentages are shown in the first and second lines, respectively..

As Tables 4.27 and 4.28 show, in the context of highest topic continuity (i.e., the continuous mention of referent), the majority of referent marking was done with zero anaphora. This result supports the findings from previous studies (e.g., Nakahama, 2003a, 2009; Nakamura, 1993; Yanagimachi, 1997, 2000; Yoshioka, 2005). In terms of the other forms used in this context, the use of NP+*ga* seemed slightly higher in the T/T narrative than the H/N narrative; thus, Repeated Measure ANOVA was conducted to determine whether or not there is a within subject difference. The results revealed that there is a statistically significant difference between the two task types ($F(1, 46) = 24.3, p = .000$), and the further multiple comparison tests showed that the difference was found with the ENG-Mid group ($p = .000$). Across groups, more particle drops were observed in the T/T than the H/N, just as was found in the context of the topic switch, but the differences were significant only at $p < .05$ level ($F(1, 46) = 6.23, p = .02$).

4.2.3.1 The use of zero anaphora in the context of continuous mention

The performance of zero anaphora will now be compared under the two task conditions. First, Figure 4.11 graphically illustrates the percentage use of zero anaphora in the context of continuous mention of referents in both the H/N and T/T narratives.

Use of Zero Anaphora in Continuous Mention

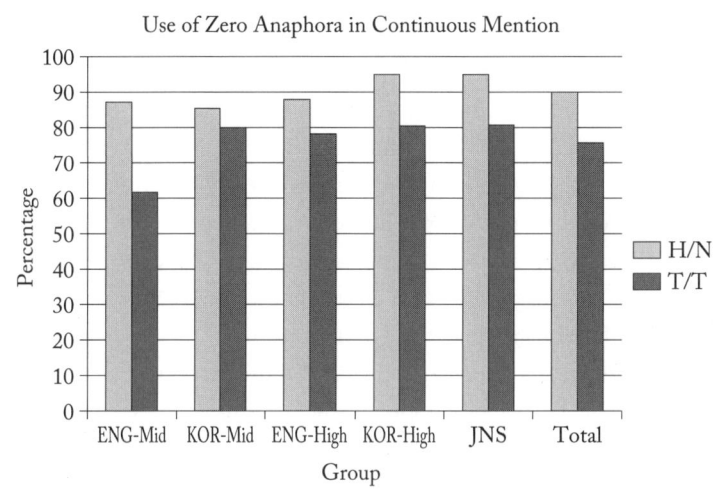

Figure 4.11 Percentage Use of Zero Anaphora in the Context of Continuous Mention of Referent

Under the H/N narrative condition, the average percentage use of zero anaphora across the five groups was 90.1%. One-way ANOVA was conducted on the performance of zero anaphora across groups in the H/N narrative, and the difference was found to be significant at $p < .05$ level ($F(4, 46) = 3.68, p = .011$), but Scheffe's multiple comparison tests did not show significant group difference probably because of relatively small sample sizes. In Nakahama (2009) which employed the same picture story book for eliciting narratives (a H/N narrative), the production of zero anaphora by both the Korean and the English speaking L2 learners of Japanese at high intermediate level (according to The ACTFL guidelines) achieved more than 80% of all the markings in the context of the continuous referent. Drawn from the results of the previous study and the current one, I argue that an appropriate marking of referents of high topicality in narrating consecutive pictures has been acquired by the time the learners achieve intermediate-mid to intermediate-high level (on the ACTFL guidelines), regardless of their L1 background. Furthermore, qualitative analysis of the learner data revealed that the vast majority of the use of zero anaphora was in reference to the main characters in both task types.

As was the case in the H/N narrative, the form most frequently used to code the referents of highest topic continuity in the T/T narrative was zero anaphora. However, the performance in the T/T seems less homogeneous among groups than the H/N narratives. One-way ANOVA was conducted on the percentage use of zero anaphora in the T/T, and it was found that the between group difference was significant at $p < .01$ level ($F(4, 46) = 4.27$, $p = .005$), and the significant difference was found between the ENG-Mid and the JNSs ($p = .037$) as well as the ENG-Mid and the KOR-High ($p = .039$).[39] This result indicates that at the level of intermediate proficiency, English speaking L2 learners of Japanese had not yet reached the target level performance in the story-retelling activity, whereas their Korean speaking counterparts had. Furthermore, the performance of zero anaphora increased with proficiency for the English L1 speaking group, in the T/T narrative.

The part of the results which found that the production of zero anaphora increased with the level of proficiency in the English L1 speakers' oral productions in the T/T narrative replicated the results found in Nakahama (2003) and Yanagimachi (1997, 2000) for their investigation of zero anaphora in Japanese as a second language, and as well those of Jin (1994) and Polio (1995) for Chinese as a second language.

With the results of the performance of zero anaphora, Hypothesis 3, that predicted that 'the target-like performance of referent introduction and tracking will increase with proficiency', was supported with regard to the English speakers in the T/T narrative. However, it was not supported in the H/N narrative, as both L1 groups already demonstrated a target-like use of zero anaphora when they reached the intermediate proficiency level. Furthermore, Hypothesis 4 which predicted that 'the Korean and English L1 speakers will display differing acquisition patterns in referent markings', was supported in terms of the use of zero anaphora in the T/T narrative.

The average percentage use of zero anaphora across groups was 76.1%, thus the percentage use was less than that found in their H/N counterpart (90.1%). Repeated Measure ANOVA was conducted on the use of zero anaphora, and it was found that the difference within subject was significant ($F(1, 46) = 42.66$, $p = .000$). Multiple comparison procedure was conducted, and the significant difference within subject was found in all the groups except for the KOR-Mid group.[40] This result suggests that task complexity has an influence on the speakers' marking of the most continuous topics regardless of the learners' proficiency level or L1 background. As was the case with the use of zero anaphora in the context of topic switch, its higher occurrence in the H/N than the T/T narratives can be explained by the fact that the speaker and the listener had shared information via the pictures that were right in front of them, in the former type of storytelling.

Follow-up interviews with some NNSs and all the JNSs revealed that the use and non-use of zero anaphora was not a conscious choice by the speakers. The consensus among the participants (both the NSs and the NNSs) from the interviews was that the speakers' main focus in re-telling a story in the T/T narrative was to make sure their narratives were easy to follow. The speakers used more explicit forms out of concern that the listeners might get confused about what and to whom the speakers were talking about, as they themselves were trying to remember while reconstructing the story. In contrast, in the H/N narratives, the burden on the speaker (and the listener as well) was greatly reduced since the pictures were right there for the listener to refer to, so the speakers could relate the events in the story without facing, or fear of imposing, a cognitive challenge. Based on the follow-up interview results, it can be argued that the speakers attempted to promote the listeners' better understanding of the story by using a full NP (rather than zero anaphora) when there was no shared information between the speaker and the listener

The higher use of zero anaphora in the H/N was not only seen in the context of continuous mention in the NNS narratives but also in the JNS, KNS, and ENS narratives as compared to the T/T narratives in each group. This cross-linguistically shared difference between the H/N and T/T tasks, in terms of the use of zero anaphora, is relevant to what Robinson (2003) explains of learner discourse. He argues that increased conceptual and/or communicative demands placed on learners under the T/T condition triggers the production of more complex discourse which was measured via lexical complexity. The higher usage of full NPs or lexical pronouns contributes to higher complexity of sentences than that which is found with the use of zero anaphora; therefore it is considered more complex. Thus it can be hypothesised that the continuous referent marking with more complex linguistic coding found in the T/T narrative is caused by the task's higher cognitive demands.

The findings in the current study can clarify what was found in the previous research in regard to the performance of zero anaphora. In Nakahama (2003), Polio (1995) and Yanagimachi (1997, 2000), which employed silent film retelling to elicit narratives (i.e., T/T narrative condition), it took the learners to achieve a sufficient proficiency level in order to achieve target-like performance of zero anaphora.[41] In Nakahama (2009) who used picture storybook to elicit data, on the other hand, the learners demonstrated appropriate marking of topic continuity with zero anaphora at an earlier stage of language development. The higher use of full NP in T/T narrative might be inevitable due to the reason stated above; however, the use of full NP decreased with proficiency and reached target-like by the time the learners reached the advanced level of proficiency.

Among the SLA studies which investigated the acquisition of zero anaphora, Polio's (1995), Nakahama's (2009) and the current study inquired whether a shared specific topic prominent feature (i.e., zero anaphora) between the learners' L1 and L2 facilitates such acquisition. Polio compared English and Japanese speaking learners of Chinese, while Nakahama (2009, the current study) compared English and Korean speaking learners of Japanese. Despite the prediction, Polio found that there were no significant differences between the English and Japanese groups, and she claimed that transfer might not be at play. Polio also found that high task complexity (film retelling task) triggered lower uses of zero anaphora, even by the speakers of Japanese, a language which employs zero anaphora for marking high topic continuity. In other words, they could not make use of the linguistic features that L1 (Japanese) and L2 (Chinese) share. In the current study, irrespective of task complexity, the Korean learners of Japanese performed target-like use of zero anaphora even at the lower proficiency level (i.e., intermediate level). The English speaking learners of Japanese, in contrast, were able to successfully mark referents of high continuity with zero anaphora in the H/N narratives; however, it took longer for them to achieve a target like level in the T/T narratives. This differing result between Polio (1995) and the current one might be explained by language distance. I argue that the language distance between Japanese and Chinese is not 'close enough' for the learners to benefit from the shared language phenomenon (+pro-drop parameter), whereas Japanese and Korean are typologically almost identical to each other, in terms of referent tracking system. Therefore, the learners' perceived similarity between two languages (i.e., psycholinguistic closeness between L1 and L2) operated favourably in the Korean learners' performance of zero anaphora in L2 Japanese (see Kellerman, 1977 for the concept of this psychotypology).

Although zero anaphora and post positional markers for NPs and passive constructions were the key features in the present investigation to examine referent tracking, the usage of pronouns was also examined in order to capture possible CLI from English. Recall that pronouns are the predominant form used to mark the continuous mention of referent in English in both types of narratives, and that the percentage use of pronouns is slightly higher in the T/T narratives than the H/N narratives. All the NNS and JNS narratives were studied in terms of the use of pronouns in Japanese [42] in the context of referent introduction, topic switch and continuous mention of referents, and the results are presented in Table 4.28.

Table 4.28 Number of the Occurrences of Japanese Third Person Pronouns

	kare/kanojo/karera H/N Switch	kare/kanojo/karera H/N Continuous	kare/kanojo/karera T/T Switch	kare/kanojo/karera T/T Continuous
ENG-Mid	1/0/0 (1)	(0)	2/2/0 (4)	2/0/0 (2)
KOR-Mid	(0)	(0)	0/1/0 (1)	(0)
ENG-High	2/0/1 (3)	2/0/0 (2)	1/1/0 (2)	6/1/0 (7)
KOR-High	(0)	(0)	0/0/2 (2)	0/1/1 (2)
JNS	(0)	(0)	1/1/0 (2)	0/0/1 (1)

The numbers of occurrence of each pronoun and the total numbers of occurrences of all pronouns were shown in the first and second lines, respectively.

All the occurrences of the third person pronouns were classified into the types of pronoun (*kare/kanojo/karera*), the types of narrative (H/N or T/T), and the context (referent introduction, topic switch, continuous mention of referent) in which the pronouns were used. As expected, the third person pronouns were not found in the context of referent introduction, as it is the least topical position of narrative discourse. Compared to the Korean learners of Japanese or the JNSs, English L1 learners of Japanese produced higher numbers of third person pronouns, which might indicate CLI from their native language (i.e., English). The speakers in the ENG-Mid group produced seven pronouns and the ENG-High group 14 pronouns. The KOR-Mid level speakers produced only one pronoun and their counterparts at higher proficiency level produced four pronouns. The speakers in the JNS group produced three pronouns.

A detailed analysis of the data showed that the pronouns tended to be used more often in the T/T narrative than the H/N narrative, irrespective of the participants' L1 (including the NSs of Japanese) or proficiency level. This finding replicates the pattern found in the English L1 data (ENS) as is shown in Table 4.15 in Section 4.1.3.3 (61.0% use of pronouns in H/N and 72.2% in T/T). Furthermore, although pronouns are normally expected to be used for marking referents of high topicality, some of them were found in the context of topic switch. For instance, in the ENG-Mid group (in H/N and T/T combined), five of the pronouns were found in the context of topic switch, while only two were found in the context of continuous mention of referent. The use of pronouns by learners in the ENG-High group, in contrast, was more conventional in that more cases of pronoun use were found in the context of continuous mentions (five cases in topic switch, and nine cases in continuous mention).

Recall that although pronouns were not the prevalent form used for indicating topic switch in the ENS narratives, as many as 35.9% (H/N) and 48.9% (T/T) of referent markings were done with personal pronouns when switching topics. Again, the T/T condition generated more percentage use of pronouns in this context as well. All the uses of pronouns in the context of topic switch went through further categorisation based on what character they correspond to. The results are summarised in Table 4.29 below.

Table 4.29 Referents that were Referred to with Pronouns in Topic Switch

	H/N	T/T
ENG-Mid	*kare* (frog) 1	*kare* (bear or rabbit) 1 *kare* (scarecrow)1 *kanojo* (sheep) 2
KOR-Mid		*kanojo* (sheep) 1
ENG-High	*karera* (boy & dog) 1 *kare* (frog) 1 *kare* (boy) 1	*kanojo* (sheep) 1 *kare* (scarecrow) 1
KOR-High		*karera* (rabbit & bear) 2
JNS		*kare* (bear) 1 *kanojo* (sheep) 1

There is a possible risk in using pronouns in the context of topic switch because the listener might be uncertain to whom the speaker switched the topic, if there is not enough contextual guidance. When *kanojo* was used in the T/T narrative, the listener would find it easy to decipher which referent it denotes, as there is only one female leading character. There were other female characters but they played insignificant roles in the story and thus were hardly mentioned in the topic switch context. In contrast, the use of *kare* in the scenes where the two leading male characters (i.e., bear and the rabbit) play together, it could be confusing. In fact, in the ENG-Mid group, the speaker uttered *kare* but it was not clear to which character the speaker was referring. In the JNS narrative, in contrast, the way in which one speaker used *kare* to indicate the bear was easy to follow. He uttered '*kuma mitai na kare ga*' (he who appears to be bear-like), thus, it was obvious he meant the bear, rather than the rabbit. When *karera* was used in the T/T, the saliency of the referent was high due to the fact the two main male characters were occasionally referred to as a pair. Likewise, in the H/N narrative, *karera* could be either the boy and the dog or the boy and the frog, and with the contextual support, it was found to be the boy and the frog in the narrative of the ENG-High group.

To summarise the referent marking in the context of highest topic continuity (i.e., continuous mention of the referent), the most prevalent form used to mark topic continuity was zero anaphora in both the H/N and the T/T narratives. In the H/N narratives, the learners showed target like performance of referent tracking by the time they reached the intermediate level, irrespective of their L1 backgrounds. However, in the T/T narratives, their performances seemed to increase with proficiency in terms of the learners whose L1 is English, and by the time they reached the advanced level, they were able to display target-like patterns in referent marking. The Korean speaking L2 learners of Japanese, in contrast, show consistently superior performance in tracking referents, regardless of their proficiency level or narrative type.

Therefore, Hypothesis 3, 'the target-like performance of referent introduction and tracking will increase with proficiency' was supported regarding the English speakers but not the Korean speakers, as they had already achieved target-like proficiency by the intermediate level. Hypothesis 4 which predicted, 'Korean speakers will achieve target-like performance earlier than English speakers due to the typological similarities shared between Korean and Japanese' was supported in terms of the T/T narrative. Hypothesis 5 that predicted more complex form choice in the T/T narrative context was supported with higher percentage use of full NPs in the context of continuous mention of referents. Hypothesis 6, which postulated that L1 Japanese speakers' narrative discourse would not be affected drastically by task complexity was not upheld in terms of the percentage use of zero anaphora, as the T/T narrative condition triggered higher use of full NPs than the H/N in JNS narratives.

To sum up the results section, it was found that the Korean and English speakers generally displayed different developmental patterns in introducing and tracking referents in L2 Japanese. The investigation of the Japanese and Korean NS narratives revealed that there are systematic similarities in how a referent is introduced, continued and discontinued as a topic in oral narratives, whereas English NS narratives display differences from both the JNSs and KNSs. As predicted, the similarities shared between the two languages facilitated the Korean learners' acquisition of referent introduction and its continuity as a topic in Japanese. In contrast, the NS English oral narratives showed striking differences with the NS Japanese narratives in terms of how referents were introduced and continued. These differences in L1 narratives appear to have created some difficulties for the English speaking participants, in performing target-like use of certain linguistic forms in their Japanese narratives. As far as English speaking participants are concerned, it appeared that CLI was more evident among the lower proficiency levels. However, it was also found that different forms generated different patterns in the acquisition processes for both L1 groups. Furthermore, conceptual differences in viewing and relating events were revealed between Japanese and English/Korean NS groups. The conceptual differences resulted in much fewer occurrences of voice alternations (thus numbers of the passive construction were less) in the learner discourse. The next chapter will summarise these results in a more systematic manner and expand discussions concerning the developmental patterns that are unique to each L1 group. The discussions will be made with regard to CLI caused by typological proximity, proficiency, conceptual differences marked between the learners' L1 and L2 (i.e., thinking for speaking in Slobin's sense), as well as the role task complexity plays in learners' performance on certain linguistic features.

Notes

23 The percentage of NP+*ga* (52.9 %) does not denote the percentage of the occurrences of NP+*ga* (34) of the sum occurrences (64) of all the linguistic features used to mark the referent introduction shown in Table 4.1. Rather, 52.9 % is the average percentage of proportional use of NP+*ga* among the 10 NSs.
24 In addition to the forms that were used frequently or provide characteristic patterns other extant forms were amalgamated into a single category called 'others' and presented together in the table.
25 The sheep character had a somewhat unidentifiable face, therefore, it was mistaken as a white bear or white fox, and some speakers referred to it as an 'unknown or unrecognizable white animal'. In Example 4.8, it is referred to as a (lit.) 'white bear-like thing'.
26 In English, when plural noun phrases are introduced into discourse for the first time, they take the form of 'bare noun phrase'. For instance, in the current study, noun phrases such as honeybees and wild animals are used for introducing some peripheral characters by the ENS. These 'determiner less' phrases are considered indefinite and coded in the same category as indefinite markers, along with noun phrases with indefinite articles (i.e., 'a' and 'an').
27 It should be noted here that the p value was close to the level of significance ($p < .05$) in the H/N narratives. Obvious differences among groups might not have reached statistical significance due to the small number of participants.
28 Although the speaker initially uttered '*ni*' to mark the bees, she self-repaired the utterance by changing '*ni*' to '*ga*' and the change the structure itself. Therefore, the marking of the bees was considered to be done with '*ga*' by this speaker.
29 As mentioned in the main text above, there were two incorrect conjugations of passive expressions (one by the KOR-Mid level in the H/N narrative and the other in the KOR-High level in the H/N narrative). These attempts were included in the count of passive expressions/constructions, as the speakers kept the main character in the topical position as a patient, and with the help of the context, the meaning got across.
30 It should be noted here that the number of participants in the ENG-Mid level is 11 and in the other group is 10, thus it cannot provide a fully fair comparison. Simple normalisation of the total count (13) to N=10 equals 12, thus one can regard the total occurrence of passive expressions to be 12 in the ENG-Mid level group.
31 One speaker produced a passive structure only once in the T/T narratives, while she produced two in the H/N narratives.
32 B&R refers to the bear and the rabbit, and B&R&S refers to the bear, the rabbit and the sheep
33 Syntactically the last half of the sentence can be interpreted as 'the bees were awakened and running'. However, semantically it is not possible for the bees to 'run', and further, based on the pictures, it was the dog that was running, not the bees. Thus, the utterance was interpreted as is shown in Example 4.34.
34 It should be recalled that the learners who were rated intermediate-mid and intermediate-high on The ACTFL guidelines were grouped as ENG-Mid level in the current study. Thus, the present ENG-Mid level learners are more proficient than Nakahama's (2009) lowest proficiency level learners.

35 In the case of the H/N narratives by the speakers in the JNS group, the percentage use of zero anaphora was higher than that of NP+*ga* or NP+*wa*.
36 Combination of the percentages of full NP and zero anaphora do not add up to the total percentages (100%). This is because the occurrences of particle drops were not included as full NPs. Inclusion of particle drops into full NPs would make the differences between full NP and zero anaphora larger than the current results.
37 The chi-square test results are as follows. H/N narratives: ENG-Mid (χ^2 (1) = 33.6, p < .001), KOR-Mid (χ^2 (1) = 67.9, p < .001), ENG-High (χ^2 (1) = 133, p < .001), KOR-High (χ^2 (1) = 64.5, p < .001), JNS (χ^2 (1) = 10.6, p = .001). T/T narratives: ENG-Mid (χ^2 (1) = 97.0, p < .001), KOR-Mid (χ^2 (1) = 62.6, p < .001), ENG-High (χ^2 (1) = 115, p < .001), KOR-High (χ^2 (1) = 92.6, p < .001), JNS (χ^2 (1) = 59.8, p < .001).
38 The production of particle drop was also found in ENG-High level learner discourse, but the percentage use was as low as 0.4%.
39 It should be noted here that the difference almost reached significant level (level of p = .05) between the ENG-Mid and the KOR-Mid as well (p = .051).
40 *P* value was as follows: ENG-Mid Level (p = .000), ENG-High Level (p = .05), KOR-High Level (p = .005), and JNS (p =.004).
41 Among the studies listed here, the measurement of learners' proficiency level varied across studies; therefore, the argument posited here cannot be conclusive.
42 Third person pronouns that can be used for animate entities in Japanese are *kare* (he), *kanojo* (she), and *karera* (they- plural of he), and *kanojotachi* (they- plural of she).

Chapter 5

Discussion and Conclusion

This chapter will summarise the results and discuss them in terms of the three major constructs that the study addressed, that is, CLI, learners' target language proficiency, and task complexity. Although all these constructs are intertwined with one another, and therefore complex to discuss separately, I will recapitulate the results and the discussion in the following manner. First, I will summarise the arguments for CLI (both positive and negative transfer) from Korean and English in learning L2 Japanese. Second, possible effects of L2 proficiency will be discussed for CLI to take place, as the relationship between proficiency and CLI has not been clearly understood in the past. Last, but not least important, task effects will be discussed for the NNSs and the NS of Japanese, as well as for the Korean and English NS narratives. While the discussion on CLI encompasses the NNSs' performances caused by the typological similarities/ differences between the learners' L1 and L2, conceptual transfer will receive central attention, as it appears to have played a major role in the speakers' selection of linguistic devices in encoding events in L2 narratives.

Some tentative hypotheses are posited to explain the differing acquisitional patterns between the two L1 groups, as well as the different levels of performance with respect to linguistic features within the same group. To be specific, I will discuss the differing rates of acquisition of NP+*ga* and other forms such as NP+*ni/kara* in marking referent introductions, NP+ *ga* for re-introduction of the frog, relating to possible positive transfer when appropriate. Then, I will discuss the distinct developmental patterns in English speaking learners of Japanese, focusing on negative transfer that is realised in the production of particle omission. The effects of task complexity will be discussed in terms of the production of passive structures, NP+*ga*, zero anaphora, and particle drops. After the discussion is presented, each research question will be revisited with answers.

In the last section of the book, I will discuss limitations of the study as well as suggestions for further research. Then pedagogical implications will be provided with the hope of helping learners to enhance their ability to create comprehensible and coherent storytelling that will lead to better understanding between the speakers and the listeners.

5.1 Discussion

5.1.1 CLI evidenced in L2 narratives by Korean L1 speakers: Accelerated acquisition of NP+*ga*

The results revealed that the Korean L1 speaking learners of Japanese showed a high percentage use of NP+*ga*, the indefinite marker in Japanese, in encoding referent introduction, irrespective of proficiency level. The average percentage of use of NP+*ga* at intermediate level proficiency by the Korean speakers already reached 63.1% in the H/N narrative and 71.8% in the T/T narrative, which were even higher percentage uses than their advanced level counterparts, or the JNSs in both cases (50.5%, 52.9% in H/N, and 65.2 %, 63% in T/T, advanced level and NSs of Japanese, respectively). It should be recalled that compared to the English L1 speaking participants at the same proficiency level, their production of NP+*ga* was significantly higher.

Further, not only the quantitative but also the qualitative results revealed that the Korean speakers had already acquired the target-like use of NP+*ga* by the time they reached an intermediate level of proficiency. It is undeniable that this remarkably successful performance of NP+*ga* (i.e., the accelerated acquisition rate of NP+*ga*) by the Korean speakers could be caused by the typologically similar features between Japanese and Korean, as has been argued throughout this manuscript. In addition, I intend to claim that this accelerated acquisition of NP+*ga* is assisted by the two following factors: 1) phonological resemblance between L1 (*ka*) and L2 (*ga*), and 2) saliency of NP+*ga* and NP+*ka* (*i*) as prototypical devices for introducing new referents into Japanese and Korean discourse, correspondingly.

First of all, in Korean, *ka* is used to encode a new referent, if it is preceded by a noun which ends in a vowel. In addition to the fact that Japanese and Korean share similar post positional marking systems, the phonological similarity of *ka* and *ga* in the two languages may also facilitate acquisition. It should also be noted that *i* is used for marking a new referent that ends in a consonant. It is assumed that even though there is no similarity in the sounds between *i* and *ga*, the learners could make use of the connection between *ka* and *ga* in their restructuring of the grammar, as well as the aforementioned shared postpositioning marking system, and make a fairly easy transition to the accurate production of *ga* in their L2 Japanese.

Second, the successful performance of NP+*ga* could be attributable to its saliency, as compared to other forms, as a prototypical encoding system for referent introduction. The majority of cases of referent introduction (56.6% in H/N, 62.6% in T/T) were marked with NP+*ka/i* in the Korean narratives in the current study. Recall that in another Korean narrative (Kim, 1989), as much as 94% of (human) referent introduction was done with NP+*ka/i*. Thus it is possible that the NSs of Korean would be more familiar with the function of *ka/i* than other forms, such as *eykey* for use as a marker of a new referent. Therefore, they drew on the most obvious option in their L1, for referent introduction in their L2 (i.e., NP+*ga*) due to its prototypicality in their first language.

Recall that, in their post study interviews, five Korean participants stated that the use of NP+*ga* and NP+*wa* were straightforward for them as the equivalent forms exist in their L1. They claimed that "*ka/i, (n)un* are two of the most commonly used or noticeable particles in daily conversation." It should be mentioned that in Nakahama (2009), some Korean informants stated that "*ga* would be a typical marker for bringing in a new referent into discourse, and it was easy for them to recognise this because they have an almost identical form, *ka*, in Korean."

However, the rapid acquisition of NP+*ga* by the Korean speakers might have its downside in that their production of NP+*ga* at the KOR-Mid level surpassed that of the JNSs in the context of referent introduction in the current study, though there were no statistical differences between the two groups (KOR-Mid: 63.1%, JNS: 52.9% in H/N, and KOR-Mid: 71.8%, JNS: 63.0% in T/T). Two possible explanations can be posited. First, somewhat overproduced NP+*ga* might well be a unique characteristic of this stage of acquisition by Korean speaking learners of Japanese, which coincides with the results of L1 acquisition of Japanese reported in Nakamura (1993). Recall that the Japanese children tended to prefer the use of NP+*ga* to NP+*wa* in her study, and NP+*wa* was hardly produced until they reached five years of age. The same pattern was found in the context of second mention of referents in Nakamura's study. While the majority of the second mentions of referents were marked with zero anaphora, younger children (3 and 4 yrs old) used NP+*ga* over NP+*wa* when they used full NPs. Nakamura argued that these children were using *ga* repetitively to ensure the salience of the referents. This claim of a 'saliency' effect of NP+*ga* might be related to the high occurrences of NP+*ga* with KOR-Mid learners and thus may deserve investigation in a follow-up study.

Another possible explanation follows. The slight overproduction of NP+*ga* by the intermediate level Korean speakers might be explicable given the underproduction of the other forms such as *ni/kara* (the agentive marker in Japanese). In fact, while the JNSs produced *ni/kara* as much as 9.9% of the time in the H/N narrative, KOR-Mid learners produced this form only 3.9% of the time. The underproduction of this particle can be explained by the lower occurrence of passive construction found in the intermediate level learners' narratives. Taking this stance, the higher percentage use of *ni/kara* (9.8%) and passive construction utilised by the KOR-High level learners should be able to explain the reduced percentage use of NP+*ga*, as compared to the production of their KOR-Mid level counterparts. However, whether or not the higher use of NP+*ga* was an artefact of the lower production of NP+*ni/kara* remains speculative, and needs to be clarified in a future research investigation. The discussion of underproduction of NP+*ni/kara* as well as passive constructions will be provided in the relevant sections in depth, as it concerns the conceptual transfer as well as possible constraints placed on CLI.

5.1.2 CLI evidenced in L2 narratives by English L1 speakers
5.1.2.1 Particle drop in referent introduction and topic switch
Recall that NPs with particle omission was the second most frequently observed form (16.5%) for referent introduction used by the intermediate level English speakers in the H/N narrative. As discussed in Chapter 4, omission of a case particle is a common practice within the frame of natural conversations in Japanese (e.g., Hasegawa, 1993; Maruyama, 1996), but not in the case of monologic discourse. Of course, some variation is expected even among the NSs' speech as Nakamura's (1993) study showed when relating that 3% of referent introduction was done by NP+particle omission, with her adult NS

participants, as opposed to zero occurrences of such an item in the current study. However, in the native English speakers' data, a frequency level of 16.5% of such usage by intermediate proficiency level learners is well above the level found in Japanese discourse, and this figure appears to be too high to represent merely a matter of chance or stylistic variation. Furthermore, a similar pattern was found in Nakahama (2009) in that the percentage use of particle drop for referent introduction by the English L1 speakers was 19.7% at the low-intermediate level, and 9.7% at the high-intermediate level.

Particle drop by the English speakers was not limited to the context of referent introduction. The percentage of referent marking with particle drop was found in the context of topic switch (11.2% in the H/H, and 11.9% in the T/T narratives by ENG-Mid level learners). A possible reason why a similar percentage use of particle drop was observed in the T/T narratives in the context of topic switch will be discussed in a later section, within the section focusing on the effects of task complexity on narrative formations. In any case, irrespective of the narrative types, the proportional use of particle drop was much higher compared to the Korean speakers or the English speakers at a higher L2 Japanese proficiency level.

Given that English uses pre-positional marking of NPs to encode the definiteness (*the*) and indefiniteness (*a, an,* or bare noun for plural forms), this NP+particle omission appears to be a potential example of negative language transfer from English. Pertinent to the current study, in their investigation of spatial reference in L2 English by Swedish and Finnish speakers, Jarvis and Odlin (2000) detected similar CLI. The Swedish language shares 'prepositional' marking features with English, while the Finnish language has a 'postpositional' marking system. The authors found that Finnish speakers (whose L1 uses postpositions and case marking) omitted prepositions, while such a tendency was not found in the Swedish (whose language uses prepositions) learner production of L2 English. Jarvis and Odlin posited that the omission of prepositions by the Finnish speakers could be attributable to simplification, transfer, or an interaction between simplification and transfer. I concur with the last possibility, i.e., interaction between simplification and transfer, as mere simplification (as a developmental path all learners go through) could be discounted by the very rare occurrences of such forms in the narratives produced by the Korean speakers. In short, I suggest that the simplification was caused by CLI in that the learners had no equivalent L1 form to draw on, and ended up omitting the form in their L2. That is, occurrences of a particle omission by the English L1 speakers seems to provide evidence for CLI which involves simplification of the target language when there is no similar construction in the L1.

In a similar vein, the findings of the difficulty of the acquisition of the English article system also support the results of particle drop in the current study. As introduced in the literature review section, Jarvis (2002) provided evidence that learners whose L1 did not have article systems took longer time to achieve the same level of performance in the use of English articles, as compared to learners with article systems. Furthermore, learners whose L1 did not have an article system often dropped articles in production of L2 English. The accelerated acquisition rate of postpositional markings such as NP+*ga* by Korean speakers, as well as particle drops by English L1 speakers, replicates Jarvis' findings.

Particle omission by young Japanese children was reported in Nakamura's (1993) study. As reviewed in Chapter 2, very young Japanese children (age 3) frequently omitted postpositional particles (54% of all cases). Omission of particles decreased, while appropriate referential marking concurrently increased, with age. Whereas Nakamura claimed the omission was attributable to a cognitive challenge that the young children were not yet capable of facing, I suggest that the results of the current study, in terms of the omission of postpositional particles by English L1 learners of Japanese, stem from the linguistic challenge caused by a lack of a similar postpositional marking system in their L1 (i.e., English). However, as a learner's linguistic capacity develops, their ability to adjust to the new concept and structure increases, and therefore the occurrence of particle omission decreases with proficiency level.

5.1.2.2 The use of definiteness marker, NP+*wa* in referent introduction

Recall that the percentage use of NP+*wa* was 12.3% by the ENG-Mid group and 10.9% by the ENG-High group in the H/N narrative and 28.6% by the ENG-Mid group in the T/T narrative. The use of NP+*ga* by ENG-Mid level was much lower compared to the other groups (28.5% in H/N, 41.5% in T/T). However, if the percentage uses of the particles are simply considered quantitatively among the English speakers' narratives, it seems as though the English L1 speakers 'acquired' the use of NP+*ga*, as it is the most frequently used form in encoding the referent introduction. However, compared to their

Korean speaking counterparts, as well as the JNSs, the percentage use of NP+*wa* in the English speakers was significantly higher in both types of narrative. The occurrence of NP+*wa* decreased with proficiency, as NP+*ga* use increased accordingly.

While the previous JSL studies were informative in terms of the acquisition order of *wa* and *ga* as measured by accuracy rate, they did not explore the distributional patterns of incorrect use of the forms qualitatively in an extended discourse. Furthermore, many of the studies (e.g., Hanada, 1993; Sakamoto, 1993; Tomita, 1997) used cloze tests as a data elicitation method, and such a method would not have displayed what learners can actually produce in real communication.

If we employ the notion of acquisition being the mere emergence/appearance of a form, it would appear that the acquisition of both NP+*wa* and *ga* has occurred by the time the English speakers reach the intermediate level. This definition of acquisition misses the important point that the ENG-Mid level learners in this case used NP+*wa* in a very different way from all of the other groups. Taking a functional/discourse analytic approach, which considers distributional factors, reveals that although the English speakers produced the *wa* form at early stages, they did not begin to master its function until the more advanced levels of proficiency. An examination of the use of NP+*wa* at a lower proficiency level failed to reveal any systematic use of the particle. In contrast, learners at the advanced level used *wa* only for referring to the main characters, just as was the case with the NSs of Japanese and the Korean speakers. In other words, an in-depth investigation of the patterns of use, i.e., the inappropriate uses of *wa* as well as the appropriate uses, reveals that the learners develop appropriate form-function mapping of the definiteness marker in Japanese concurrent with a general increase in proficiency.

The same argument would explain higher usage of NP+*wa* in the H/N narrative than in the T/T narrative, except for the case of the ENG-Mid level speakers. Recall that the ENG-Mid level speakers produced a higher percentage use of NP+*wa* in their T/T narratives than in their H/N narratives and that this might be indicative of their inability to linguistically differentiate the information status of the characters, with or without the pictorial support. In other words, while the JNS, ENG-High, KOR-Mid, and KOR-High level learners managed to differentiate the ways in which they mark the characters based on their importance within a story, as well as with regards the condition of narrative elicitation (i.e., H/N and T/T settings), ENG-Mid level learners' choice of NP+*wa* was not systematic. This qualitative analysis reveals that the English L1 speakers have not gained the appropriate form-function mapping at the intermediate proficiency level. The performance of the use (or non-use) of NP+*wa* increased with proficiency in terms of English groups, however. It should be recalled that the native like performance on NP+*wa* by the Korean learners appeared at the intermediate level proficiency. Thus, the data suggests that it might take longer for the English L1 speakers to identify the discoursal functions of NP+*wa* than their Korean counterparts. I argue that the fact there is a shared notion of postpositional markings of NPs and their corresponding form with NP+*wa* to denote exact same function (i.e., known topical referents) in Korean, facilitated the form-function mapping skills exhibited by Korean speakers in their L2 Japanese production.

Higher percentage use of NP+*wa* by ENG-Mid level than any other group was also found in the context of continuous mention of referents. Whereas over 80% of the referent marking in the context of continuous mention was done with zero anaphora by the other groups, ENG-Mid level learners produced only 61.7%. Their percentage use of NP+*ga* and NP+*wa* was as high as 20.7% and 13.0%, respectively. The ubiquitous (and inappropriate) appearance of NP+*wa*, regardless of the discourse context, suggests an overgeneralisation of the form by the English intermediate learners (and a concomitant underutilisation of target-like forms such as NP+*ga* in referent introduction, and zero anaphora in continuous mention of referents). Comparing the different contexts of referent introduction and continuous mention, overuse of NP+*wa* was observed in the lower proficiency level; this replicates the findings of Nakahama (2009) in that her intermediate level English L1 speakers overproduced NP+*wa* regardless of context.

Nakahama (2009) found that the acquisition order of NP+*wa* preceded NP+*ga*, based on the order of appearance of these forms. This acquisition order of definiteness preceding indefiniteness by the English speaking participants in Nakahama replicated not only the previous L2 Japanese studies (e.g., Doi and Yoshioka, 1990; Sakamoto, 1993) but also L2 English acquisition studies (see e.g., Andersen, 1977; Huebner, 1985). The current study did not produce the same results of the previous studies in that the percentage use of NP+*wa* did not exceed that of NP+*ga* in either narrative type. Furthermore, given that the lower proficiency level speakers did not have the appropriate form-function mapping of NP+*ga* or NP+*wa*, it could be said that English L1 speakers have acquired neither of the forms at the intermediate level of proficiency. This differing result between the current study and my previous one (Nakahama, 2009) might be caused by the differing proficiency levels between the studies.[43] Therefore, it could be posited that English L1 speaking learners might be able to start producing NP+*ga* somewhere between the intermediate to high-intermediate level, though they might not have the competence to fully manage form-function mapping.

As discussed in Chapter 2, there are two different accounts of the early acquisition of definiteness marking, as compared to indefiniteness marking. Some researchers (e.g., Huebner, 1983; Rutherford, 1983) claim that the appearance of definiteness markers is attributable to a learners' L1, while others (e.g., Fuller and Gundel, 1987) argue that topic prominence is a part of the universal developmental stage that all learners go through. Nakahama (2009) revealed that definiteness marking preceded indefiniteness marking by English speakers, but that such a predisposition was not found among the Korean speakers. This result tends to weaken the universal theory of early acquisition of definiteness marking, as there was no clear shared pattern between the two different L1 groups regarding the performance of definiteness marking. Instead, these results lead to the hypothesis that even if a universal developmental stage exists, the rate of acquisition could be accelerated by positive language transfer from a learners' L1. Although the current study did not show the prevailing use of definiteness marking over indefiniteness marking, *per se*, it revealed that the Korean learners of Japanese had already grasped both types of marking at the intermediate proficiency level. Therefore, with the results of the current study and those of Nakahama (2009), I claim a faster acquisitional speed of L2 Japanese by Korean L1 speakers, than English L1 speakers.

Though the acquisition order of *wa* preceding *ga* was rationalised by Doi and Yoshioka (1990) based on developmental sequences (Meisel, Clahsen and Pienemann, 1981), the order of instruction cannot be completely ruled out as a cause or factor. An examination of several leading Japanese textbooks showed that *wa* marking is introduced first (e.g., *Basic Functional Japanese*, Kawai et. al, 1987; *Nakama*, Makino, Hatasa and Hatasa, 1998; *An Introduction to Modern Japanese*, Mizutani and Mizutani, 1977; *Japanese for Everyone*, Nagara, 1990).[44] The relationship between the order of introduction of forms and accuracy rate was investigated by Sakamoto (1985). He examined beginning level students who learned Japanese using the textbook (*Learn Japanese* by Young and Nakajima-Okano, 1984), which, contrary to most Japanese texts, introduces *ga* prior to *wa*. The results indicated that the accuracy rate of the production of *ga* was 90.5%, while that of *wa* was 78.1%; this result contradicts the findings of other studies (e.g., Russell, 1985). Sakamoto argues that the production of *ga* and *wa* is influenced by the order in which they are introduced to learners.

It is expected that the Korean learners in the current study have presumably been exposed to the same kinds of instructional patterns. However, it is likely that the English L1 learners of Japanese, who had no concept of new-old information being marked in a similar structural model in their L1, might have much more difficulty in distinguishing these two forms compared to their Korean counterparts. Therefore, as far as the current study is concerned, even if there was a relationship between the acquisition order and the order of introduction of these forms, the instructional order seems not to have had the same impact on the development of *ga* and *wa* in the case of the Korean learners of Japanese.

Thus far we have seen how CLI (both negative and positive transfer) has an effect on learners' performance of referent introduction and somewhat on their performance of continuous mention of referents. However, regarding the production of NP+*ni/kara* and passive constructions, both learner groups displayed different performance from the JNSs. Furthermore, there is no vast difference between the learner groups of the two different L1 backgrounds. An earlier development of target-like performance by the Korean speakers would have been expected, due to the corresponding marking system for referring to equivalent entities in their L1. However, this was not the case, and this brings to the fore: How come NP+*ga* is easy to acquire for Koreans while NP+*ni/kara* is not? In other words, we are left with uncertainty as to why sharing the comparable linguistic feature in their L1 facilitates the use of *ga* but not *ni/kara*? A possible explanation for this perplexing result will be attempted below.

5.1.3 Proficiency and CLI: Constraints on transfer
5.1.3.1 The use of NP+*ni/kara* and the passive constructions by Korean L1 speakers
In contrast to their early target-like production of NP+*ga*, it took the Korean speakers longer to develop a target-like use of NP+*ni/kara* for introducing a referent into a narrative discourse (increase from 3.9% at the intermediate level

to 9.7% at the advanced level, while 9.8% was produced in the NSs narratives under the H/N condition). Recall that while NP+*ni/kara* can appear independently, in Japanese narratives it is closely tied to the passive construction and serves to mark the demoted agent. As the Korean learners produced fewer passives (as indicated by the absence of passive verb morphology or passive expressions) than the JNSs, the low total frequency of the use of NP+*ni/kara* appears to be related to the low passive production at the lower proficiency level.

The use of NP+*ni/kara* increased with proficiency and by the time they reached the advanced level, the percentage use of the form reached the NS level. The rather few occurrences of NP+*ni/kara* may be attributable to the fact that this particle is not a prototypical marker for referent introduction as NP+*ga* is in Japanese, as discussed above. Another possibility of the fewer occurrences of NP+*ni/kara* is that it seems that the learners have not fully acquired the passive constructions at the intermediate level, and therefore opted not to use this agentive particle, as part of the passive structure. Constructing passive structures includes complex verbal morphology, and as Pienemann (1998) maintains, the acquisition of the passive emerges in a late stage of learning, therefore, it did not happen until the Korean learners reached the advanced level. As was indicated in the results section concerning the use of NP+*ni/kara*, one learner from the KOR-Mid level used NP+*ni/kara* in the passive construction, but with an incorrect conjugation of the verb. As was shown in the results section, even two advanced learners made some erroneous passive sentences (one speaker made correct conjugation of the wrong verb, while the other incorrectly conjugated the right verb).

As discussed in earlier chapters, voice alternation (active vs. passive) plays a very crucial role in topic continuity. The NSs of Japanese in the study switched back and forth between active and passive voice to maintain the topic of discourse; in the native Japanese speakers' discourse, the main characters were maintained in the focus position with the use of the passive form and the peripheral characters were described with *ni* (by) in the less topical position. The alternation of voice was not observed much until the Korean learners reached the advanced level, indicating their gain in the ability to control the formal aspects of the construction, which could then be used to express topic continuity in a more native-like manner. The difficulty in producing passive constructions by the Korean learners, despite having similar features of passivisation in their native language, indicates that CLI is not a simple phenomenon to explain. The difficulty of realising CLI in the production of passive forms and NP+*ni/kara* seems to have been caused by the fact that the learners had to do more than merely substituting postparticiple markers (e.g., *ka/i* with *ga*). They had to keep the main character in the topical position as the patient, conjugate the verb, and (if necessary) place the agent before the agentive marker (*ni/kara*). It is possible to claim that because of the complex process of voice alternation, the Korean speakers did not benefit from typological similarities between the two languages, in this instance.

Lastly, it could be plausible that the learners produced fewer numbers of passives and NP+*ni/kara* because they may have exercised their L1 conception of the configuration of passives in their L2 Japanese narratives. To clarify this possibility, it is repeated here that Korean speakers tend to place more focus on what happens in each scene with neutral perspective, while Japanese NSs centre their attention on the main characters and tell the story from their perspectives. As a result of these differing ways in which the two groups view the unfolding of an episode, it can be understood why the Korean speakers produced fewer passive constructions in their L2 Japanese narratives, as compared to their Japanese NS counterparts. This last possible cause will be discussed, in conjunction with the results of the English speakers' data, in the separate section on conceptual transfer.

All the above possibilities or some combination thereof, seem probable in explaining the Korean learners' frequency of production of NP+*ni/kara* as well as passive constructions. To clarify the certainty of these claims in future studies, it is suggested that a combination of different types of methods for eliciting passives be used — one type which gives learners options to use or not use passive structures (such as the series of pictures or silent film used for this study), and the other type which requires passive constructions (such as more controlled grammar tests).

To sum up, within the current study there was evidence that showed how the learners' proficiency places constraints on positive transfer taking place in terms of the passive structures produced by Korean learners of Japanese. What follows next is a discussion of how task complexity has an effect on form selections in storytelling in L1 and L2 Japanese. The relationship between task effects and the learners' L1, as well as their proficiency levels, will be explored.

5.1.4 Task complexity and its effects on L1 and L2 storytelling

As I showed in the results section, many observable facts appeared to be affected by the task complexity of the narrative. To be specific, the production of NP+*ga*, particle drop, erroneous referent marking, and zero anaphora seem to have been influenced by the condition under which narratives were told. Task complexity effects were mainly found on the NNSs of Japanese and some were found only in the English speakers' narratives. Further, proficiency level played some role in task effects taking place. Task complexity also had an effect on the JNSs' form selections, of which some NNS groups shared the pattern.

I will discuss how task complexity influenced the L1 and L2 narrative discourse in the following order. First, I will make a case for how it affected the accuracy of the particle usage of L2 Japanese; the cases of NP+*ga*, particle drop, and erroneous particle marking in the context of referent introduction, will be presented. Task effects on particle drop found in the T/T narratives by the NNSs and NSs will also be discussed in the context of topic switch, although the claim might not be conclusive. Then, the relationship between task complexity and the speakers' choice of full NP and zero anaphora will be discussed. Robinson's (2001, 2003) Cognition Hypothesis is referred to in order to explain the effects of task complexity on the accuracy and complexity of L2 discourse.

5.1.4.1 Task complexity and accuracy of referent marking

In the context of referent introduction, the percentage use of the prototypical referent marker, NP+*ga*, by the ENG-Mid group learners was significantly lower than the JNS group in the H/N narrative. However, the percentage use of the form by the same group vastly increased in the T/T narratives and there was no difference among all five groups. Although qualitative analysis revealed that the form-function mapping is not as skilfully done as their advanced level counterparts, the Korean speakers or the JNS, the accurate marking of the referent introduction was achieved in the T/T narrative. Furthermore, the same tendency was found in terms of particle drop between the two narrative types. After NP+*ga*, the most frequently used form by the ENG-Mid group for encoding referent introduction was particle drop (16.5%) in their H/N narrative; however its percentage use in the same group drop to 3.8% in the T/T narrative. As discussed previously in the manuscript, particle drop was considered ungrammatical in a monologic narrative discourse.

While briefly discussed in the results section, it should be repeated here that there were some grammatical errors in marking referent introduction in the NNSs data. The occurrences of error was collapsed into another variable 'others' along with NP+copula, *ni* (at, to, with), *to* (with), *no* (possessive), due to its few frequencies. Errors in marking referent introduction were only found in ENG-Mid level and the percentage was 6.1% in the H/N narrative. The speakers in the ENG-Mid level did not produce errorneous marking in the T/T narrative. Thus, it appears the grammatical accuracy within the ENG-Mid group increased in the T/T narrative, which was indicated by the increased use of NP+*ga* and the decreased use of particle drop and errorneous marking.

The increased accuracy with more complex storytelling task (i.e., T/T narrative condition) in the current study supports the findings of the previous studies that showed significant effects for task complexity measured by error free T-unit (Iwashita, et.al, 2001; Rahimpour, 1999), and target-like use of articles (Ishikawa, 2007; Robinson, 1995). The increased accuracy in the current study and the previous ones under the T/T narrative condition can be explained by Robinson's Cognition Hypothesis (2001, 2003). The Cognition Hypothesis claims that as increased cognitive demands on the tasks should promote learners to pay more attention to features of the L2 system, and as a result, L2 learner discourse should become more grammaticised and complex.

The T/T task requires the learners to store the information on the characters and the events, put them together and reconstruct the story, therefore places higher cognitive demands on the learners. I claim that the higher cognitive demands involved in narrative telling under the T/T condition pushed the L2 learners to greater accuracy, in terms of the use and nonuse of NP+*ga* and particle drop/errorneous marking, respectively.

However, it should be noted that high complexity of task also triggered some instances of particle drop in the context of topic switch. I argue that switching topic is more intricate than referent introduction, as the speakers need to consider the competition of topicality between the two referents in switching the topic. This complex procedure led the speakers to confusion as to which particle to use and they ended up dropping the particles. Therefore, the effect of task complexity on the accurate grammaticisation was realised in the referent introduction context but not in topic switch.

5.1.4.2 Task complexity and production of attenuated form

In the context of topic switch and continuous mention of referents, the less complex narrative task (i.e., H/N narrative) generated the higher percentage use of zero anaphora than the T/T narrative. This result applies to all the learners as well as the JNS, KNS and ENS thus suggests that less demanding task triggered the speakers' choice of attenuated form regardless of the proficiency level and L1 background. On the structural markedness scale (Chaudron and Parker, 1990), zero anaphora is considered to be the least marked form. Therefore it is claimed that less demanding narrative task generated the less complex structures in the current study. This result supports the previous hypothesis made by Robinson (2001, 2003) that increased conceptual/communicative demands placed on the learners triggers more complex learner discourse. Moreover, the relationship between the more complex syntactic structures in marking topic switch and continuation in more complex task can be explained by the argument posited by Givon (2009). In explaining the possible correlation between linguistic and cognitive complexity, Givon argues that 'the more complex mentally-represented events are coded by more complex linguistic/syntactic structures' (2009: 10).

The participants in the current study applied the higher percentage use of marked syntactic coding to the referent such as NP+*ga* and NP+*wa* in the T/T narrative than the H/N. The follow-up interviews revealed that this choice of applying more complex form in the more complex narrative task was not a conscious one. However, all the participants who were interviewed stated that they tried to be more explicit regarding about what and whom they were referring to, as they struggled with remembering the storyline in the T/T task. In the H/N narrative, the speakers did not have the sole pressure placed on them, as the listeners had the pictures if they chose to look at in the case of the occurrence of non-understanding. The speakers form choice of full NPs in the T/T narrative is related to what Clancy (1997) found in two very young children's acquisition of Korean. As was discussed in the literature review section, at the very young age of less than two, they already managed to differentiate the use of full NP and zero anaphora based on the presence of the referents they were referring to. On the whole, the results of the current study reinforced the claim made by the previous studies that the more complex task gerenrate more complex syntactical form.

5.1.5 Conceptual transfer

Thus far, I demonstrated how typological similarities between the learners' L1 and L2 affected the way in which the learners encode the introduction and the tracking of referents in L2 narrative discourse under the H/N and T/T conditions. To be specific, negative transfer was observed in the L2 narratives at lower proficiency level (i.e., intermediate) of English L1 speakers, whereas positive transfer was found in Korean learners' L2 narratives. Furthermore, the relationship between proficiency and CLI was discussed in explaining the Korean learners' underproduction of passive structures and NP+*ni/kara* in referent introduction. Qualitative examinations enabled us to discover that there are cases of positive and negative transfer that could be caused by resembling or differing conceptual prototypes in depicting experiences between the learners' L1 and the L2. First, I will show how patterns of event construal in the learners' L1 emerged in their L2 narrative discourse by discussing the case of voice alternation.

As emphasised throughout the manuscript, previous literature revealed that English and Korean speakers tend to take more neutral perspective in construing events than Japanese, as they place focal point on the 'fact' rather than 'standpoint' (Jung, 2002; Kim, 2001; Kurihara and Nakahama, 2010; Mizutani, 1985; Yanagimachi, 2000). An important consequence of this difference in focus is the tendency for Korean and English NSs to change discoursal topics more than Japanese NSs, which was evidenced in both the KNS and the ENS narratives in this study. Japanese NSs, on the other hand, have a propensity to adhere to the main characters as discourse topics by placing them in the subject position. When Japanese speakers introduce peripheral characters, those characters appear in less topical positions, such as agents in passive structures. In the current study, more instances of passive morphemes were produced by the Japanese NSs than by the KNS or the ENS, and the differences were more apparent in the T/T narrative than H/N. The same tendency was found in the NNSs narrative both by English and Korean speakers. Even at the advanced level, the Korean and English speakers' L2 Japanese contained fewer instances of passive constructions than was the case with the NSs of Japanese in the H/N narratives (18 times each in the ENG-High and the KOR-High groups and 27 times by the JNS) and in the T/T narrative (9 times in the ENG-High, 7 times in the KOR-High, and 27 times in the JNS).

These differing conceptualisation patterns through which speakers express their viewpoints in perceiving and describing events in L1 and L2 seem to have hindered both Korean and English speakers from achieving target-like performance in terms of formation of passive structures.

What was most noteworthy was that task complexity did not affect the speakers' production of passives in the JNS group, whereas higher task demands (i.e., referring to events in 'there-and-then' context) contributed to reducing the occurrence of passive structures in all the other groups, including the ENS and the KNS. I will repeat the frequencies of passive forms for all the groups in both narrative types.

Table 5.1 Number of the Occurrences of Passive Expressions by All Groups

	H/N	T/T	Total
ENG-Mid	4	9	13
KOR-Mid	7	5	12
ENG-High	18	9	27
KOR-High	18	7	25
JNS	27	27	54
ENS	21	6	27
KNS	17	2	19

As is shown in Table 5.1, the total numbers of the occurrences of passives by the Korean and English L1 and L2 speakers were slightly lower than the JNS except for the lower proficiency learners in the H/N narrative. However, the episodes of passives were rather scarce across group except for the JNS in the T/T narrative. If all the groups, including the JNS displayed differing patterns between the two tasks, the effect of high task demands or differing story plots on the formation of passive would be verified; however, that was not the case.

As discussed in the results section, the actions/events delineated in the series of pictures in the H/N story provide more salient contexts to generate passive structures, as compared to the story plot in the T/T narrative. However, in spite of this difference between the two tasks, the JNS produced as many passive constructions/expressions in their T/T narrative, and the patients of the passive sentences were all main characters in both the H/N and the T/T narratives.

This is what Slobin (1991) calls 'thinking for speaking' case in point, as the Japanese speakers' thought was induced into the systematic manifestation that was available in Japanese (i.e., voice alternation in order to topicalise the main characters). The speakers of Korean and English produced passive structures with the guidance of pictures that clearly trigger voice alternation in the H/N narrative. However, when they have more liberty regarding the way in which the story can be construed, they opted not to employ voice alternation unlike their Japanese NS counterparts.

While this circumstance constituted a case of negative transfer caused by differing concepts, there was also a pattern in which Japanese and Korean shared a conceptual notion and the way in which shared notion is realised in language which facilitated the production of target-like performance in the Korean speakers' L2 Japanese. Recall that most of the Japanese and Korean NSs used NP+*ga* and NP+*ka/i* in the existential sentence structures for re-introduction of the frog toward the end of the story. It was argued that the speakers were trying to emphasise the reappearance of the frog (i.e., the significance hierarchy) and/or re-establish or raise the frog's role as a member of the frog family (i.e., the animacy hierarchy), rather than just a pet of the boy, by utilizing the new information markers in both languages. Among the English NSs, on the other hand, some speakers used the conventional prototype, *the*, i.e., the definite article, while others use indefinite marking, as some speakers re-introduced the frog in conjunction with his family members which were new information in the discourse. The majority of the ENS introduced the frog as the object of the verb, *to find*, or *to see*, in the less topical position in the sentence.

In short, the three groups of NS narratives (Japanese, Korean and English) demonstrated the distinctive ways in which different languages display differing coding schemes that are available in each language for marking the same referent in the same event. In other words, the different manners in which this highlight of the story was encoded between the English and Japanese/Korean speakers provide another case of evidence of how differently language works as a "filter" regarding how people interprete and describe the events (see Berman and Slobin, 1994). This conceptual diversity between Japanese/Korean and English became visible in the L2 learners' encoding of the same episode. As was shown in the results section, the majority (5 out of 11) of the marking of the re-introduction of the frog was done with NP+*o* by the lower proficiency level English speakers' narratives. With proficiency, the use of NP+*o* decreased greatly, and most of the speakers in the ENG-High group marked the frog with NP+*ga* (7 out of 10 speakers) in the existential sentence construction. The majority of the Korean speakers (70% in the KOR-Mid, and 90% in the KOR-High), marked the same referent in the same context with NP+*ga*, irrespective of their proficiency.

With these results, I argue that CLI derives not only from the typological similarities and differences but also from conceptual conversion and diversion between the learners' L1 and L2. With regard to the marking of the finding of the pet frog in the H/N narrative, the English speakers acquired the target like conceptualisation of the event and grammaticisation of it accordingly by the time they reached the advanced level proficiency. In other words, as Cardierno and Lund (2004) puts it, employing the interpretation of Slobin's language learning, the English speaking learners acquired another way of 'thinking for speaking'.

Besides this occurrence of transfer, as I have shown throughout this manuscript, some typological similarities and dissimilarities found in Japanese and the learners' L1s (Korean and English) seemed to either facilitate or hinder L2 learning. Kellerman (1995) states that some grammatical features such as closed class morphemes are not easy to acquire, especially if their equivalents are not found in the learners' L1. However, it is even more difficult to 'notice' the subtly differing ways in which events are encoded into language between the learners' L1 and L2. He called this notion the 'transfer to nowhere' principle, a concept meant to express the claim that differences in the way speakers have been predisposed to conceptualise knowledge and experience in L1 and L2 might go unheeded and thereby cause difficulties in learning. This hypothesis is basically in accordance with the claims of Odlin (1990). He argues that implicitness of discourse awareness, as opposed to some obvious metalinguistic knowledge such as word order, makes language learning more challenging. This theory concerning the difficulty of 'conceptualising' discourse level differences between L1 and L2 offers an explanation for the under-performance of passive constructions by the Korean learners and the manner in which the English speakers re-introduced the frog in their L2 narratives at the lower proficiency level.

The difficulty of learning (or more precisely put, being aware of) another way of 'thinking for speaking' is confirmed with the results of post-task interviews collected from several L2 learners. Regardless of the learners' proficiency levels, the learners knew the function of passive forms, they were not aware of the protocol of voice alternation in order to keep the focus on the main speaker. What is more, the learners did not know this particular way of setting the speakers' perspective on the main characters and describe the events from their point of views in storytelling in Japanese.

As was revealed from the interview data and claims made by Kellerman and Odlin above, it should be maintained that how to capture the world and convey thought through the means that are made available in the speakers' L1 is not easily altered to the conceptual norm of the target language. In other words, as Odlin (2005) rightly argues, even learners of high proficiency may never entirely be able to divest themselves of the "binding power" of language on thought in L1 (see Whorf (1956) for linguistic relativity). Language is more than just a mere channel for expressing thought; it is, rather, constitutes an important element in the formation of thought. As Odlin maintains, the relationship of this concept of linguistic relativity and CLI is extremely important, and whereas there is increasing evidence in L2 studies to explicate conceptual transfer (see Jarvis and Pavlenko, 2010; Odlin, 2005), it is still under explored domain in CLI, and thus deserves further investigations in the field of SLA (Odlin, personal communication, March 28, 2005).

5.2 Conclusion

5.2.1 Answers to the research questions

Research Question 1: What kinds of referential devices are used by NS of Japanese, Korean and English for introducing and tracking referents in oral narratives?

As predicted in Hypothesis 1 (a) and (b), Japanese and Korean NSs marked referent introductions with NP+*ga* and NP+*ka/i*, respectively, and zero anaphora was the canonical form used to mark the highest topic continuity in both languages. Hypothesis 1 (c) was also supported, as the English NSs used indefinite markings to encode referent introduction, and pronouns to encode topics with high continuity. Furthermore, as predicted, in marking referents in the context of topic switch, full NP was preferred over attenuated forms (zero anaphora for Japanese/Korean and pronoun for English) in all three languages.

Topic continuity was achieved via voice alternation in the NS narrative discourse of Japanese, Korean and English. Japanese narratives generated more passive structures (27 times each in both H/N and T/T narratives) as compared to the Korean narratives (17 times in H/N and 2 times in T/T) and the English narratives (21 times in H/N and 6 times in T/T) therefore, Hypothesis 2 was supported, particularly in the T/T condition narratives. Higher use of passive forms in the JNS were triggered by the differing ways in which NSs of Japanese perceive the events in the story from Korean and English and how Japanese language acted as a filter on the ways in which they related to the events (i.e., keeping the focus on the main protagonist via voice alternation).

Research Question 2: Are there any developmental patterns in acquiring referent marking strategies in L2 Japanese narratives? If so, does the pattern of learning differ between the Korean and English L1 speakers due to CLI?

The ability to appropriately mark referent introduction and tracking increased with proficiency with regard to the English L1 group. The Korean learners of Japanese, on the other hand, already performed a target-like use of referent introduction and tracking by the time they reached the intermediate proficiency level, except for passive forms and NP+*ni/kara*. Therefore, Hypothesis 3 which states, 'the target-like performance of referent introduction and tracking will increase with proficiency' was fully supported for the English L1 group and partially supported for the Korean L1 group. Hypothesis 4 which predicted differing acquisition rate of referent markings between Korean and English was supported with the Korean learners' faster acquisition of appropriacy of form-function mapping of referent markings with one exception of the passive constructions. It was argued in the study that the typological similarities between Korean and Japanese facilitated learning of appropriate marking of story characters in the context of introducing and tracking of referents in L2 narrative discourse.

Research Question 3: Does task complexity affect referent markings in oral narratives? Also, does task complexity affect L1 and L2 narrative formation Japanese differently?

As Hypothesis 5 predicted, more accurate form choice was observed in the T/T narratives. Accuracy was measured by the increased use of indefinite markings and decreased erroneous markings and particle drop in the context of referent introduction by the English L1 speakers. The increase in the use of indefinite markings was also detected in the L2 narratives by the Korean speakers and the JNS. Although the percentage was rather small, particle drop was found in the context of topic switch in all the L1 and L2 Japanese groups. Therefore, Hypothesis 5 was not borne out in terms of the ungrammatical marking of the topic switch with particle drops. The T/T narrative generated structurally more complex marking of referents in the context of topic switch and continuous mention, thereby support Hypothesis 5 with regard to the positive correlation between the task complexity and complexity of L2 narratives.

With regard to the production of passives, high task complexity triggered fewer occurrences of such structure. It was argued that the fewer episodes of passives can be explained by the followings: 1) storyline in the T/T narrative did not induce passivasion of the actions and/or 2) the learners tell the story while struggling to retrieve a plethora of information from their memory, therefore, they focus on depicting each episode by naturally set their viewpoint on the action doers in each scene. Hypothesis 6 which states 'L1 Japanese speakers' narrative discourse will not be affected drastically by task complexity' was supported in terms of the passive formation, but not regarding the complexity measured by the higher use of full NP in topic switch and continuous mention.

5.2.2 Summary of findings

The study was able to demonstrate differing patterns in the acquisition of the management of referent marking in oral narratives between different L1 groups, and hence it rejects the notion that CLI has no role to play due to language universals that govern language acquisition processes. Furthermore, within the framework of a functional approach, the study was able to answer some of the unanswered issues of CLI in the field of SLA at least in the following ways.

1) Interlanguage grammar (e.g., syntax and bound morphology) has been considered more impervious to CLI, as compared to other areas of language such as phonology and lexicon. However, the present study was able to provide abundant evidence of CLI in grammar and contributed to the current understanding of CLI and interlanguage grammar. It was found that there

were differing patterns in the acquisition of postpositional markers between the Korean and English L1 speakers. It is claimed that the concept of, or lack thereof, marking a new referent postpositionally in their L1s influenced the interlanguage of Japanese by the Korean and English speakers, respectively. The production of particle drop and low percentage use of NP+*ga* by the English L1 group at the lower proficiency level provided the clearest example of negative transfer. Such a trend was interpreted as negative transfer or simplification resulting from the lack of postpositional marking systems in their L1.

2) Conducting not only quantitative but also qualitative analyses of oral production data enabled us to see how speakers (NSs and NNSs) manage form-function mapping while telling a story, and thus contributed to a better understanding of discourse-grammar interface in learner language. The ability to perform target-like form-function mapping generally increased with proficiency, and the tendency of the increase with proficiency was especially obvious with the English speakers. With regard to the performance by the English group, for instance, NP+*ga* was used unsystematically by the English speaking lower proficiency learners, while the usage was restricted for reintroducing the main characters (which replicates the performance in the JNS group and Korean speaking learners at both proficiency levels) as proficiency increased. While the Korean speakers generally performed better than their English counterparts at the intermediate proficiency level, their performance increased with proficiency with regard to the use of NP+*ni/kara* and as well as of morphological changes (passivisation) in the verbs.

3) It has been pointed out in the literature that CLI is not easily detected possibly because many of the CLI studies examine learner productions at rather high proficiency levels (Kellerman, 1995; Odlin, 1990). In response to this concern, the current study included learners with both intermediate and advanced levels in hopes of discovering any relationship between proficiency and CLI. The results showed that L1 influence was evident among the English speakers at the lower proficiency level (i.e., intermediate level), but as proficiency increased, their performance on most of the grammatical features improved. Whereas postpositional markings seemed troublesome for the lower level English L1 speakers, they showed slightly more target-like performance in the use of zero anaphora, especially in the narrative task with lesser cognitive demand.

As far as the Korean speakers are concerned, it appears that positive transfer facilitated the performance of certain linguistic forms, while it did not assist the acquisition of others as greatly. Some unexpected results regarding the performance of passivisation of verbs between the two L1 groups (i.e., Korean L1 speakers and English L1 speakers showed very similar developmental patterns) might be explained by linguistic constraints lower level learners of both groups experienced. The lower-level learners of both groups tended to switch topic of discourse in order to avoid voice alternation, whereas their higher proficient counterparts managed to skilfully alternate active and passive voices if the scenes trigger such actions. With this result, it was argued that positive transfer is difficult to take place when linguistic constraint exists, i.e., lack of morphological knowledge.

4) The study extended the notion of conceptual transfer from the lexical level to the discourse level in L2 narrative studies. Previously, some researchers (e.g., Helms-Park, 2001; Jarvis, 1998, 2000; Ringbom, 1987) in their systematic investigation of CLI have shown that conceptual knowledge in L1 does transfer to L2 in the form of lexicon. Jarvis (1998) showed that a choice of L2 vocabulary is largely influenced by what is available in L1; the researcher claimed that how speakers depict events in their native language has effects on L2 production. Jarvis explained this circumstance as conceptual transfer, adapting the transfer to nowhere principle of Kellerman as mentioned previously.

In the current study, the manner in which experiences are filtered (cf. Berman and Slobin, 1994; Slobin, 1996) in their L1 seems to have a large effect on L2 discourse in the production of passive constructions among the Korean and English speakers' L2 Japanese and on the different re-introduction strategies used with the frog as encoded by the Korean and English speakers in their Japanese L2. Using Slobin's terminology, the 'thinking for speaking' that the learners established in their L1 shaped their L2 discourse, and this conceptual transfer at the discourse level would add to the body of knowledge in the discipline of L2 oral narrative discourse.

5) Lastly, the current study confirmed the findings of the previous studies (e.g., Robinson, 1995; Ishikawa, 2007) with regard to how task complexity influences the accuracy and complexity of the L2 narrative discourse. In the study, the accuracy was measured with the proper marking of the referents in the context of referent introduction. The complexity of the discourse was measured in terms of the use of zero anaphora versus full NP. It was found that

more complex narrative task generated the more accurate marking of referents in the English speaking L2 Japanese discourse. The reason the task effects were not observed in the increase in accuracy of L2 Japanese by the Korean speakers in the T/T task was that they already demonstrated the target-like performance in introducing a new referent into discourse by the time they reached the intermediate level proficiency. In regard to the English speakers' narratives, task effects on accuracy were noted with the increased use of NP+*ga* and decreased use of particle drop and erroneous referent markings in the context of referent introduction. Regarding the task effect and complexity of L2 discourse, fewer occurrences of zero anaphora were found in both contexts of topic switch and continuous mention of referents, across all the learner groups and the JNS. In short, by implementing the narrative tasks of different complexities in a single study clarified the varied results of the performance of zero anaphora in the preceding studies (see e.g., Nakahama (2009) for the H/N setting, and Nakahama, 2003; Polio, 1995; Yanagimachi, 1997, 2000 for the T/T setting).

5.2.3 Limitations and suggestions for further research

In this section, I discuss several limitations of the current study and recommendations for further research in the related field. First of all, it is realised that the study was carried out with a relatively small number of participants, mainly due to practical limitations, such as locating certified raters of the SOPI, as well as learners of Japanese at the optimal level of proficiency projected for the study. Although careful scrutiny was attempted in terms of the statistical analyses, i.e., implementation of both ANOVA and chi-square, depending on the nature of the data, it would be premature to claim definitive conclusions based solely on this study due to the limited number of participants.[45]

Secondly, in this study, a limited number of linguistic features were the target of investigation (i.e., various postpositional markers, passive morphology and zero anaphora). However, topic continuity can be studied in a plethora of ways. For instance, definiteness marking could be indicated by demonstratives (*kore* and *are/sore* in Japanese, referring to 'this' and 'that', respectively) along with *wa*. In addition, considering Givón's (1983) iconicity principle which states "the more disruptive, surprising, discontinuous or hard to process a topic is, the more coding material must be assigned to it," an introduction or re-introduction of a referent would be expected to require the most complex linguistic marking such as an existential structure or complex relative clauses (see e.g., Chaudron and Parker, 1990; Nakahama, 2003).

The results of the studies by Chaudron and Parker and by Nakahama showed that the new context enhanced the utilisation of more complex coding of the referent, and appropriate coding improved with proficiency in investigation of English by Japanese speakers and Japanese by English speakers, correspondingly. These studies concerned the notion of markedness and its relation to the ease and difficulty of acquisition of noun referential forms. In both of these studies, the learners of the same L1 background served as participants, therefore transfer effects could not be appropriately investigated (without comparison to learners of different L1 backgrounds) with respect to the complexity of noun modification and its development. A study of more refined coding of referential markings (especially in rather understudied languages) might provide further information that leads to a better understanding of how form-function mapping is implemented by L2 learners, and thus make a contribution to the SLA within the framework of markedness and transfer.

Viewpoint setting was examined in terms of voice alternation in the present study. However, other linguistic features might serve as clues to understanding the speaker's viewpoint (Kurihara and Nakahama, 2010; Nakahama and Kurihara, 2007; Yanagimachi, 2000). For instance, Nakahama and Kurihara (2007) and Kurihara and Nakahama (2010) considered viewpoints via giving- and receiving-related expressions, motion verbs, voice alternation, self expressions, sub-emotive expressions and emotive expressions. By broadening the ways to measure how the speakers express their viewpoints, the L1 and L2 narratives by Korean and English speakers might be projected differently.

Other important implications for relevant SLA research include implementation of different data elicitation methods since differing methods themselves might have an effect on the results of NP marking, as found in Yoshioka (1991). Similarly, Aramaki (2003) reports differing results of auxiliary verbs of giving/receiving in L2 Japanese in knowledge based and performance based tasks. Her study showed that the learners' grammatical knowledge does not necessarily equate their ability to use the form in the context where the use of such a form is expected. The current study did not incorporate grammar test of postpositional markings as well as passive construction; therefore, we are left with uncertainly as to whether or not the learners had the knowledge of the forms when they did not use them. With the findings of Aramaki's and the current study in mind, incorporation of multiple tasks might be recommended to gain better access to the learners' capacity in terms of knowledge and use.

The current study analysed monologic discourse, focusing on the product by the L2 learners. However, as Mitchell and Myles (2004) pointed out, within the framework of 'functional approaches' to understanding language learning, many studies have focused on describing the final products, not the processes that lead to it. In other words, interactions between the speaker and the listener tend to get overlooked in describing the form-function relationship in learner discourse. In reality, storytelling is facilitated by collaboration between the speaker and the listener. And this 'collaboration can be realised for example as feedback between participants in the form of completions, clarifying questions, or other types of acknowledging that the participants have understood what their fellow communicators were saying (Tanskanen, 2006: 24). In other words, storytelling is not solely a work of the teller, but it is the end results of co-construction of the story between the speaker and the listener. Many different forms of meaning negotiations can be expected to appear in storytelling activities even among the NSs. Incomprehensibility of stories told by L2 speakes might be remedied by meaning negotiations such as clarification requests and confirmation checks. On the whole, we would benefit from a study that examines not only the final products but the processes in order to understand how learners manage effective storytelling (Nakahama, 2011). Some studies have been conducted to explore interactional moves which arise while narrating a story (see e.g., Gilabert et al., 2009; Nuevo, 2006). These studies will be discussed, within the context of task complexity, in the next section.

Lastly, in the field of SLA, there are increasing amounts of research that test interventional effects on language development (e.g., Larsen-Freeman and Long, 1991; Ellis, 1994). Kitajima's (1997) study is one of the few studies in Japanese L2 research that showed that instruction has effects on learning referential markings. In his study, Kitajima first provided an explanation of the differing roles of referents in Japanese and English to the experimental group, and later demonstrated reading strategies to them. More importantly, the researcher showed learners not only syntactic, but also discoursal techniques to alleviate the difficulty of reading comprehension related to referential use. After the treatment, the learners were asked to read a Japanese story and they had to rewrite the contents in their L1 (English). It was found that the experimental group comprehended the story on the macro level much better than the control group, and the results suggest that strategy training leads to the learners' better understanding of the referential processes in reading comprehension of Japanese. Given the findings of the present study relating to developmental sequences in referent markings, studies to test various types of instructional effects would merit further consideration.

In the field of the acquisition of JSL, research by Kida and Kodama (2001) also deserves a mention here. Though the focus of their investigation was not on referent markings, their study examined instructional effects on L2 Japanese storytelling within the context of conversational interaction. They found that after receiving the instruction, the learners employed evaluative devices such as the use of historical present and direct quotes in their storytelling. It was argued that these devices were used by a storyteller in order to frame and excentuate the importance of the content of the story, and its use is supposed to help the listener to better understand the story, or be drawn into it. While the number of the learners for which the researchers presented the results, was rather small (N=3), the study's contribution to the current understanding of L2 learners' language use should be noted, due to the fact that the topic is understudied, and this study directly offers pedagogical propositions.

5.2.4 Pedagogical implications

The study was able to show the differing developmental patterns of referent marking in L2 Japanese narrative discourse between Korean and English L1 speakers. Most notably, it was found that typological closeness between L1 and L2 in terms of morphology and syntax does not guarantee the way in which thoughts are organised into a story if cultural worldview differs considerably in the two languages. The analysis of L2 narrative discourse at two different proficiency levels has helped us understand what kind of route learners take to ultimately make coherent utterances. Furthermore, comparing two different types of narratives has enabled us to see how complexity of given tasks affects the ways in which the speakers select linguistic forms in relating events.

Overall, the findings of the current study suggest the importance of providing instructions on not only grammar but also how to use the language in a culturally convincing way. Recall that Aramaki (2003) revealed that grammatical knowledge by itself does not warrant the production of contextually appropriate giving/receiving auxiliary verbs. The researcher rightly suggests that not only the instruction of grammar but also guidance in how to use the form in contextually appropriate ways (i.e., form-function mapping) is needed. Though the learners at higher proficiency level in the current study were able to produce passive forms, the total number of forms did not reach the same level as the NSs of Japanese. Furthermore, the speakers told the story from the perspective of the main characters in the H/N narrative but not to the extent to which the NSs did. In the T/T, the passive forms were hardly used irrespective of the learners' proficiency level, whereas an equal amount of passivisation was observed in the JNS narratives. As discussed before, more uses of the passive structures in the H/N were instigated by the salient cause and effect relationship for passivisation depicted in the picture. Given that the learners were not 'aware' of Japanese being a position centred language, consciousness-raising activities might be essential, as well as instruction into how to express the feature via voice alternation.

However, learners' proficiency levels need to be carefully assessed in terms of the content of instruction. With regard to viewpoint setting, Wei (2010) found that guiding the learners to fix their viewpoint on the main characters helped them to produce target-like narratives with the use of linguistic devices such as passivisation of verbs, and auxiliary verbs of giving/receiving. However, those whose proficiency level was not high enough did not get enough benefit of consciousness-raising of viewpoint setting, as they could not overcome the linguistic challenge of producing related expressions.

On the whole, in conjunction with the recommendation posited by the previous related studies, the results of this study can provide pedagogical suggestions for language teachers, assist in the development of teaching materials, and provide input in setting goals for a curriculum. Although it would not be expected that target-like coherent narratives could be mastered until the learners reach certain proficiency levels, some explicit instruction (along the lines of Kitajima, 1997), as well as consciousness-raising of various kinds (e.g., Rutherford and Sharwood Smith, 1985), might facilitate the development of referent markings, such as deciphering the use of *wa*, *ga* and zero anaphora, in terms of information status of referents in a narrative discourse.

Some complicated passive structures cannot be expected to be mastered in the beginning levels, as they are subject to processing constraints as noted by (Pienemann, 1998), and later supported by Wei's (2010) study of L2 Japanese. However, it might be possible to teach learners at the beginning level some of the appropriate external elements of coherence (i.e., contextualisation cues) as replacement of the passivisation of verbs through means such as circumlocution with an interlocutor participating in dialogic story exchanges. For advanced level learners, it would be reasonable to expect that they would be ready to learn how to make their narratives coherent in a variety of ways, including passive structures (see Pienemann, 1983, for learnability hypothesis).

The follow-up interviews revealed that the English-speaking learners at the lower proficiency level in this study revealed that they were not aware of the differing functions of NP+*wa* and NP+*ga*. Furthermore, among these participants, the choice of *wa* and *ga* over other forms in introducing a referent seemed random. Therefore developing more effective ways of teaching the 'function' of these particles is crucial. As was sensibly suggested by Sakamoto (1997), successful acquisition of *wa* and *ga* cannot be accomplished without understanding their functions regarding information status (new and old), focus within discourse, and discourse flow itself. It goes without saying that mere explanation of grammar at the sentence level would not enhance real understanding of the function of these forms, and the importance of explicating the ways in which forms function in discourse, should be understood by teachers, and reflected in teaching methods. The function of *ga* and *wa*, as well as the ellipsis of subject and object, might be mentioned briefly in Japanese language textbooks at the metalinguistic level. However, the roles they play in creating coherence in discourse are seldom discussed. One solution for filling the void between the issues raised in language research and pedagogy can be found in Fujiwara and Yamura-Takei (2002). That study presents a computer-assisted program that helps learners to become familiar with the 'use' of zero anaphora in discourse.

Lastly, it is essential to recognise that the sequence of not only the introduction of the linguistic elements, but also the task type should be taken into consideration. The ultimate goal of foreign language teaching is for learners to acquire the ability to use language in real contexts, and that can only be achieved by implementing real world tasks in foreign language classroom activities. Furthermore, such tasks need to be carefully assessed based on the learners' proficiency level. In other words, so as to implement authentic tasks, a series of pedagogic tasks should be introduced and practiced beforehand, or at least concomitantly.

As discussed throughout this manuscript, H/N tasks are considered less complex compared to T/T condition narratives, and thus it is naturally expected to introduce H/N tasks first and then T/T. On the other hand, as the current study, as well as previous ones (e.g., Gilabert, 2007; Ishikawa, 2007; Robinson, 1995) showed, increasing cognitive demands could push learners to more accurate and/or complex L2 production. Therefore, having in mind that complex tasks can potentially push the learners to execute the best of their capacity, appropriate advancement from less complex tasks to more complex ones should be emphasised.

In sequencing tasks on the basis of their complexity, Robinson (2001) argues that three groups of factors need to be identified. These are: task complexity, task conditions, and task difficulty. Task complexity is concerned with cognitive factors as discussed throughout this manuscript, while task conditions relate to interactive factors, which Robinson further divides into two types of variables, participation and participant variables. Participation variables include whether the task requires one-way or two-way communication, whereas participant variables can be influenced by elements such as gender and familiarity between interactants. Finally, task difficulty relates to how learners perceive task demands, and it is argued that affective and ability variables constitute this factor. For instance, motivational and anxiety factors are categorised as the former type, whilst learners' aptitude and intelligence factors belong to the latter.

According to Robinson (2001), task condition is controlled by the type of designated task, and thus, "participation and participant factors are unlikely to be a useful basis for *a priori* sequencing decisions" (Robinson, 2001: 295). Additionally, the researcher continues that learners' affective variables cannot be predicted prior to their engagement with a given task, thus this aspect needs to be monitored on-line during the task implementation. With this premise in mind, it is imperative for language teachers to appreciate cognitive complexity as one of the important elements in designing and sequencing tasks, in conjunction with consideration of linguistic complexity in L2 classrooms, based on the learners' proficiency levels.

There are several ways in which cognitive complexity can be controlled. While the current study monitored task complexity in terms of one aspect of resource-directing dimension, i.e., +/- here-and-now factor, other variables of the same dimension also have been reported to have effects on L2 production. To be specific, task complexity determined in a resource-directing dimension tends to trigger more accurate and complex, but less fluent, L2 production. On the other hand, the more complex task in terms of the resource-dispersing dimension, (e.g., familiarity (+/- prior knowledge)) negatively affects L2 production in terms of fluency, accuracy, and complexity (Robinson, 2001). Thus, for instance, teachers can conceivably have lower proficient learners start on tasks with which they have more familiarity, and gradually proceed to tasks on less familiar topics.

In terms of storytelling activities, in Section 5.2.3 above, I made a case for the importance of examining interaction in storytelling, as an area of improvement that can be made in future studies of L2 narrative discourse. Gilabert et al. (2009) investigated the relationship between task complexity and interactional moves the learners make by comparing three different types of task: a narrative task, an instruction giving task, and a decision making task. They divided interactional moves into three types: recasts, negotiation of meaning, and language related episodes. Language related episodes refer to remarks learners make during interaction regarding their own utterances, or the asking of questions on language use, as well as the conducting of self- or other-repairs. They found that in comparing two types of narrative of different complexity (+/- here-and-now condition), the more complex task generated significantly higher occurrences of recast and a strong trend toward higher use of confirmation checks, as well as language related episodes. Besides Gilabert et al.'s (2009) study, Nuevo (2006) also revealed that a more complex task triggers conversational adjustments, such as confirmation checks and comprehension checks. To date, several studies have shown that interactional modification facilitates L2 language development (see Mackey, 2007 for a compilation of studies). Therefore, exposing learners to opportunities to negotiate meaning with each other by having them engage in a complex task is unquestionably beneficial to the L2 learning processs.

The current study's focus was placed on investigating how L2 speakers manage referent introduction and tracking, and thus, minimal interruption was imperative. Therefore, the listeners were instructed to give minimal interaction except for back channelings. However, in a real world context, storytelling almost always entails conversational interactions between the storyteller and the listener. Nakahama (2011) embarked on an exploratory study, the qualitative analysis of which revealed that ESL learners use various interactional strategies to tell their life stories, and not only the teller of the story, but also the listener joined in co-constructing the stories. Nakahama compared learners from ESL with EFL backgrounds and found that the EFL learners were less interactive than their ESL counterparts. Furthermore, though proficiency level was the same between the two groups, the EFL learners tended to appeal for help from NSs, whereas ESL learners asked for agreement from the NS listeners, instead of their assistance. All in all, while Nakahama's study examined real life stories of the L2 speakers in a T/T context (- here-and-now task), as opposed to simulated picture description narration tasks, it generally supported the findings of Gilabert et al. (2009) in that there were many interactional moves, especially by the ESL learners.

In designing a task, it is important to keep in mind that the final goal for the learners is to be able to use the language in the real world. Narration of a series of pictures or film retelling might be realistic enough exercises in a language classroom, as in a real life someone might watch a movie and later tell his/her friends its storyline. Still, more authentic storytelling activities with a range of complexity might be useful for learners. Taking into account the issues of task sequencing, interaction, CLI (especially conceptual transfer discussed in the manuscript), as well as insights that stem from my own experience as a language teacher, I attempt to share with the reader some pedagogical suggestions that might promote effective L2 storytelling.

Suggested Activities of Storytelling

As discussed above, appropriate task sequencing plays an important role in bringing about successful L2 development. As Robinson (2001) argues, while foreign language teachers should move from a simple task to a more complex one, they should monitor on-line participant factors (e.g., whether the same or opposite gender pair might be more appropriate for certain tasks) and affective variable (e.g., whether the learners' motivation are kept intact while doing a task). Teachers should be flexible to modify the complexity of tasks on-line, if necessary.

An exercise that might be a simple but practical activity for a novice learner is stating a story in + here-and-now setting. As many of us experienced when we were at primary school, 'show and tell' exercises might also be useful in the L2 classroom. Such an exercise can bring out rich L2 production. The task can be simplified by giving the learners instruction to bring something that they can 'talk about' in the present tense. For instance, a learner can bring CDs of their favorite singers and talk about when they listen to the music, as well as plans of going to their concert (in non-past tense). Since the learners have the familiarity with the theme or the topic, task complexity is considered low, and therefore appropriate for even novice learners.

The same activities can easily be made complicated by having them talk about an item and tell the past history behind it. This activity can be done in groups or pairs, especially since pair or group work would trigger many instances of interaction. If there are only a few students in class and learner proficiency level might not be high enough, one student at a time can present in front of class as a more monologic storytelling exercise, while the rest of class write down questions to ask after the narration has ended. As monologic storytelling is supposed to be cognitively less complex than dialogic one, this can be better suited for lower proficiency levels. If the activity is done in pairs (as a dialogic storytelling), a teacher can select one learner in each pair and have him/her report to the class about the item that his/her classmate introduced. In so doing, the listener of the storytelling can test hypothesis about the lexicon, morphology, and grammar in the retelling the story behind his/her partner's item, and thus, L2 learning can be facilitated.

In addition, since the speaker will be talking about someone else's story, the discourse topic shifts to the third person singular, from the first person. Recall that Yanagimachi's (2000) study revealed that positioning perspective is found to be difficult for L2 learners of Japanese in the third person narratives, as compared to first or second person narratives. Therefore, a retelling activity of someone else's story can be challenging enough even for more seasoned language learners, in terms of providing opportunities to 'notice' and practice perspective setting in L2 Japanese.

If the learners are of intermediate level or higher, they can be asked to tell real life stories (if they feel comfortable doing so). For this activity, they could bring family video clips, and show them to the class. After showing a short video clip, without any additional visual support, he/she can explain what it was about, when and why the event took place, and what he/she thought of it. To reduce task complexity, the task can be simplified by having the learners show several consecutive pictures of family activities and tell the story while showing the pictures, using the present tense (i.e., + here-and-now condition narrative). Again, if the teacher wants to make this activity more complex, dialogic interaction, as well as reporting someone else's life story, can be arranged.

I have shown two possible storytelling activities that can be made simple or complex by manipulating simple design factors. In designing tasks, I intend to value organic relationships between learners and what surrounds them, rather than placing the entire focus on what learners can or cannot produce. This outlook resembles the concept of *affordance* found in the field of ecological linguistics, as "it (*affordance*) denotes a relationship of possibility between a learner and something in the environment" (van Lier, personal communication, April 13, 2011). In this approach, the appropriate integration of learners and authentic activities is of value, especially in an EFL environment, where L2 input is rather limited.

Last but not least important, based on the findings of the current study, I suggest the importance of providing the learners not only the grammatical guidance but also instruction on how different perspective alignments are displayed in their L1 and L2, in relating events. In so doing, language distance can be discussed by providing abundant examples, be it in terms of word order or morphology. More importantly, learners can be taught that typological similarity does not necessarily constitute similarity of discourse formation, as was evidenced in Korean L2 narratives found in the current study. Consciousness-raising activities can be planned to teach learners how Japanese speakers place their focus in relating events, and this can be done either explicitly (see e.g., Wei, 2010) or implicitly. Moreover, as a teacher, it is crucial to keep in mind that a group of learners should not be forced to alter how they view the world, by acquiring another way of 'thinking for speaking' in their L2.

This final section 5.2.4 was intended to show how research findings can be implemented in foreign language instruction. It is hoped that increasing efforts will be made to link research with practice, in order to enhance foreign language learning in the years to come.

Notes

43 Nakahama (2009) compared three different proficiency levels; low-intermediate, high-intermediate, and advanced. The intermediate level in the current study would be approximately equivalent to the high-intermediate level in Nakahama (2009).

44 It should be noted that there are, in fact, books which introduce *wa* and *ga* concurrently (see e.g., *Japanese the Spoken Language*, 1987 written by Jorden and Noda).

45 It should be noted here that it is quite possible that the statistical significance could not be found on certain linguistic items, due to the small number of sample size.

Bibliography

Andersen, R. (1977). The impoverished state of cross-sectional morpheme acquisition/accuracy methodology. *Proceedings of the Los Angeles Second Language Research Forum* (pp. 308–319). Los Angeles: Department of English, University of California at Los Angeles.

Andersen, R. (1983). Transfer to somewhere. In S. Gass & L. Selinker (eds.), *Language transfer in language learning* (pp.177–201). Rowley, MA: Newbury House.

Aramaki, T. (2003). The relationship between ability of composing sentences using benefactive expressions and ability in situation judgement: An error analysis of benefactive expressions by a survey. *Nihongo Kyooiku (Journal of Japanese Language Teaching)*, 117, 43–52.

Bamberg, M. (1987). *The acquisition of narratives: Learning to use language*. New York: Mouton de Gruyter.

Bamberg, M. (1994). Development of linguistic forms: German. In R. Berman & D. Slobin (eds.), *Relating Events in Narrative: A crosslinguistic developmental study* (pp. 189–238). Hillsdale, NJ: Lawrence Erlbaum Associates, Inc.

Bar-Lev, Z. (1986). Discourse Theory and "Contrastive Rhetoric". *Discourse Processes*, 9, 235–246.

Berman R. & Slobin, D. (1994). *Relating Events in Narrative: A crosslinguistic developmental study*. Hillsdale, NJ: Lawrence Erlbaum Associates, Inc.

Birdsong, D. (1992). Ultimate attainment in second language acquisition. *Language*, 68, 706–755.

Blum-Kulka, S. (1982). Learning to say what you mean: A study of speech act performance of learners of Hebrew as a second language. *Applied Linguistics*, 3, 29–59.

Butler, G. Y. (2002). Second language learners' theories on the use of English articles. An analysis of the metalinguistic knowledge used by Japanese students in acquiring the English article system. *Studies in Second Language Acquisition*, 24, 451–480.

Byrnes, H, Child, J., Levinson, N., Lowe, Jr., P., Makino, S., Thompson, I., and Walton, A. R. (1986). ACTFL Proficiency Guidelines. In H. Byrnes & M. Canale (eds.), *Defining and developing proficiency: Guidelines, implementations, and concepts*. Yonkers, NY: ACTFL.

Cardierno, T., & Lund, K. (2004). Cognitive linguistic and second language acquisition: motion events in a typological framework. In B. VanPatten., J. Williams., S. Rott., & M. Overstreet (eds.), *Form-meaning Connections in Second Language Acquisition* (pp. 139–154). Mahwah, NJ: Lawrence Erlbaum Associates, Inc.

Chafe, W. (1987). Cognitive constraints on information flow. In R. Tomlin, (ed.), *Coherence and Grounding in Discourse*. Amsterdam and Philadelphia: John Benjamins.

Chafe, W. (1994). *Discourse, Consciousness, and Time. The Flow and Displacement of Conscious Experience in Speaking and Writing*. Chicago and London: The University of Chicago

Press.

Chaudron, C. & Parker, K. (1990). Discourse markedness and structural markedness: the acquisition of English noun phrases. *Studies in Second Language Acquisition*, 12, 1: 43–64.

Chen, P. (1986). Referent introducing and tracking in Chinese narratives. Unpublished doctoral dissertation, University of California, Los Angeles.

Clancy, P. (1980). Referential choice in English and Japanese narrative discourse. In W. Chafe (ed.), *The pear stories: Cognitive, cultural, and linguistic aspects of narrative production* (pp. 127–202). Norwood, NJ: Ablex.

Clancy, P. (1985). The acquisition of Japanese. In D. I. Slobin (ed.), *The crosslinguistic study of language acquisition*, Vol. 1 (pp. 373–524). Hillsdale, NJ: Lawrence Erlbaum Association.

Clancy, P. (1992). Referential strategies in narratives of Japanese children. *Discourse Processes*, 15, 441–467.

Clancy, P. (1997). Discourse Motivations for Referential Choice in Korean Acquisition. In H. Sohn, & J. Haig (eds.), *Japanese/Korean Linguistics*. Volume 6. CSLI Publications.

Clancy, P. & Downing, P. (1987). The use of *wa* as a cohesion marker in Japanese oral narratives. In J. Hinds, S. Maynard & S. Iwasaki (eds.), *Perspectives of topicalization: The case of Japanese wa*. John Benjamins Publishing Co. Amsterdam/Philadelphia.

Cohen, A. & Olshtain, E. (1981). Developing a measure of sociocultural competence: The case of apology. *Language Learning*, 31, 113–134.

Comrie, B. (1989). *Language Universals and Linguistic Typology*. 2nd ed. Oxford: Basil Blackwell.

Cooreman, A. (1983). Topic continuity and the voicing system of an ergative language: Chamorro. In T. Givón (ed.), *Topic Continuity in Discourse. A Quantitative Cross-Language Study*. Amsterdam: John Benjamins.

Cooreman, A. (1987). *Transitivity and Discourse Continuity in Chamorro Narratives*. Berlin: Mouton de Gruyter.

Coppieters, R. (1987). Competence differences between native and near-native speakers. *Language*, 63, 544–573.

Corder, S. P. (1967). The significance of learners' errors. *International Review of Applied Linguistics*, 5, 161–169.

Cortazzi, M. & Jin, L. (1994). Narrative analysis: Applying linguistics to cultural models of learning. In D. Graddol, D. & J. Swann (eds.), *Evaluating Language*. Clevedon: Multilingual Matters Ltd.

Dik, S. C. (1987). Some principles of functional grammar. In R. Dirven & V. Fried (eds.), *Functionalism in linguistics* (pp. 101–134). Amsterdam: John Benjamins.

Doi, T. & Yoshioka, K. (1990). Speech processing constraints on the acquisition of Japanese particles: Applying the Pienemann-Johnson model to Japanese as a second language. *Proceedings of the 1st Conference on Second Language Acquisition and Teaching*, 23–33. International University of Japan.

Dulay, H. & Burt, M. (1974a). Errors and strategies in child second language acquisition. *TESOL Quarterly*, 8, 129–136.

Dulay, H. & Burt, M. (1974b). Natural sequences in child second language acquisition.

Language Learning, 24, 37–53.
Dulay, H., Burt, M. & Krashen, S. (1982). *Language Two*. New York: Oxford University Press.
Ellis, R. (1985). *Understanding second language acquisition*. Oxford, UK: Oxford University Press.
Ellis, R. (1994). *The study of second language acquisition*. Oxford, UK: Oxford University Press.
Faerch, C. & Kasper, G. (1989). Internal and external modification in interlanguage request realization. In S. Blum-Kulka, J. House & G. Kasper (eds.), *Cross-cultural pragmatics: request and apologies* (pp. 21–247). Nowrood, NJ: Ablex.
Fakhri, A. (1989). Variation in the use of referential forms. In S. Gass, C. Madden, D. Preston, & L. Selinker (eds.), *Variation in second language acquisition: Vol. II Psycholinguistic issues*. (pp. 189–201). Clevedon, UK: Multilingual Matters.
Foreign Service Institute. (1985). *Schedule of Courses, 1985–1986*. Washington, DC.: U. S. Department of State.
Fox, B. (1987). *Discourse structure and anaphora in written and conversational English*. Cambridge University Press.
Fujiwara, M. & Yamura-Takei, M. (2002). Analysis of Japanese zero anaphora and its application for a CALL program (Zero Checker). *Paper presented at Third International Conference on Practical Linguistics of Japanese*. San Francisco State University.
Fuller, J. W. & Gundel, J. K. (1987). Topic prominence in interlanguage. *Language Learning*, 37, 1–18.
Gass, S. & Selinker, L. (1983). *Language Transfer in Language Learning*. Rowley, Mass.: Newbury House.
Gilabert, R. (2007). The simultaneous manipulation of task complexity along planning time and +/- Here-and-Now: effects on L2 oral production. In Maria del Pilar Garcia-Mayo (ed.), *Investigating Tasks in Formal Language Learning* (pp. 44–68). Clevedon, UK: Multilingual Matters.
Gilabert R., Barón, J., & Llanes, A. (2009). Manipulating cognitive complexity across task types and its impact on learners' interaction during oral performance. *IRAL*, 47, 367–395.
Givón, T. (1978). Definiteness and referentiality in J. Greenberg (ed.), *Universals of human language*, Vol.4, Syntax, Stanford: Stanford University Press.
Givón, T. (1979). *On understanding grammar*. NY: Academic Press.
Givón, T. (1983). *Topic continuity in discourse: Quantitative cross-language studies*. Amsterdam: John Benjamins.
Givón, T. (1984). Universals of discourse structure and second language acquisition. In W. Rutherford. (ed.) *Language universals and second language acquisition* (pp. 109–136). Amsterdam: John Benjamins.
Givón, T. (1995). *Functionalism and grammar*. Amsterdam: J. Benjamins.
Givón, T (2009). Introcution. In T. Givón & M. Shibatani (eds.), *Syntactic complexity: Diachrony, Acquisition, Neuro-cognition, Evolution*. Amsterdam John Benjamins.
Gumperz, J. (1982). *Discourse strategies*. Cambridge: Cambridge University Press.
Gumperz, J. (1992). Contextualization and understanding. In A. Duranti & C. Goodwin

(eds.), *Rethinking context* (pp. 229–252). Cambridge: Cambridge University Press.

Gundel, J. K. & Tarone, E. (1983). "Language transfer" and the acquisition of pronominal anaphora. In S. Gass & L. Selinker (eds.), *Language transfer in language learning* (pp. 281–296). Rowley, MA: Newbury.

Hakuta, K. (1978). A report on the development of the grammatical morphemes in a Japanese girl learning English as a second language. In E. Hatch (ed.), *Second Language Acquisition* (pp. 132–147). Rowley, MA.: Newbury House.

Halliday, M. A. K. (1985). *An introduction to functional grammar*. London: Edward Arnold.

Hanada, A. (1993). The acquisition of *wa* and *ga* by foreigners. *Japanese Education*, 6, 27–43. Fukuoka YWCA.

Harwell, M. R., Rubinstein, E. N., Hayes, W. S. & Olds. C. C (1992). Summarizing Monte Carlo results in methodological research: The one-and two-factor fixed effects ANOVA cases. *J. Educ. Stat.*, 17: 315–339.

Hasegawa, Y. (1993). The Function of the "Zero Particle" in Conversational Japanese. *Nihongo Kyooiku (Journal of Japanese Language Teaching)*, 80, 158–168.

Hattori, S. (1959). *Nihongo no keito*. Tokyo: Iwanami

Hawkins, J. A. (1985). *A comparative typology of English and German; Unifying the contrasts*. Austin: University of Texas Press.

Hedberg, N., & Fadden, L. (2007). The information structure of It-clefts, Wh-clefts and Reverse Wh-clefts in English. In N. Hedberg & R. Zacharski (eds.), *The Grammar-Pragmatics interface: Essays in honor of Jeanette K. Gundel* (pp. 49–76). Amsterdam/Philadelphia: John Benjamins. Pragmatics & beyond New Series.

Helms-Park, R. (2001). Evidence of lexical transfer in learner syntax. The acquisition of English causatives by speakers of Hindi-Urdu and Vietnamese. *Studies in Second Language Acquisition*, 23, 71–102.

Hendriks, H. (2000). The acquisition of topic marking in L2 Chinese and L2 and L2 French. *Studies in Second Language Acquisition*, 22: 369–397.

Hinds, J. (1980). Japanese conversation, discourse structure, and ellipsis. *Discourse Processes*, 3, 263–286.

Hinds, J. (1983). Topic continuity in Japanese. In T. Givón (ed.), *Topic continuity in discourse: Quantitative cross-language studies*. Amsterdam: John Benjamins.

Hinds, J. (1984). Topic maintenance in Japanese narratives and Japanese conversational interaction. *Discourse Processes*, 7, 465–482.

Hinds, J. (1987). Thematization, assumed familiarity, staging, and syntactic binding in Japanese. In J. Hinds, S. K. Maynard, & S. Iwasaki (eds.), *Perspectives on topicalization: The case of Japanese 'wa'* (pp. 83–106). Philadelphia: John Benjamins.

Huebner, T. (1983). *A longitudinal analysis of the acquisition of English*. Ann Arbor, MI: Karoma.

Huebner, T. (1985). System and variability in interlanguage syntax. *Language Learning*, 35, 141–163.

Hwang, M. (1983). Topic continuity and discontinuity in Korean narrative. *Korean Linguistics*, Vol. 3, 47–79.

Ishikawa, T. (2007). The effect of manipulating task complexity along the [+/- Here-and-Now] dimension on L2 written narrative discourse. In Maria del Pilar Garcia-Mayo (ed.), *Investigating Tasks in Formal Language Learning* (pp. 136–156). Clevedon, UK: Multilingual Matters.

Iuchi, M. (1995). The process of acquisition of *wa*, *ga*, and *o*. *Japanese culture and Japanese Language Education*, Volume 9, 246–256. Ochanomizu Women's College.

Iwashita, N., McNamara, T., & Elder, C. (2001). Can we predict task difficulty in an oral proficiency test? Exploring the potential of an information processing approach to task design. *Language Learning*, 51, 401–436.

Jarvis, S. (1998). *Conceptual transfer in the interlingual lexicon*. Bloomington, IN: IULC Publications.

Jarvis, S. (2000). Methodological rigor in the study of transfer: Identifying L1 influence in the interlanguage lexicon. *Language Learning*, 50, 245–309.

Jarvis, S. (2002). Topic continuity in L2 English article use. *Studies in Second Language Acquisition*, 24, 387–418.

Jarvis, S. (1998). *Conceptual transfer in the interlingual lexicon*. Bloomington, IN: IULC Publications.

Jarvis, S. & Odlin, T (2000). Morphological type, spatial reference, and language transfer. *Studies in Second Language Acquisition*, 22, 535–556.

Jarvis, S. & Pavlenko, A. (2010). *Crosslinguistic influence in language and cognition*. New York: Routledge.

Jung, H. (2002). The use of personal reference terms in Japanese and Korean: Based on the analysis of original and translated novels. *Nihongo Kyooiku (Journal of Japanese Language Teaching)*, 114: 30–39

Jin, H. G. (1994). Topic-prominence and subject-prominence in L2 acquisition: Evidence of English to Chinese typological transfer. *Language Learning*, 44: 1, 101–122.

Jorden, E. H. & Noda, M. (1987). *Japanese: The Spoken Language, Part 1*. Yale Univ Press.

Kajiwara, M. & Minami, M. (2008). Narrative construction by bilingual children: Referential topic management. In T. Ogura, H. Kobayashi, S. Inagaki, M. Hirakawa, S. Arita, & Y. Yasui (eds.), *Studies in Language Sciences 7*, Tokyo: Kurosio Publishers.

Kaplan, R. B. (1966). Cultural thought patterns in inter-cultural education. *Language Learning*, 16, 1–20.

Kasper, G. (1992). Pragmatic Transfer. *Second Language Research*, 8, 203–231.

Kasper, G., & Schmidt, R. (1996). Developmental issues in interlanguage pragmatics. Studies in Second Language Acquisition, 18, 149–169.

Kawai, K., Miura, K. & Suzuki, H. (1987). *Basic Functional Japanese*. Tokyo: The Japan Times.

Kellerman, E. (1977). Towards a characterization of the strategies of transfer in second language learning. *Interlanguage Studies Bulletin*, 2, 58–145.

Kellerman, E. (1983). Now you see it, now you don't. In S. Gass & L. Selinker (eds.), *Language transfer in language learning* (pp. 112–134). Rowley, MA: Newbury.

Kellerman, E. (1995). Crosslinguistic influence: Transfer to nowhere? *Annual Review of Applied Linguistics*, 15, 125–150.

Kenyon, D. M. & Malobonga, V. (2001). Comparing examinee attitudes toward computer-assisted and other oral proficiency assessments. *Language Learning and Technology*, Vol. 5, No. 2, 60–83.

Kida, M. & Kodama, Y. (2001). An analysis of the oral narrative competence of advanced-level Japanese language learners: Toward inputs on discourse level to learners' experiential narratives in an informal situation. *The Japan Foundation Japanese Language Institute, Urawa Bulletin,* Vol. 11, 31–49.

Kim, H. (1989). Nominal reference in discourse: Introducing and tracking referents in Korean spoken narratives. *Harvard Studies in Korean Linguistics* III (pp. 431–444) Proceeding of the 1989 Harvard Workshop on Korean Linguistics.

Kim, K. (2001). The expression of viewpoint in discourse by learners and native speakers: Contrasting the choice of subjects and verbs between Japanese and Korean. *Nihongo Kyooiku (Journal of Japanese Language Teaching),* 109: 60–69.

Kinsui, S. (1993). Gengogaku no saishin joohoo: 'Nihongogaku'. *Gekkangengo,* 22 (4), 118–121.

Kitajima, R. (1997). Referential strategy training for reading comprehension of Japanese texts. *Foreign Language Annals, 30,* (1), 84–97.

Klein, W. (1986). *Second Language Acquisition.* Cambridge: Cambridge University Press.

Klein, W. (1990). A theory of language acquisition is not so easy. *Studies in Second Language Acquisition,* 12, 219–231.

Koike, I. (1983) *Acquisition of grammatical structures and relevant verbal strategies in a second language.* Tokyo: Taishukan.

Kondo, J. (2004). Japanese Learners' Oral Narratives:Linguistic Features Affecting Comprehensibility. *Japanese Language Education around the Globe,* 14, 53–74.

Krashen, S. (1981). *Second language acquisition and second language learning.* Oxford: Pergamon Press.

Kubota, M. (1996). Acquaintance or fiancee: Pragmatic differences in requests between Japanese and Americans. *Working papers in Educational Linguistics,* 12 (1), 23–37.

Kumpf, L. (1992). Preferred argument in second language discourse: A preliminary study. *Studies In Language,* 16, 369–403.

Kuno, S. (1973). *The structure of the Japanese languages.* Cambridge, MA: MIT Press.

Kurihara, Y. & Nakahama, Y. (2010). Sutoorii ni okeru shiten: Nihongo washa to jookyuu nihongo gakushuusha to no hikaku kara. In M. Minami (ed.), *Linguistics and Japanese Language Education VI: New Directions in Applied Linguistics of Japanese* (pp. 141–156). Tokyo: Kurosio Publisher.

Labov, W. (1972). *Language in the inner city.* Philadelphia, PA: University of Pennsylvania Press.

Lado, R. (1957). *Linguistics Across Cultures.* Ann Arbor: University of Michigan Press.

Landis, J. R. & Koch, G. G. (1977). The measurement of observer agreement for categorical data. *Biometrics,* 33, 159–174.

Larsen-Freeman, D. & Long, M. (1991). *An introduction to second language acquisition research.* London: Longman.

Lee, H. S. (1987). Discourse Presupposition and the discourse function of the topic marker *nun* in Korean. *IULC,* Indiana University.

Li, C. & Thompson, S. (1976). Subject and topic: A new typology of language. In C. N., Li (ed.), *Subject and topic: Symposium on subject and topic,* University of California, Santa Barbara (pp. 457–489). New York: Academic Press.

Li, C. & Thompson, S. (1979). Third-person pronouns and zero anaphora in Chinese discourse. In T. Givón (ed.), *Syntax and semantics* (Vol. 12, pp. 311–355). New York: Academic Press.

Liu, D. & Gleason J. L. (2002). Acquisition of the article THE by nonnative speaker of English. An analysis of four nongeneric uses. *Studies in Second Language Acquisition*, 24, 1–26.

Mackey, A. (Ed.) (2007). *Conversational interaction in second language acquisition: A collection of empirical studies.* Oxford: Oxford University Press.

Maeshiba, N., Yoshinaga, N., Kaspter, G. & Ross, S. (1996). Transfer and proficiency in interlanguage apologizing. In S. Gass & J. Neu (eds.), *Speech acts across cultures* (pp. 155–187). Berlin: Mouton.

Major, R. C. (1986). The ontogeny model: Evidence from L2 acquisition of Spanish r. *Language Learning*, 36, 453–504.

Makino, T. (1979). English morpheme acquisition order of Japanese secondary school students. *TESOL Quarterly*, 13, 428.

Makino, S., Hatasa, Y. & Hatasa, K. (1998). *Nakama 1: Japanese communication, culture, context*, Houghton Mifflin Co.

Martin, C. G. & Games, P. A. (1977). ANOVA tests for homogeneity of variance: Nonnormality and unequal samples. *Journal of Educational Statistics*, 2 (3), 187–206.

Maruyama, N. (1996). Joshi no datsuraku genshoo (The phenomenon of particle drop). *Gekkan Gengo* (Language Monthly), 25, 74–80.

Master, P. (1987). *A cross-linguistic interlanguage analysis of the acquisition of the English article system.* Unpublished doctoral dissertation, University of California, Los Angeles.

Master, P. (1997). English Article System: Acquisition, function and pedagogy. *System*, 25, 2, 215–232.

Master, P. (2002). Information structure and English article pedagogy. *System*, 30 (3) 331–348.

Mayer, M. (1969). *Frog, where are you?* New York: Dial Press.

Meisel, J., Clahsen, H. & Pienemann, M. (1981). On determining developmental stages in second language acquisition. *Studies in Second Language Acquisition* 3, 109–135.

Milon, J. (1974). The development of negation in English by a second language learner. *TESOL Quarterly* 8: 137–143.

Mitchell, R. & Myles, F. (2004). *Second Language Learning Theories.* 2nd edition. Arnold Publication.

Mizutani, N. (1985). *Nichiei hikaku hanashi kotoba no bunpoo.* Tokyo: Kurosio Publishers.

Mizutani, O. & Mizutani, N. (1977). *An Introduction to Modern Japanese.* Tokyo: The Japan Times.

Muñoz, C. (1995). Markedness and the acquisition of referential forms. The case of zero anaphora (Replication Study). *Studies in Second Language Acquisition*, 17 (4), 517–527.

Nagara, S., Ed (1990). *Japanese for everyone.* Tokyo: Gakken.

Nagatomo, K. (1991). The acquisition of *ga* and *wa* in discourse. Systematic Variation Model. *Proceedings of the Japanese Symposium: Interaction of Linguistic Theory and Japanese Language Education*; 10–24. Tsudajuku Japanese Education Center.

Nagatomo, K., N., Hoki, N. & Hajikano, A. (1993). Longitudinal study of SLA:

Investigation of interlanguage of beginning level Japanese learners. *Proceeding of the Conference of Japanese Language Education*, 149–159.

Nakahama, Y. (1999). Requests in L1/L2 Japanese and American English: A crosscultural investigation of Politeness. In L. Bouton (ed.), *Pragmatics and language learning monograph* (pp. 1–29) Volume 9. Urbana: IL. University of Illinois at Urbana-Champaign.

Nakahama, Y. (2003). Development of referent management in L2 Japanese: A film retelling task. *Studies in Language and Culture* Vol. XXV No. 1 pp. 127–146. Graduate School of Languages and Cultures. Nagoya University.

Nakahama, Y. (2004). Dainigengo to shite no monogatari hatsuwa ni okeru shiji taishoo no topikku kanri no hattatsu pattan. In M. Minami & M. Asano (eds.), *Linguistics and Japanese Language Education III: New Directions in Applied Linguistics of Japanese* (pp. 77–96). Tokyo: Kurosio Publisher.

Nakahama, Y. (2009). Cross-linguistic influence on referent introduction and tracking in Japanese as a second language. *Modern Language Journal*, Vol. 93 (2), 241–260.

Nakahama, Y. (2010). L2 acquisition of English referential strategies. *Paper presented at the 18th Pragmatic Language Learning Conference*. Kobe, Japan.

Nakahama, Y. (2011). Co-constructing narratives in L2 conversation. *Paper presented at Hawaii International Conference of Arts and Humanities*. Honolulu, HI.

Nakahama, Y. and Kurihara. Y. (2007). Viewpoint setting in L1 and L2 Japanese narratives. In H. Sirai, S. Arita, M. Hirakawa, S. Inagaki, M.Minami, Y. Oshima-Takane, Y. Shirai & Y. Terao (eds.), *Studies in Language Sciences* (6). Tokyo: Kurosio Publishers.

Nakamura, K. (1993). Referential Structure in Japanese Children's Narratives: The Acquisition of *wa* and *ga*. In S. Choi (ed.), *Japanese/Korean Linguistics*. Volume 3. CSLI Publications.

Nuevo, A (2006). Task complexity and interaction. Unpublished doctoral dissertation, Gerogetown University.

Odlin, T. (1989). *Language transfer: Cross-linguistic influence in language learning*. Cambridge, UK: Cambridge University Press.

Odlin, T. (1990). Word order transfer, metalinguistic awareness, and constraints on foreign language learning. In B. VanPatten & J. F. Lee (eds.), *Second language acquisition/foreign language learning* (pp. 95–117). Clevedon, UK: Multilingual Matters.

Odlin, T. (2001). Language Transfer and Substrate Influence. In R. Mesthrie (ed.), *Concise Encyclopedia of Sociolinguistics* (pp. 499–503). Amsterdam: Elsevier.

Odlin, T. (2002). Language transfer and cross-linguistic studies: Relativism, universalism, and the native language. In R. Kaplan (ed.), *The oxford handbook of applied linguistics*. New York: Oxford University Press.

Odlin, T. (2003). Cross-linguistic influence. In C. Doughty & M. Long (eds.), *Handbook of SLA*. Oxford: Blackwell

Odlin, T. (2005). Cross-Linguistic Influence and Conceptual Transfer: What are the Concepts? *Annual Review of Applied Linguistics* 25, 3–25.

Odlin, T. (2006). Continuity and Change in Language Transfer Research. In Nakahama, Y. (ed) The Influence of Learners' L1 on L2 Acquisition: A Functional Approach to Understanding Language Learning (pp. 75–96). Report of the Grant-in-Aid for

Scientific Research (C) Supported by Japan Society for the Promotion of Science. Project No. 15520330.
Olshtain, E. & Cohen, A. (1989). Speech act behavior across languages. In Dechert & Raupach. (eds.), *Transfer in language production*. Norwood, NJ: Ablex.
Orr, G. (1987). *Aspects of the second language acquisition of Chichewa noun class morphology* Unpublished doctoral dissertation, University of California, Los Angeles.
Peck, S. (1978). Child-child discourse in second language acquisition. In E. Hatch (ed.), *Second Language Acquisition: A Book of Readings*. Rowley, Mass.: Newbury House.
Pienemann, M. (1983). Learnability and syllabus construction. In K. Hylternstam & M. Pienemann (eds.), *Modeling and assessing second language development* (pp. 23–75). Clevedon, Avon: Multilingual Matters.
Pienemann, M. (1998). *Language processing and second language development: processability theory*. Amsterdam: John Benjamins.
Polio, C. (1995). Acquiring nothing? The use of zero pronouns by nonnative speakers of Chinese and the implications for the acquisition of nominal reference. *Studies in Second Language Acquisition*, 17, 353–377.
Rahimpour, M. (1999). Task complexity and variation in interlanguage. In N. Jungheim & P. Robinson (eds.), *Pragmatics and pedagogy: Proceedings of the 3rd Pacific Second language Research Forum, Vol 2* (pp. 115–134). Tokyo: PacSLRF.
Riessman, C. K. (1993). *Narrative analysis: Qualitative research methods*. Vol. 30 Mewbury Park, London: Sage Publications.
Ringbom, H. (1987). *The role of the first language in foreign language learning*. Clevedon, U. K.: Multilingual Matters.
Robinson, M. A. (1992). Introspective methodology in interlanguage pragmatics research. In G. Kasper (ed.), *Pragmatics of Japanese as native and target language (Second Language Teaching and Curriculum Center Technical Rep*. No.3, pp. 27–82). Honolulu: University of Hawaii Press.
Robinson, P. (1995). Task complexity and second language narrative discourse. *Language Learning*, 30, 397–416.
Robinson, P. (2001). Task complexity, cognitive resources and syllabus design: A triadic framework for examining task influences on SLA. In P. Robinson (ed.), *Cognition and second language instruction* (pp. 185–316). New York: Cambridge University Press.
Robinson, P. (2003). The cognition hypothesis, task design, and adult task-based language learning. *Second Language Studies*, 21 (2), 45–105.
Robinson, P. (2007). Task complexity, theory of mind, and intentional reasoning. Effects on L2 speech production, interaction, uptake and perception of task difficulty. *IRAL*, 45, 193–213.
Russell, R. A. (1985). An analysis of student errors in the use of Japanese- WA and–GA. *Papers in Linguistics*, 18 (2), 197–221.
Rutherford, W. (1983). Language typology and language transfer. In S. Gass & L. Selinker (eds.), *Language transfer in language learning* (pp. 358–370). Rowley, MA: Newbury House.
Rutherford, W. & Sharwood Smith, M. (1985). Consciousness-raising and universal grammar. *Applied Linguistics*, 6, 274–282

Sakamoto, T. (1985). *Acquisition of wa and ga among the beginning level learners of Japanese*. Paper presented at Summer Japanese Language Research Seminar at Middlebury University.
Sakamoto, T. (1993). On acquisition order: Japanese particles WA and GA.*Proceedings of the 3rd Conference on Second Language Acquisition and Teaching*, 105–122. International University of Japan.
Sakamoto, T. (2000). The acquisition of wa and ga: Comparison of Korean, Chinese and English speakers. *Nihon Bunka Gakuhoo*, 8, 69–81.
Sato, C. (1988). Origins of complex syntax in interlanguage development. *Studies in Second Language Acquisition* 10: 371–395.
Schachter, J. (1974). An error in error analysis. *Language Learning*, 27, 205–214.
Schmidt, R. (1990). The role of consciousness in second language learning. *Applied Linguistics*, 11, 129–158.
Schumann, J. (1987). The expression of temporality in basilang speech. *Studies in Second Language Acquisition* 9: 21–41.
Selinker, L.(1969). Language transfer. *General Linguistics*, 9, 67–92.
Selinker, L. (1992). *Rediscovering interlanguage*. London: Longman
Sharwood Smith, M. & Kellerman, E. (1986). Crosslinguistic influence in second language acquisition: an introduction, in E. Kellerman & M. Sharwood Smith (eds.), *Crosslinguistic influence in second language acquisition* (pp. 1–9). Oxford: Pergamon Press.
Shibatani, M. (1985). Passives and related constructions: A prototype analysis. *Language*, 61 (4), 821–848.
Shibatani, M. (1990). *The languages of Japan*. Cambridge, England: Cambridge University Press.
Shimojo, M. & U, Lee. (2010). Nihongo no shudai maakaa 'wa' ni tsuite- danwa ni okeru kankokugo to no hikaku bunseki. Paper presented at CAJLE 2010 Annual Conference, University of British Columbia, Canada.
Shotter, J. (1989). Social accountability and the social construction of 'you'. In J. Shotter & K. Gergen (eds.), *Texts of identity*. London: Sage Publications.
Slobin, D. (1991). Learning to think for speaking: Native language, cognition, and rhetorical style. *Pragmatics*, 1, 7–25.
Slobin, D. (1993). Adult language acquisition: A view from child language study. In C. Perdue (ed.), *Adult language acquisition: Cross-linguistic perspectives* (pp. 239–252). Cambridge, UK: Cambridge University Press.
Slobin, D. (1996). From "thought and language" to "thinking for speaking" In J. Gumperz & S. Levinson (eds.), *Rethinking linguistic relativity* (pp. 70–96). Cambridge, UK: Cambridge University Press.
Sohn, H. (1994). *Korean*. London; New York : Routledge.
Sohn, H. (1999). *Korean Language*. New York: Cambridge University Press
Spada, N. & Lightbown, P. M. (1999). Instruction, first language influence, and developmental readiness in second language acquistion. *Modern Language Journal*, 83, 1–22.
Stockwell, R., Bowen, J. D. & Martin, J. (1965). *The grammatical structures of English and*

Spanish. Chicago: University of Chicago Press.
Swain, M. (1995). Three functions of output in second language learning. In G. Cook & B. Seidlhoffer (eds.), *Principle and practice in applied linguistics: Studies in honour of H. G. Widdowson* (pp. 125–144). Oxford: Oxford University Press.
Takahashi, T. (1984). *A study on lexico-semantic transfer*. Unpublished doctoral dissertation, Columbia University, New York.
Takahashi, S. (2000). Transfer in interlanguage pragmatics: New research agenda. *Studies in Languages and Cultures*, 11, 109 – 128.
Takahashi, T. & Beebe, L. (1987). The development of pragmatic competence by Japanese learners of English. *JALT Journal*, 8, 131–155.
Takana, M. (1996). The acquisition of viewpoint and voice: Cross-sectional and longitudinal studies of sentence construction tests. *Nihongo Kyooiku (Journal of Japanese Language Teaching)*, 88, 104–115.
Tannen, D. (1980). A comparative analysis of oral narrative strategies: Athenian Greek and American English. In Chafe, W. (ed.), *The pear stories. Cognitive, cultural, and linguistic aspects of narrative production*. New Jersey: Ablex.
Tanskanen, S. K. (2006). *Collaborating Towards Coherence*. Amsterdam & Philadelphia: John Benjamins
Tashiro, H. (1995). Problems with writing styles by intermediate learners of Japanese-Investigation of the cause of unnaturalness and incomprehensibility. *Journal of Japanese Language Teaching*, 85, 25–37.
Taylor, B. (1975). The use of overgeneralization and transfer learning strategies by elementary and intermediate students of ESL. *Language Learning*, 25, 73–107.
Thomas, J. (1983). Cross-cultural pragmatic failure. *Applied Linguistics*, 4, 91–112.
Thomas, M (1989). The acquisition of English articles by first- and second-language learners. *Applied Psycholinguistics*, 10, 335–355.
Thomason, S. & Kaufman, T. (1988). *Language contact, creolization, and genetic linguistics. Berkeley*: University of California Press.
Tomita, H. (1997). The L2 acquisition of *wa* and *ga*. The difficulty caused by competing 'cues'. *Japanese Language Education around the Globe*, 7, 157–174.
Tomlin (1987). Linguistic reflections of cognitive events. In R. Tomlin (ed.), *Coherence and grounding in discourse* (pp. 455–480). Amsterdam: John Benjamins.
Tomlin, R. (1990). Functionalism in second language acquisition. *Studies in Second Language Acquisition*, 12, 155–177.
Toyama, C. (2006). The acquisition of Japanese discourse as a second language – Within the framework of cognitive pragmatics- In Y. Sasaki (ed.), *The state of art in second language acquisition and instruction research -2006 version-* Tokyo: Bonjinsha.
Traugott, E. & Heine, B. (1991). *Approaches to Grammaticalization*. TSL #19. 1/2, Amsterdam: J. Benjamins.
Tran-Chi-Chau. (1975). Error analysis, contrastive analysis and students' perceptions: a study of difficulty in second language learning. *International Review of Applied Linguistics*, 13, 119–43.
Tsujimura, N. (1996). *Introduction to Japanese Linguistics*. Cambridge, MA: Blackwell Publishers.

Tyler, A. (1995). Co-constructing Miscommunication: The Role of Participant Frame and Schema in Cross-cultural Miscommunication. *Studies in Second Language Acquisition*, 17, 129–152.

Wardhaugh, R. (1970). The contrastive analysis hypothesis. *TESOL Quarterly*, 4, 123–30.

Watanabe, A. (1996). *Chu jokyu nihongo gakushusha no danwa tenkai*. Kurosio Publishers.

Watanabe, F. (2003). Nihongo bogowasha to hibogowasha no katari no danwa ni okeru shijihyoogen to danwa no matomari. *Proceedings of Japanese Language Teaching Autumn Conference*, pp. 236–238.

Watanabe, F. (2004). On use of "wa" in Japanese narrative discourse pp. 3–15. *Bulletin of Graduate School of Social & Cultural Systems at Yamagata University*

Watanabe, F. (2011). Katari no danwa, bunshoo ni okeru shudai hyooshiki ni kansuru nikkan taishoo kenkyuu. *A paper presented at Seventh International Conference on Practical Linguistics of Japanese*. San Francisco State University.

Wei, C. (2010). The expression of viewpoint in narrative discourse by Taiwanese learners of Japanese: the correlation with learners' Japanese proficiency. *Nihongo Kyooiku (Journal of Japanese Language Teaching)*, 144, 133–144.

Weinreich, U. (1953). *Languages in Contact*. The Hague: Mouton.

White, L. (1985). The pro-drop parameter in adult second language acquisition. *Language Learning* 35: 47–62.

Williams, J. (1988). Zero anaphora in second language acquisition: A comparison among three varieties of English. *Studies in Second Language Acquisition*, 10, 339–370.

Williams, J. (1989). Pronoun copies, pronominal anaphora, and zero anaphora in second language production. In S. Gass, S., D. Madden., D. Preston., & L. Selinker (eds.), *Variation in Second Language Acquisition, Vol. I: Sociolinguistic Issues* (pp. 153–189). Clevedon, Avon: Multilingual Matters.

Williams, J. (1992). Planning, discourse marking, and the comprehensibility of international teaching assistants. *TESOL Quarterly*, 26 (4), 693–711.

Wode, H. (1978). The L1 vs. L2 acquisition of English negation. *Working Papers on Bilingualism*, 15, 37–57.

Wode, H. (1983). Contrastive analysis and language learning. In H. Wode (ed.), *Papers on language acquisition, language learning and language teaching* (pp. 202–212). Heidelberg, Germany: Groos.

Yamamoto, M. (1996). *Animacy and Reference. A Cognitive Approach to Corpus Linguistics*. Amsterdam: John Benjamins.

Yanagimachi, T. (1997). The acquisition of referential form use in L2 oral narrative discourse by adult English-speaking learners of Japanese. Unpublished doctoral dissertation, University of Minnesota.

Yanagimachi, T. (2000). JFL learners' referential-form choice in first-through third-person narratives. *Japanese Language Education around the Globe*, 10, 109–128.

Yoshioka, K. (1991). Elicited imitation test for oral production assessment. *Working Papers*, 127–140. International University of Japan.

Yoshioka, K. (2005). Linguistic and gestural introduction and tracking of referents in L1 and L2 discourse. Groningen Dissertations in Linguistics 55.

Young, J. & Nakajima-Okano, K. (1984). *Learn Japanese: New College Text*. University of

Hawai'i Press.
Zobl, H. (1979). Nominal and pronominal interrogation in the speech of adult francophone ESL learners: Some insights into the workings of transfer. *SPEAQ Journal* 3, 69–93.
Zobl, H. (1986). Word order typology, lexical government, and the prediction of multiple, graded effects in L2 word order. *Language Learning*, 36, 159–183.
Zobl, H. (1995). Markedness aspects of case-marking in L1 French/L2 English interlanguage. In L. Eubank, L. Selinker, & M. Sharwood Smith (eds.), *The current state of interlanguage: Studies in honor of William E. Rutherford* (pp.197–203). Amsterdam/Philadelphia: John Benjamins.

Index

a
accuracy 10, 11, 16, 63, 64, 158, 159, 195–196, 204, 206, 207, 214
the ACTFL guidelines 15, 69, 81
the animacy hierarchy 59, 88, 89, 200

c
the Cognition Hypothesis 62, 65, 196
cognitive demands 62–64, 175, 196, 213
coherence 1, 36, 211, 212
complexity 11, 16, 62, 64, 170, 195–197, 204, 206–208, 210, 213–215
conceptual transfer 194, 198, 202, 206, 215
continuous mention of referent 14–15, 79–80
contrastive analysis hypothesis (CAH) 4, 19–22
cross-linguistic influence (CLI) 1–7, 13, 19–20, 23, 25–34, 54, 184, 186, 192, 198, 203, 205–206

f
film retelling 10, 14, 62, 77
form-function mapping(s) (form-function relationship(s)) 7–8, 15, 97, 111, 128, 131, 189–191, 203, 205
functional approach(es) 8, 12, 16, 19, 38, 40

h
here and now (H/N) 10, 14, 16, 64, 75–77, 195–197, 203, 211–213

l
L1 background(s) 1–3, 5, 7, 45–46, 57, 69, 192, 197, 208
L2 narrative(s) 1, 34, 36–38, 62, 64, 184, 186, 203
language distance 3, 13–14, 20, 72, 176
language transfer (L1 transfer) 1, 4–5, 13, 20, 24, 26, 28–29, 31, 33

m
markedness 53, 55–56, 197, 208

n
narrative formation 12, 43, 65
negative transfer 7, 11, 13, 22, 26–27, 31–32, 71, 198, 200, 205

o
Oral Proficiency Interview (OPI) 49, 74
overgeneralisation 28, 135, 190

p
particle drop 108, 110, 125–127, 154, 160, 166, 186–188, 195–196, 204–205, 207
passive structure(s) 38, 42, 45, 60, 80, 90, 107, 118, 141, 147–150, 152, 193–194, 198–200, 203
perspective(s) 33–34, 36, 41–43, 45, 107, 140, 152–153, 168, 170, 198, 202, 211, 217
picture description 10, 54, 62, 215
positive transfer 2, 3, 5, 13, 32, 47–48, 54–56, 192, 194, 198, 205–206
postpositions (postpositional) 9, 30, 48, 51, 80, 98, 104, 155, 157, 187–188, 205
prepositions (prepositional) 13, 30–31, 187
proficiency level 6, 15, 26–28, 70, 72–74, 127, 158–159, 179, 184, 187–191, 193, 195, 197, 198, 201, 203, 205, 211, 212
pronoun(s) 40, 41, 49, 52, 61, 62, 65, 119–122, 124, 168, 177–179, 202–203

q
quantity universal 38–39, 41

r

referent introduction 9, 10, 14–15, 19, 64–65, 78
referent marking(s) 11–12, 14, 40, 48, 58, 61, 64–65, 158–159, 179, 187, 190, 195, 203–204, 207, 210–211

s

the significance hierarchy 89, 200
Simulated Oral Proficiency Interview (SOPI) 12, 15, 70, 74
storytelling 7, 14, 34, 35, 209–210, 214–216

t

task complexity 10–12, 16–17, 62–63, 65, 170, 180, 195–197, 203–204, 213–214, 216
there and then (T/T) 10, 14, 16, 63–65, 73, 75–77, 195–197, 203–204, 211–213, 215
thinking for speaking 33, 107, 153, 180, 200–201, 206, 217
topic continuity (discontinuity) 9, 14, 40–41, 61, 65, 77, 80, 124, 179, 193, 202–203
topic switch 14–15, 65, 76, 78–79
typological difference(s) 4, 13
typological similarity (similarities) 3–4, 13, 65, 183, 194, 201, 203

v

voice alternation 41–44, 65, 147, 193–194, 198, 200, 202–203

z

zero anaphora 40–41, 45–54, 65, 77, 79, 98–99, 101, 104, 108, 110, 119, 122, 123, 161–162, 164, 172, 190, 197, 202, 205–206

235

Appendix

Frog, where are you? Mercer Mayer (1969)

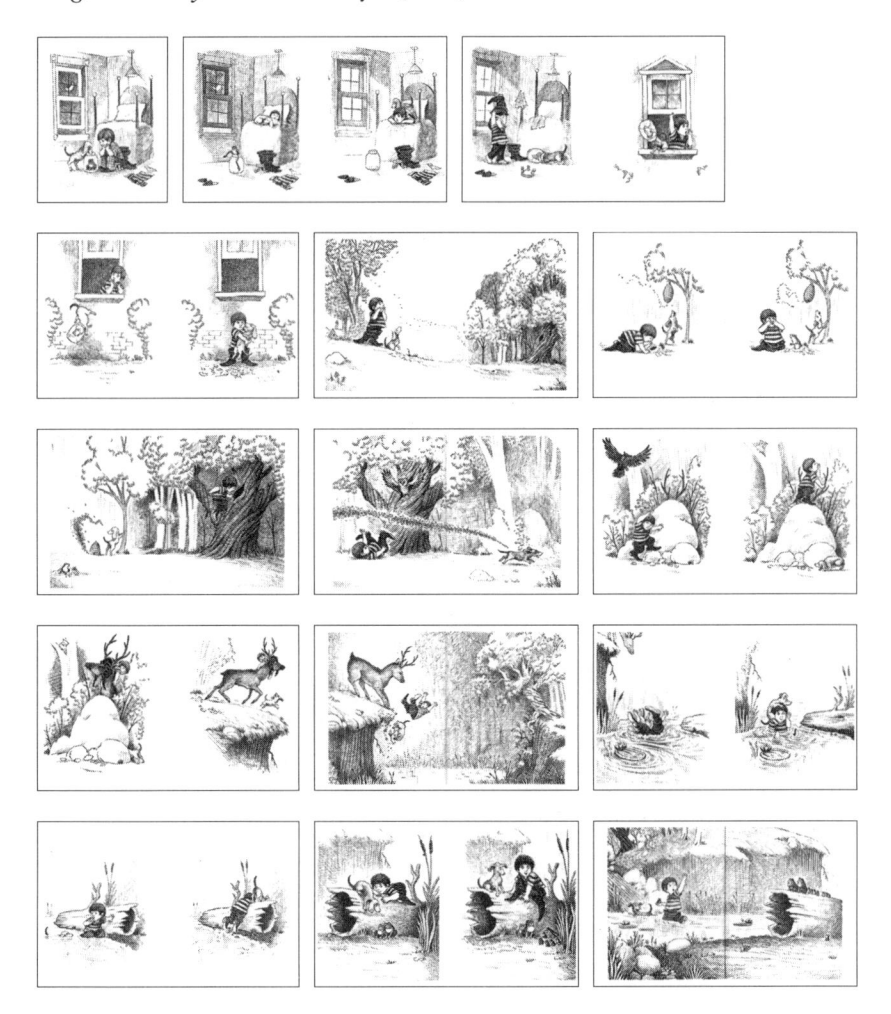

【著者紹介】

中浜 優子（なかはま ゆうこ）

2003年米国ジョージタウン大学博士課程修了(Ph.D)。米国バージニア大学、ノートルダム大学専任講師、名古屋大学大学院助教授、東京外国語大学大学院准教授を経て慶應義塾大学環境情報学部教授。

［主要論文］Cross-linguistic influence on referent introduction and tracking in Japanese as a second language (*Modern Language Journal*, 2009年 Vol. 93:2)、「ストーリー構築における視点：母語話者と上級日本語話者の比較から」(『言語学と日本語教育VI』南雅彦(編)2010年、共著)

Referent Markings in L2 Narratives
Effects of Task Complexity, Learners' L1 and Proficiency Level

発行	2011年3月31日　初版1刷
定価	12000円＋税
著者	©中浜優子
発行者	松本 功
印刷所	三美印刷株式会社
製本所	田中製本印刷株式会社
発行所	株式会社 ひつじ書房
	〒112-0011 東京都文京区千石2-1-2 大和ビル2F
	Tel.03-5319-4916　Fax.03-5319-4917
	郵便振替 00120-8-142852
	toiawase@hituzi.co.jp　http://www.hituzi.co.jp/

ISBN978-4-89476-535-1　　C3080

造本には充分注意しておりますが、落丁・乱丁などがございましたら、小社かお買上げ書店にておとりかえいたします。ご意見、ご感想など、小社までお寄せ下されば幸いです。